Rese

John Fitzmaurice

LIVERPOOL HOPE UNIVERSITY STUDIES IN ETHICS SERIES
SERIES EDITOR: DR. DAVID TOREVELL
SERIES DEPUTY EDITOR: DR. JACQUI MILLER

VOLUME ONE:
ENGAGING RELIGIOUS EDUCATION
Editors: Joy Schmack, Matthew Thompson and David Torevell with Camilla Cole

VOLUME TWO:
RESERVOIRS OF HOPE: SUSTAINING SPIRITUALITY IN SCHOOL LEADERS
Author: Alan Flintham

Reservoirs of Hope:
Sustaining Spirituality in School Leaders

By

Alan Flintham

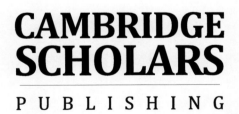

Reservoirs of Hope: Sustaining Spirituality in School Leaders, by Alan Flintham

This book first published 2010. The present binding first published 2011.

Cambridge Scholars Publishing

12 Back Chapman Street, Newcastle upon Tyne, NE6 2XX, UK

British Library Cataloguing in Publication Data
A catalogue record for this book is available from the British Library

ISBN (10): 1-4438-3182-4, ISBN (13): 978-1-4438-3182-6

For Jean, Andrew and Martin

TABLE OF CONTENTS

LIST OF FIGURES AND TABLES

PREFACE

In the 1986 film 'Clockwise', the manic headteacher played by John Cleese utters the memorable words: "It's not the despair. I can cope with the despair. It's the *hope* I can't stand". This book is about hope, and how it can be sustained by and in the leaders of our schools. It argues that a personal spirituality, be it sacred or secular, is the means by which that hope may be sustained. It demonstrates the outworking of that spirituality as spiritual and moral leadership in the face of critical incidents and challenging pressures. It offers the engaging metaphor of 'reservoirs of hope' to promote reflection on these issues and offers a theological underpinning to it. It captures the authentic voices of practitioners as they engage in reflection on what drains and replenishes their personal reservoir of hope.

Like ripples in a reservoir, the research on which this book is based has continued to spread. It was initially conceived as a small-scale piece of practitioner research involving 25 headteachers under the National College for the Leadership of Schools and Children's Services (formerly the National College for School Leadership, NCSL) research associate scheme. Encouraged by a remarkable 97% willingness to participate and the enthusiasm of the wider practitioner community for the metaphor of 'reservoirs of hope', and supported by funding from the East Midlands Leadership Centre (EMLC), Liverpool Hope University, ACU National (the Australian Catholic University), the Roman Catholic Diocese of Parramatta and a Winston Churchill Travelling Fellowship, the scope of the research grew to encompass interviews with 150 school leaders and 40 supporting educationists in the United Kingdom, Australia and New Zealand (as acknowledged in the Appendix). My sincere thanks go to all these colleagues who so willingly and enthusiastically agreed to be interviewed, for their warmth of welcome and openness of response. Without such ready co-operation from often hard-pressed and time-pressured colleagues, this research could not have been possible.

My thanks also go to colleagues at the National College who supported the initial research associate opportunity and colleagues at Liverpool Hope University, in particular to Dr David Torevell as series editor, together with Professor Gerald Grace of the London Institute of Education, for their encouragement and support in converting the research into a book.

Particular thanks must go to the two colleagues who supervised the research: Professor John Sullivan for his conscientious and detailed critique of my work, and Professor John West-Burnham for his insightful overview and kind permission to use, adapt and develop his original phrase 'reservoir of hope'. Any errors, omissions or infelicities remain clearly mine, however.

Above all, my thanks are due to my long-suffering family: my wife Jean and my sons Andrew and Martin, for their understanding, advice and support which have sustained me through the production of this book and ensured that my own personal 'reservoir of hope' has never run dry.

INTRODUCTION

Jack Straw, long-serving British politician and erstwhile government minister, has suggested that successful survival in political leadership is a question of possessing a number of professional characteristics:

> You have got to have *a clear agenda*, but equally you've got to be ready to have your mind changed...

> You've got to be able intellectually to do the job. You've got to be able to turn the paper round. That may sound bureaucratic, but you have got to *keep the show on the road.*

> Keeping the show on the road is also dealing with *stuff that comes out of a clear blue sky...* Dealing with what is apparently routine...you've got to have a sixth sense...to spot things that are small but could turn big. Then when an emergency does arise, working out what the angles are and how you deal with them. (Straw 2010, 9; emphasis added)

And all this is clearly as applicable to the task of leading a school as it is to running a political system.

When constant revisions of national education policy threaten to cause change overload and system malfunction, it is to the headteacher that colleagues look to preserve *a clear agenda*, a coherence of vision and direction underpinned by integrity of values. When day-to-day pressures threaten to overwhelm the smooth running of a school, it is to the headteacher that colleagues look '*to keep the show on the road*'. When critical incidents and emergencies hit a school '*out of a clear blue sky*', it is to the headteacher that colleagues look '*to deal with all the angles*' and to keep the school on course.

And colleagues look to their leaders not only for *what* they do in such circumstances—the leadership actions they take together with *how* they do it and the skills, processes and relationships on which they draw—but also *why* they do it—the values and vision which underpin their actions and the moral imperative of their leadership.

Teaching at its core is a profession built on moral values—"scratch a good teacher and you will find a moral purpose" (Fullan 1993, 12)—and the same is surely equally true of school leaders. The research on which this book stands (Flintham 2009) is based on interviews with 150 headteachers from a range of personal faith perspectives both sacred and secular, and a variety of school contexts, including community schools, schools of a religious character and schools facing particularly challenging social circumstances, across the United Kingdom, Australia and New Zealand. It captures practitioner reflections on the personal value systems, leadership styles and sustainability strategies of headteachers in such circumstances: the 'why' as well as the 'how' and 'what' of their leadership.

Its findings demonstrate that *all* school leaders can readily articulate a moral purpose: their core moral and ethical value system or 'spirituality', the 'lived faith' which underpins their leadership actions, particularly when the going gets tough. That spirituality may be substantially secular (as outlined in Chapter Three) or sacred (as described in Chapter Four). It is seen demonstrated in practice especially when critical incidents hit the school community 'out of a clear blue sky', or in facing the day-to-day pressures of leading a school facing particularly challenging circumstances (as described in Chapter Five), when spiritual and moral leadership is displayed as 'a lived faith in action'.

The research has used the metaphor *'reservoirs of hope'* to promote practitioner reflection on these issues. The metaphor of the school leader as a 'reservoir of hope' has been found to be a useful one by practitioners working in the challenging and demanding contexts of school leadership (Flintham 2003a, 2003b). The successful school leader, by providing the calm centre at the heart of the storm when critical incidents and incessant pressures hit a school, is called on to act as the *'external reservoir of hope'*, because hope is what drives the school forward towards delivering its vision whilst allowing it to remain true to its fundamental values, and "without hope the people perish".

Napoleon Bonaparte described leaders as "dealers in hope", an appellation which requires them not only to maintain reserves of inner self-belief and personal resilience when faced with challenging circumstances, but also to inspire and imbue those they lead with that same spirit of hope in the prospect of a better future. And the school leaders of today are equally required to be the harbingers of hope, the messengers who continue to bring to school communities buffeted by the pressures of external events, that enduring spirit of hope, "a hope that is about the potential for the future...about growth and resilience" (West-Burnham 2009, 86).

But to maintain that resilience in demanding circumstances demands the school leader drawing on an *'internal reservoir of hope'* (the phrase is from West-Burnham 2002, and is used by kind permission): a reservoir which provides the calm centre at the heart of the individual leader, which preserves their personal values and vision and which continues to allow effective inter-personal engagement and sustainability of self-belief in the face of external pressures. To successfully maintain that internal reservoir of hope requires two things:

- firm *foundations of faith* to preserve moral purpose in the face of constant pressures;
- robust *sustainability strategies* of replenishment and renewal to ensure that the reservoir of hope does not run dry.

'Faith' should not necessarily be construed solely in the religious terms of sacred spirituality but viewed as a universal concept of *'secular spirituality'* wherein the leader's actions are seen to rest explicitly or implicitly on the foundation of an embedded personal moral and ethical value system, the fundamental motivation and purpose that distinguishes leaders from mere efficient functionaries. This foundation of deeply-held beliefs and code of moral values not only provides a personal paradigm for living, but also gives an innate philosophy of practice which comes into play not only in the face of the day-to-day experiences of school leadership, but also when that leadership is tested by the unexpected pressures of critical incidents and external events. In the context of such circumstances:

> The notion of 'an innate philosophy of practice' is a powerful one; and both heads with and without formal religious faith will find themselves on common ground. Very few school leaders follow a codified rule of practice in such circumstances: *what they believe is seen in what they do, how they respond to people and to situations.* (Caperon 2007b, 2; emphasis added)

Those leadership actions, engagements and responses to critical situations, when underpinned by a firm moral purpose, thereby demonstrate the definition, developed from a survey of a range of writings on leadership and spirituality in Chapter Two and used throughout this book, that *spiritual and moral leadership is 'a lived faith in action'.*

However, the constant coping with such pressures can threaten to drain the personal reservoir of hope to dryness and destruction. Without robust sustainability strategies such as space for reflection, networks of supportive relationships, and engagement with the world beyond education, which maintain and replenish inner self-belief and emotional reserves, the reservoir of hope can run dry, there will be burn out or drop out and school leaders will withdraw from the change arena, and in the memorable words of one primary school headteacher: *"you will die a lingering death through managing the stock cupboard"*.

How successful school leaders avoid that 'lingering death' is a function of both professional experience and personal characteristics (as explored in Chapter Five). A questionnaire survey for the National College of over 300 English school headteachers deemed 'outstanding' in their leadership and management by the school inspection agency, Ofsted, found that "outstanding headteachers are confident in their beliefs, secure in rich relationships and develop professional knowledge and skills but, pivotally, are also reflective learners" (NCSL 2009, 14).

This book seeks to capture the authentic voices of serving headteachers and analyse the learning from such reflections on their spiritual and moral leadership. It thereby generates key messages for both practitioners and policy makers regarding the importance of maintaining *a constant vision of hope* which informs and maintains moral purpose, the value of *structured reflection opportunities* in codifying it, and the necessity for the continual renewal of it through engagement in *sustaining networks of mutual support*.

But in addition to capturing that reflective learning, this book also offers in Chapter Six a theological reflection on the spiritual and moral leadership of headteachers, applying the concepts of kerygma, kenosis and koinonia to such leadership. It further analyses the leadership stories of headteachers by offering a theological reflection on their leadership as viewed not only through a secular educational lens but also through the theological concepts of kerygma as the essential message of hope that their leadership conveys, kenosis as they act as the self-draining reservoir of hope for their schools when confronted with critical incidents and systemic pressures, and koinonia as they refill and sustain their personal internal reservoirs by seizing opportunities to engage in individual reflection and networked support. Through applying a capacity for 'bilingualism' to enable and inform dialogue, it thereby seeks to offer a groundbreaking connecting bridge between the worlds of educational leadership and theology, to the mutual benefit of both.

And given the growing interest in 'spirituality at work' and its impact on spiritual leadership development across the business world (Tourish and Tourish 2010), described by Aburdene (2005) as a 'Megatrend 2010', these generic bridging concepts of kerygma, kenosis and koinonia and the metaphor 'reservoirs of hope' could also profitably be transferred to studies of leadership in other professions where there is a perceived and identified need for the promotion of reflection and support opportunities, to ensure that the reservoir of hope of leaders in whatever context does not run dry but can overflow in a 'triumph of hope over experience'.

CHAPTER ONE

OUTLINE OF A STUDY OF SPIRITUAL AND MORAL LEADERSHIP

This introductory chapter first outlines the aims of the research study on which this book is based, the research questions that were posed and the research samples used to investigate them. Second, it identifies the need for this study both in drawing on a wider empirical base than previous extant research and also in offering a connecting bridge between the worlds of educational leadership and theology, through the application of a capacity for 'bilingualism' to enable and inform dialogue. Third, it outlines the assumptions made in constructing this study, namely the applicability of a universally applicable concept of 'secular spirituality', the value of the metaphor 'reservoirs of hope' in promoting practitioner reflection on spiritual and moral leadership and the validity of the methodological approach used. Finally, it offers an outline of the organisation of the research findings as set out in the remainder of the book and describes the conceptual framework that has been applied throughout.

1. The aims of this study

This book explores the spirituality of headteachers and how it is sustained and demonstrated as spiritual and moral leadership when exposed to critical incidents and day-to-day leadership pressures. Whilst recognising that school leadership is a distributed function and not simply the sole preserve of the headteacher, it argues that particularly when faced with critical incidents, it is to the headteacher above all that the school community looks for spiritual and moral leadership, in addition to the management and public relations skills necessary to mitigate any consequential negative impact. This function can be potentially draining of personal leadership energy and self-belief, and can require access to replenishing sustainability strategies and support structures.

The following research questions are considered:

- What are the spiritual and moral bases on which headteachers stand, from whence are they derived and how do they impact on leadership?
- What value has the opportunity for headteachers to reflect on critical incidents when spiritual and moral leadership was tested?
- What sustainability and support structures are deployed and valued by headteachers?
- What key messages may be drawn to influence the formation, development and support of existing and future headteachers?

These research questions were explored through a qualitative phenomenological study, using data primarily gained from one-to-one semi-structured reflective interviews carried out by a fellow practitioner headteacher using an ethnographic approach and applying the metaphor 'reservoirs of hope' as an aid to promoting reflection. A cross-sectional sample of 150 serving and former headteachers, balanced in terms of phase, gender and context and drawn from the UK, Australia and New Zealand was used, and triangulated with interviews with 40 supporting local, diocesan and national educationists.

As a phenomenological study, the research sought to focus on the lived experience of the headteachers interviewed and to express it in a language that is as loyal to that lived experience as possible (Polkinghorne 1989). It allowed those interviewed particularly to reflect on and analyse their experience of critical incidents in their leadership story (Flanagan 1954), defining 'critical' as not necessarily high level but as a testing occurrence from which learning had ensued, and thence to enable the making explicit of the underpinning value system which governed their leadership actions. It has captured and elucidated that experience from the guided reflections of practitioners obtained in the naturalistic setting of the school environment and their articulation in an authentic rendering of practitioner voice, through the use of direct quotations from those interviewed.

The headteachers interviewed had a significant range of leadership experience within a variety of school contexts, including schools of a specific religious character and those facing particularly challenging circumstances. The study sought to illuminate differences between these sub-groups, to identify any development of leadership capacity linked to length of experience and to consider whether there were any specific clusters of professional characteristics dominant in leaders of schools facing particularly challenging circumstances.

Within the three main data chapters of this book, entitled 'Reservoirs of hope', 'Foundations of faith' and 'Labours of love' respectively, the headteacher research sample is consequently divided into:

- A total of 50 interviews with representative samples of 25 serving headteachers and 15 headteachers who left headship early in advance of the normal retirement age in England, together with a further 10 Australian school principals. Those interviewed were perceived as apparently 'successful' headteachers leading predominantly secular schools as *'reservoirs of hope'*, or conversely those who left their headships early, possibly 'when reservoirs ran dry'. It is recognised, however, that "often what is regarded as successful leadership can be seen in retrospect to be deeply flawed, while leadership which may appear poor can often have within it a wisdom or insight which is only valued much later" (Hanvey 2008, 32), and that significant lessons may be drawn from both categories.
- A total of 60 headteachers interviewed in England, Australia and New Zealand who were leading schools from an individual religious faith perspective which provides personal *'foundations of faith'* in leadership. Such leadership may be exercised in a school associated with a similar faith perspective to that personally held, one distinct from it, or one purely secular.
- A total of 40 headteachers leading schools in the UK facing particularly challenging circumstances of context or social deprivation, or failing to meet academic 'floor targets', where such service may be seen as *'labours of love'*. Sub-sets of this sample were studied in terms of professional characteristics of leaders and the value of sabbatical support.

These samples of headteachers, as detailed in the Appendix, have been balanced as far as possible in terms of both school phase and leadership gender. Individual quotations from headteachers, as shown in italics in the text, are where necessary appropriately attributed in this latter regard. However, in the interests of economy and clarity, in the remainder of the text, leadership references should be considered as gender-neutral.

2. The need for this study

This research therefore stands on a solid empirical base of data drawn from the leadership stories revealed in interviews with a total of 150 headteachers from the UK, Australia and New Zealand (a remarkable 97%

participation rate from those approached), and triangulated against the views of 40 local and national educationists. Woods (2007, 135) has indicated that whilst there has been a growing concern to emphasise the moral, ethical and emotional aspects of leadership, and that some literature about spirituality and leadership exists (as will be described in Chapter Two), there is relatively little empirical work in this area. Although Caperon (2007a, 3), writing from an Anglican perspective, goes so far as to describe the research underpinning this book as "the only recent empirical work I am aware of which looks seriously at the spiritual dimension of school leadership", this view takes no cognisance of studies such as Grace (2002) on 60 headteachers of Catholic secondary schools in deprived urban communities in three English cities and Reed et al (2002), who studied the role of the headteacher in leading transformation in three Church of England secondary schools compared to three community schools, nor of Woods (2007), who studied spiritual experience in educational leadership by analysing questionnaire returns from 244 headteachers (a 43% response rate) across three English local authorities. Equally, account must be taken of individual headteacher studies such as Luckcock (2004) on the distinctiveness and inclusiveness of Anglican church school headship, and Bracken (2004) on the principal's leadership role in spiritual formation in Australian Catholic schools. Other relevant research in the field includes the study by Day et al (2000) on leading schools in times of change, which explored 12 case study schools of varying phase and context in terms of the metaphors used to describe the leadership role of the headteacher, triangulated against the views of staff and the wider school community including students. Recent small-scale practitioner research for the National College for Leadership of Schools and Children's Services (formerly the National College for School Leadership, NCSL) has also considered how leaders and teachers in five primary schools have dealt with critical incidents and episodes (Mander 2008), and how leadership capacity to do this is seen to develop over time in six secondary headteachers (Ingate 2006). However, the author is unaware of any empirical interview-based research that has studied either the range or variety or number of headteachers involved in this present study.

This study applies the metaphor 'reservoirs of hope' to the spiritual and moral leadership of headteachers. If writings on spirituality and leadership are under-represented in the canon, so too are writings on leadership based on hope. Indeed Godfrey (1987, ix, cited in Halpin 2003, 12) has observed that, "as a topic for study, hope has been largely left to psychologists and theologians". Halpin (2003, 12) points out that "it is also a neglected concept in the academic study of education". The research described in this book contributes towards redressing this by exploring the concept of hope as an essential component of spiritual and moral leadership of schools, especially when facing pressures of critical incidents and challenging circumstances. Its particular contribution is to be found not only in the extent of its empirical base, nor simply in its sampling of a range of headteachers from a variety of geographical and faith perspectives and contexts. Rather it is also to be found in the authentic rendering of practitioner voice regarding spiritual and moral leadership and the application of a lens of theological reflection to it. One purpose of the book is to provide an analysis which offers a bridge to enable dialogue between these different groups, particularly those who are comfortable with expressing concepts in the theological language of the religious sphere and those who are more fluent in the secular language of education, a connectivity of 'engaged pluralism' which allows translation and communication rather than 'neutral pluralism' which seeks a common standard language acceptable to all.

Cardinal Cormac Murphy-O'Connor (2008) has counselled against the exclusive use of what he terms the "enclosed" or "insider" language of faith, with its taking for granted of agreed belief structures and familiarity with biblical stories and concepts, arguing instead the need to be able to communicate matters of faith "in the language of the world". In this book, the necessity is argued for a 'bilingual' capacity in a mixed economy with no readily shared language, regarding such bilingualism as the ability to be fluent in and comfortable with both the theological language of the faith community and the professional language of the education leadership sphere, and the capacity to translate generic concepts between them to facilitate not only discourse within the specialist community but also dialogue beyond it. The author's own background and experience spanning 26 years of senior leadership roles (11 as a deputy headteacher and 15 as a headteacher) in secular secondary education in socially challenged areas and over 22 years of concurrent non-stipendiary ministerial service in the Church of England (12 as a lay reader and 10 as a priest) has equipped him to act in this bilingual capacity in conducting and analysing interviews with such a varied range of headteachers.

From an analysis of the leadership stories of those interviewed and the authenticity of practitioner voice displayed in them, generic key messages may be drawn which will hopefully inform dialogue between those at local, diocesan and national level charged with the ongoing professional support and development of headteachers and those responsible for the formation and induction of future generations of school leaders at a time of significant recruitment and retention need.

3. The assumptions of this study

In embarking on this study, three assumptions have been made: that the concept of 'spirituality' is a universally applicable one in a secular as well as a sacred sense; that the metaphor 'reservoirs of hope' has value for headteachers in promoting their reflection on their spiritual and moral leadership; and that the outcomes which have emerged from promoting such reflection have validity and value within and beyond the practitioner community. These assumptions are now considered in turn.

3.1. A concept of 'secular spirituality'

In this book, the word 'spiritual' is used without a necessarily religious connotation. Rather 'spirituality' is regarded as a universal overarching concept which generates for each individual of whatever perspective a personal world-view which enables them to create meaning and purpose in their lives, affects their espoused values and subsequent behaviours and relationships based on them, and impacts on their wellbeing. That world-view may be linked to a particular religious tradition, have evolved from it or be completely independent of it. Indeed it can be asserted that *all* school leaders display what might be termed a 'secular spirituality', wherein their leadership actions are based on readily articulated foundations of ethical belief from whatever source.

Whilst the author's own background is as a practising Anglican, this book is written with a view to offering insights across a range of faith perspectives, both religious and secular, and to be accessible and of interest to those of whatever persuasion. Therefore the use of the term 'secular spirituality' within an examination of the spiritual and moral leadership of headteachers is designed to accommodate this by allowing the argument to be meaningful for those for whom a religious commitment is anathema, or who wish to distance themselves from the perceived limitations and problems of institutional religion (Hanvey 2008, 16) yet who would still resist being described as "not a spiritual person" (Harries 2002, x) or as lacking in some degree of spiritual awareness, even if embarrassed to admit to it (Hay and Hunt 2000, 14). A consideration of secular spirituality can thus provide a bridge to engagement with, for example, the sceptical school leader who when interviewed said of the National College research study *Reservoirs of Hope: Spiritual and Moral*

Leadership in Headteachers (Flintham 2003a), which was the original genesis of this book: *"I downloaded it but haven't read it because of the word 'spiritual' in the title; I'm not religious"*.

Spirituality, be it linked to a particular religious tradition or determinedly secular, is, however, more than simply possessing and articulating a static set of ethical and moral values from whatever source; rather it is a commitment to their dynamic application in the leadership challenges of life in the real world, so that belief becomes action, words become deeds, and 'the talk is walked'. Spirituality thus becomes "a lived faith" (Wakefield 2000, 686), and spiritual and moral leadership can thus be conceived of as 'a lived faith in action', an operational definition which underpins this present research study throughout.

3.2. The metaphor 'reservoirs of hope'

Personal 'foundations of faith' anchor spiritual and moral leadership actions in a framework of belief to ensure a coherence of vision and integrity of values when the leader is faced with critical incidents and systemic pressures which threaten to blow the school off course. This research tests the value of the metaphor 'reservoirs of hope' in promoting practitioner reflection and analysis of such experiences. It argues that in such circumstances the school community looks to the headteacher to be the 'external reservoir of hope' for the institution, for 'hope' is what drives the school forward towards the delivery of the collective vision in the face of such external pressures, whilst allowing the school to remain true to its fundamental values. To act in a spiritual and moral leadership role, however, also requires the headteacher to have an 'internal reservoir of hope'. This internal reservoir provides more than what Hanvey (2008, 18) has termed "a space of resistance—a safe zone, free from demands and pressures; a sort of retreat at the end of the garden for the soul or the self", or what Lee (2005) calls "strategic sanctuary, far from the madding crowd" to provide space for strategic reflection. Rather it is the calm centre at the heart of the individual leader from which their vision and values flows, which motivates leadership actions, allows the continuance of effective inter-personal engagement and sustains personal and institutional self-belief in the face of external pressures.

This personal 'reservoir of hope' has to be periodically refilled by a variety of replenishment and sustainability strategies without which there will be burn out or drop out and headteachers will withdraw from the leadership arena 'when reservoirs run dry'. This research explores with the sample of 150 headteachers from a range of school contexts, including schools facing challenging circumstances and those of a religious character, the applicability of this metaphor 'reservoirs of hope' in promoting reflection on the value systems on which they base their leadership actions, the sustainability strategies and support structures on which they rely and the key messages which need to be transmitted to those charged with their ongoing professional development and support. From interviews and discussions with these 150 headteachers and 40 supporting educationists, it is possible to capture *inter alia* an authentic rendering of practitioner voice which, it can be argued, has value, significance and relevance both for fellow practitioners and educationists.

3.3. Validity and value

The research stands on an empirical base of interviews with 150 headteachers. It must be recognised, however, that the sample, whilst constructed to be as cross-sectionally representative as possible, nevertheless is an 'opportunity sample' gained from personal knowledge and peer recommendation. It is assumed, however, that this sample, which had a remarkable 97% positive participation response rate from a time-stressed profession not renowned for its collective enthusiasm in contributing to academic research, is at least as representative as one which might have been constructed by other means such as random postal sampling, where experience has shown considerably less willingness to engage. Equally, the main methodological tool was that of a one-to-one open-ended semi-structured interview with a fellow practitioner. Guided by the researcher as an erstwhile headteacher, these non-judgemental interviews promoted reflection on leadership journey, and espoused value system and critical incidents when that value system was tested under pressure. Unlike other studies previously referred to (Grace 2002; Day et al 2000), no formal attempt was made to triangulate the findings against the views of other members of the school community for whom the headteacher had accountability, because of concerns over confidentiality and openness of response, particularly as regards the often painful memories of critical incidents and the deep personal feelings of vulnerability which arose out of them. However, the views of some 40 supporting local, diocesan and national educationists were also sought in order to offer perspectives from beyond the headteacher community, together with informal triangulation from school observation visits, and the analysis of documentation such as school prospectuses and Ofsted inspection reports. In the case of a sub-set of those leading schools facing challenging circumstances, a small-scale quantitative analysis of dominant professional characteristics was also carried out to support the emerging findings from interview. Overall therefore, the validity of the data is assumed with some confidence.

Equally, the value of the emerging findings to the practitioner community is confidently asserted. Whilst the outcomes from the 150 non-triangulated headteacher interviews may be challenged as personalised and consequently the findings drawn from them as potentially less rigorous as a result, an account of the initial *Reservoirs of Hope* research associate report having received the 'accolade' of a press description from a former Chief Inspector of Schools as "pretty banal" research (Woodhead 2003), their capturing and analysis of practitioner voice has received significant and enthusiastic validation from both participants in the study and a wide cross-section of the headteacher and education community. Participants consistently reported, in respondent validation of the interview findings, the cathartic value of the guided reflection on critical incidents and the personal leadership journey that the interview process had offered, and appreciated the opportunity of cross-reference with the experience of others. This was rather sadly summed up in the words of one experienced male secondary headteacher (a genus not renowned for self-reflection and revelation) serving a challenging socially deprived area:

> *"It's very rare in a lonely job to have the time and be encouraged to talk about yourself, and not to an inspector or advisor or deputy, but to a fellow head...and for the first time in over 16 years of headship to feel that it's legitimate to do so."*

It is recognised, however, that the primary purpose of this research was not to provide catharsis for hard-pressed participating headteachers, but to generate messages on leadership that may be of value to the wider education community. Across that community there has been resonance with the findings as promulgated through articles and conferences. The original *Reservoirs of Hope* research associate report that provided the genesis of this present study is "amongst the most downloaded of all NCSL's research associate publications" (Coleman 2008), and feedback from subsequent conferences on it has shown that the metaphor on which it is based has become a valuable unifying concept in the promotion of headteacher reflection strategies. For example, one serving headteacher, a female primary headteacher, was moved to remark: *"I started reading it [the original* Reservoirs of Hope *report] and I couldn't put it down. The words leaped off the page because I could hear myself saying that"*. Equally the associated terminology has clearly entered the collective leadership vocabulary to the extent that a paper outlining it in the journal *Management in Education* (Flintham 2004) presently still remains as one of the 50 most cited articles from that publication (Sage Publications 2010).

To sum up, therefore, the present research study in its genesis, implementation and promulgation appears to have significant perceived value: on participants in providing cathartic reflection opportunities which have influenced subsequent leadership practice; on the wider practitioner community through the cross-fertilisation of leadership experiences and the lessons learned from them; and hopefully on policy makers through highlighting the importance of reflection opportunities, the power of networking strategies and the necessity for the legitimisation, facilitation and funding thereof.

4. The organisation of this study

4.1. Conceptual framework applied

The conceptual framework which underpins this study is that spiritual and moral leadership is the summation of three aspects: the 'what', 'how' and 'why' of leadership. The successful exercise of that leadership will clearly also require "contextual literacy" (NCSL 2007, 5), dependent on the socio-economic, demographic, cultural or historical parameters of the 'where' of the particular situation. The concern, however, is not only to capture the 'what' of school leadership, the implementation of leadership actions by headteachers as they operate within the specific contexts in which they are set, and the 'how' of school leadership as leaders deploy their management, teamworking and communication skills in the role of headteacher, but also the 'why' of school leadership, its motivation, meaning and purpose which underpins leadership action and which reveals the character and personal authenticity of the individual leader.

The leadership identity of the headteacher, his or her personal authenticity both in the eyes of self and others, is to be found at the confluence of context, role and character, in the synthesis of an internal harmony between the 'how' and the 'why', which is revealed in the 'what' of leadership actions as 'the talk is walked'. Such leadership actions need to be underpinned by both 'brains, heart and spirit' (developing Starratt 2003, 242), requiring not only cognitive intelligence—an ability in numerical, verbal and logical reasoning, honed by study and experience, which effectively enables the 'what' of delivery—but also emotional intelligence—a capacity to relate to, empathise and engage with the feelings of others whilst remaining in control of one's own emotions, the 'how' of leadership which enables effective inter-personal engagement to occur through caring relationships. Above all, however, there needs to be an underpinning of spiritual intelligence that allows a making sense of the world and one's role and purpose within it, and generates a set of values to inform and imbue leadership actions by providing the reason 'why'.

Spiritual and moral leadership, defined as 'a lived faith in action', also lies at the confluence of the 'why', the 'how' and the 'what'. The spirituality of an individual is formed by the 'why' of whatever faith system provides meaning and purpose to existence, 'how' that faith system is worked out in the relationships of life, and emanates in the 'what' of actions and experiences. Spirituality, which may be tethered to a particular tradition, untethered from it or determinedly secular, is therefore the admixture of 'being', 'relating' and 'doing'. Spiritual and moral leadership then draws on that spirituality as its 'why', is concerned with the sustainability of self and others as its 'how' and results in a strategy for 'what' should be done not only to deal with the immediate impact of critical incidents but also to make progress towards the achievement of the school's long-term goals, and to ensure the ongoing personal and corporate support of the leader and his or her colleagues as they continue to work towards that end. 'Being' is informed by faith and informs meaning and purpose, sustains values and is sustained by spiritual intelligence: the 'foundations of faith' of the leader. 'Relating' is informed by relationships that in turn inform the leader's role, and is sustained by emotional intelligence, the 'reservoir of hope' of the leader. 'Doing' draws on contextual awareness to inform leadership action and sustain progress and is sustained by self-belief as leaders serve their schools as 'labours of love'. This conceptual framework is summarised as Figure 1.1.

Osmer (2008) similarly identifies what he terms the 'descriptive-empirical task' of the leader with 'what' is going on in a particular situation, and the 'interpretative task' as 'why' it is going on, so that the 'pragmatic task' of leadership becomes 'how' the leader might respond. However, he also identifies the 'normative task' of what *ought* to be going on: a comparison of the complex and messy realities of actual leadership actions in the cockpit of events against the demands of trying to remain true to an espoused value system. It is therefore through a retelling of leadership story, and in particular a consideration of how personal value systems have been tested, deconstructed and reconstructed through the pressure of events, that leadership learning can occur. Opportunities for such consideration may be provided through the capacity regularly to be prepared to step back from the daily cascade of 'crises' and systemic pressures which are the school leader's lot and engage in reflection on critical incidents and epiphanies within personal leadership story.

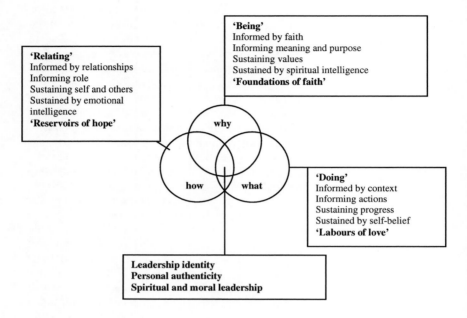

Fig. 1-1. Conceptual framework applied to spiritual and moral leadership

Such reflection opportunities may be self-generated but are better if facilitated by the support of a peer practitioner in a symbiotic model of mutually beneficial support. Starratt (2003, 236) sums this up well:

Learning takes place through storytelling… Learning the art of storytelling provides continuous practice of the grammar and rhetoric not only of one's language but also of the construction of one's life. Listening to the stories of others allows bridges to be built across the existential and cultural distances between the other. Their stories reveal the common human journey…nurture the development of imagination and the use of images and metaphors for understanding the human and natural worlds. Most of all, storytelling provides a foundation for conveying and exploring meaning…

Data collection for this research has captured the leadership stories of practitioners through semi-structured interviews that have encouraged guided reflection on the leadership journey, its meaning and purpose and the value system that has motivated and defined it. Interviews have had a reflective focus on critical incidents within individual leadership stories, stressing that such incidents are not necessarily of high level (although many selected by participants clearly were) but were of significance to the teller. In the daily life of the school leader, 'incidents' happen all the time but they only come to be regarded as 'critical' when those involved attach a particular significance to them, a significance engendered because the individual's value system has been put to the test, and from which leadership learning is seen to have occurred. As Tripp (1993, 8) has put it:

> Incidents happen, but critical incidents are produced by the way we look at a situation: a critical incident is an interpretation of the significance of an event. To take something as a critical incident is a value judgement we make, and the basis of that judgement is the significance we attach to the meaning of the incident.

Tripp (1993) suggests that a focus on such incidents in a structured and reflective way can facilitate the development of a personal 'grounded theory' (Glaser and Strauss 1967) which allows increased understanding to emerge from the analysis of the data revealed in story. In the interviews conducted for this research, the use of the metaphor 'reservoirs of hope' has both met this point by encouraging reflection on and analysis of critical incidents of significance to the practitioner, but also Starratt's point (2003, 13) referred to previously, that the use of images and metaphors can particularly promote understanding. From such analysis of leadership story can be drawn details of the effectiveness of the support and sustainability strategies used by practitioners in various school contexts in coping with both critical incidents and the equally challenging cumulative effects of day-to-day pressures.

4.2. An overview of the layout of the book

Chapter One: Outline of a study of spiritual and moral leadership

This chapter has set the scene for such an analysis of leadership story. It has identified in outline the concept of 'secular spirituality' as 'a lived faith', so that spiritual and moral leadership can be conceived of as 'a lived faith in action', a concept which can be used to engage in a discussion of such spiritual and moral leadership with practitioners of whatever faith perspective. It has indicated the perceived potential value of guided reflection in capturing from such discussions the detail of leadership story, and in particular the potential power of the metaphor 'reservoirs of hope' in facilitating such reflection by offering a ready visualisation of leadership behaviours and motivations. It has set out a conceptual framework based on the 'why', 'how' and 'what' aspects of leadership, which will be applied throughout the remainder of the book.

Chapter Two: Leadership and spirituality

This chapter reviews the literature in order to locate the research within the present canon of writings on school leadership and spirituality. It considers first various types of leadership in order to locate spiritual and moral leadership within a typography of leadership styles. It then explore definitions of spirituality in order to reach a generic concept of spirituality as "a lived faith" (Wakefield 2000, 686) from which can be developed the operational definition of spiritual and moral leadership as 'a lived faith in action' used throughout this book. Applying the overarching conceptual framework, it can be shown that this definition can be broken down into three components: faith as meaning which informs values (the 'why'); living as relationships informed by language (the 'how'); and the actions and experiences which inform the leadership story (the 'what') and how this can be related to leadership identity and personal authenticity. The concepts of leadership and spirituality are then brought together in a consideration of the spiritual and moral leadership of headteachers and the value of practitioner reflection on experience, facilitated through the medium of metaphor and story.

Chapter Three: Reservoirs of hope

In this chapter, the first of the three data chapters drawing on practitioner interviews that capture the leadership stories of headteachers, the focus is on the metaphor 'reservoirs of hope', arguing that spiritual and moral leadership is motivated by a spirituality of hope which results in an espoused value system which is sustained by reflection opportunities and underpinned by networks of belief and support, and which emanates in strategies to cope with critical incidents, day-to-day pressures and the vulnerabilities of school leadership over time. It contrasts virtues, the eternal verities that underpin existence, with contextual values and pragmatic vision. It considers how these are laid down in upbringing, formed by experience and influenced by habitus, habitat and hinterland, and how they are tested by critical incidents encompassing community tragedies, personnel problems and organisational crises. It identifies three categories of headteachers who have left headship early either as 'striders', 'strollers' or 'stumblers', and postulates a new category of 'sprinter' post-modernist portfolio headteachers. It explores the belief networks, support networks and external networks which headteachers use to sustain themselves in spiritual and moral leadership as they pay the 'price' of the 'privilege' of school principalship.

Chapter Four: Foundations of faith

This chapter explores the 'foundations of faith' of samples of school leaders who lead their schools from a personal perspective of faith, ranging from Anglican to Atheist, Buddhist to Humanist, Catholic to Charismatic. It considers those intra-faith leaders working in schools that are of a similar religious tradition to their own, those inter-faith leaders who operate within a different faith milieu and those whose extra-faith role is in the secular sphere. It investigates the sense of call to service in particular communities and the bases of belief in inclusion, invitation and social justice, respect, redemption and renewal on which that service stands. It codifies the attributes that are seen to be required, namely courage, vision and capacity together with 'reserves of resilience'. It explores the motivational driver of the 'passion' to make a difference, the leadership 'power' that can be applied, and the 'progress' outcomes that ensue. However, it is argued that it is in the motivation, or the reason 'why', drawn from the espoused individual faith perspective and the fluency with which it is expressed in the language of faith, that provides the essential difference in such leaders.

Chapter Five: Labours of love

In this chapter, the focus is on those who feel called to the leadership of schools facing particularly challenging circumstances as 'labours of love'. It shows that these leaders are motivated above all by a set of core values that are people-centred and founded on moral purpose. These values inform a leadership approach which is based on challenge and collaboration, respect and relationships. Such leaders place a high value on the pursuit of excellence no matter what the circumstances. They are motivated by a strong belief system and a vision of a better future, a passion to see progress, a tenacity in pursuing it and a willingness to take calculated risks to bring it about. From both qualitative interview and quantitative professional characteristics data, it is possible to show that the leaders of such schools are highly self-confident and have highly developed inter-personal skills of teamworking, trust and empathy, which generate small but highly significant incremental steps of successful progress, representing 'success against the odds'.

Chapter Six: Hope springs eternal

This chapter offers a theological reflection on hope as revealed in the spiritual and moral leadership of headteachers that has been explored in the preceding three data chapters. This is done through the lens of practical theology to show that a 'theology of hope' looks not only towards future things but also informs leadership actions in the present. Applying the theological concepts of kerygma, kenosis and koinonia to the central metaphor 'reservoirs of hope', it argues that a message of hope is the essential motivation for spiritual and moral leadership, the source reservoir of leadership action as the leader is prepared to empty himself or herself in the service of others, but is replenished by the development of a network of sustaining relationships. It explores concepts of the Golden Rule, redemption and covenantal relationships, and the need for a bilingual capacity in expressing them.

Chapter Seven: Last things

In the concluding chapter, three key messages are identified which have emerged from the research regarding spiritual and moral leadership; namely, the importance of vision in providing the motivational 'why' of leadership, the value of reflection as a mechanism to maintain the vision and faith of the school leader and the necessity for renewal from sustainability strategies predicated on networks of support which build community. It concludes by arguing that, given present recruitment and retention pressures in school headship, a focus on the importance of spiritual and moral leadership, driven by hope, underpinned by faith and sustained by networks of love, is timely in supporting and developing both the school leaders of the present generation and those who are to come after them.

Running throughout this book, however, is the theme of 'hope', as an essential component of and motivator for spiritual and moral leadership as headteachers act as 'reservoirs of hope' for their schools. Hope provides for the hard-pressed headteacher not only a source of support when faced with critical incidents and day-to-day disturbances, but is also a powerful antidote to the systemic pressures of an accountability culture which threatens to squeeze them into what Hargreaves (2003, xvi-xvii) has called "the tunnel vision of test scores, achievement targets and league tables... obsessed with improving and micro-managing curriculum uniformity...in place of ambitious missions of comparison and community". Hope in a vision of a better future, "not in terms of great projects but in its vision of and attention to the human person" (Hanvey 2008, 35), springs eternal from the 'foundations of faith' of school leaders, and informs their leadership 'labours of love' in the present, no matter what its challenging circumstances. The leadership stories and life histories of the 150 headteachers interviewed which are drawn on in the chapters which follow are imbued with such hope, making, in Seamus Heaney's powerful words (1990, 80), "hope and history rhyme".

CHAPTER TWO

LEADERSHIP AND SPIRITUALITY

Introduction

This chapter seeks to locate the concept of spiritual and moral leadership within the context of present thinking regarding both school leadership and spirituality, by drawing on a wide range of writings on these topics from the UK, USA and Australia. The first part of this chapter begins by considering various *types of leadership*, in order to locate moral leadership within a typography of leadership styles ranging from instructional leadership to participative leadership. It then develops an understanding of moral leadership as being rooted in the values and ethics of leaders themselves, which results in leadership behaviours consistent with those values. Finally, it suggests that such moral leadership may be infused with a spiritual dimension, which can be enhanced by reflexive practice and is seen to emanate in effective inter-personal relationships.

The second part of the chapter moves on to explore *definitions of spirituality*, with four stages in this part of the argument. First, it considers the difficulties of arriving at an agreed definition of the term. It then draws a distinction between spirituality and religious belief, arguing for a concept of 'secular spirituality' that is not grounded in a particular theological perspective or faith community but is the basic framework of belief and understanding of reality held by the individual, irrespective of its source. It explores metaphors that may be used to illuminate this concept of spirituality. Finally, it arrives at a working definition of spirituality as 'a lived faith', and explores this in terms of its three facets of meaning, relationships and experiences, and shows how these reinforce each other to generate the *gestalt* of personal authenticity.

In the third part of the chapter the concepts of leadership and spirituality are brought together by considering the *spiritual and moral leadership* of headteachers. First, it is argued that the essence of such leadership can best be captured by practitioner reflection on experience that is facilitated through the medium of metaphor and story. Second, the metaphor 'reservoirs of hope' to facilitate such reflection is developed, by considering both the requirement on the school leader to act as the 'external reservoir of hope' for the institution, preserving the coherence of its vision and values, its raison d'être or meaning, in the face of challenging experiences, and the necessity for the leader to sustain and replenish an 'internal reservoir of hope' in order to maintain personal authenticity and integrity of self-belief in the face of external pressures. Third, it explores the outworkings of spiritual and moral leadership as shown in relationships within the school community, drawing a distinction between contractual relationships and covenantal relationships within a 'community of connectivity'. Finally, it is argued that reflection on leadership stories and in particular on critical incidents within them is not only a source of professional learning for the individual concerned, but also that when couched in appropriate professional language, it can reveal the underlying values base, support structures and nexus of relationships from which personal and collective sustainability can be drawn, to the benefit of other school leaders and those charged with their professional development and support.

1. Leadership

It has been alleged that there are more than 350 extant definitions of leadership but no clear and unequivocal understanding of what distinguishes leaders from non-leaders (Cuban 1988, 190). Indeed, some have argued that as leadership is such a complex human activity, it might actually be unwise to narrow its scope unnecessarily by attempting too prescriptive a definition (Leithwood et al 1999). Fortunately, in exploring what has been termed "the swamp of literature on leadership" (Hodgkinson 1993, cited in Day et al 2000, 7), it has proved possible to categorise this plethora of definitions into a number of broad themes (Bush and Glover 2003) within a typography of leadership definitions. This builds on the work of Leithwood et al (1999) that argues that all such definitions have in common the two core functions of leadership—that of determining direction and exercising influence. Direction is determined by the synthesis and maintenance of a collective vision for the development of the organisation; influence is exercised through mobilising and working with others to achieve shared goals.

1.1. Types of leadership

The following leadership types, within which can be located the area of spiritual and moral leadership (which is the focus of this present study) demonstrate the two core functions of direction and influence in varying balance and degree.

Instructional leadership is defined as being concerned primarily with impacting directly on the *behaviour* of teachers as they engage in activities that affect student growth (Leithwood et al 1999, 8). This behaviour can be defined in the narrow sense of activities directly related to teaching and learning within the classroom. However, it also has the broader sense of encompassing the impact of organisational variables such as school culture, the interlocking organisational system of beliefs, ideas, values, attitudes, meanings, symbols, rituals and behaviours (Tuohy 1999, 10) that may be summed up as "the way we do things round here" (Day et al 2000, 20). The concept of instructional leadership can also include a concern for the professional learning of teachers as well as students (Southworth 2002), and its scope can be widened to include a strategic perspective on all leadership activities and the deployment of the resources to underpin them (Geltner and Shelton 1991, 339).

However, within an educational climate in which there is a dominant concern for standards and the meeting of accountability targets laid down by externally imposed policy decisions, the role of instructional leader may transmute into that of 'managing director', with parents seen as 'consumers' and the educational outcomes as 'product' (Grace 1995, 21). The possibility then arises of the growth of *managerial leadership* within the skills-based approach to leadership as critiqued by Sullivan (2003), and an overriding concern for operational and systems issues: for 'doing things right' rather than 'doing the right things' (West-Burnham 1997).

Transformational leadership is the means by which leaders exert their *influence* on teachers so as implicitly to impact on student learning. Such leadership seeks to build a unified common interest between leaders and so-called 'followers' (Gunter 2001, 69) in which leaders seek to capture the support of teachers for their vision for the school, and to engage and mobilise their efforts towards its realisation by enhancing the collective capacity to achieve it. Whilst not in direct opposition to *transactional leadership*, which is based on what has been called the exchange relationship between leader and follower (Leithwood 1992) in which there is an exchange of services for rewards within a structured system, memorably summarised in the term 'leadership by bargaining' (Sergiovanni 1991, 125), transformational leadership builds on and raises the concept beyond that of reward to that of motive. Thus the characteristics of transformational leadership are seen (Yukl 2002) to be focused around the concept of *vision* and how it might be achieved and the necessity to articulate that vision in a clear and compelling manner, to explain to colleagues how it can be attained and to empower them to achieve it. It should be noted, however, that even when collectively subscribed to, the genesis of the vision and its communication remains with the leader, and might therefore be seen as a vehicle of control rather than empowerment, more likely to be accepted by the leader than by those being led.

Northouse (2000) sees transformational leadership as a personality trait rather than a behaviour that can be learned, and Coleman (1996, 2002), researching gender differences in headteachers of English secondary schools, concludes that women headteachers are more likely than men to display the behaviours associated with transformational leadership. However, Baron-Cohen (2003) argues not in terms of sexual identity but in relation to perceived type of brain, drawing the distinction between empathising brains, on average but not exclusively found in females, and systematising brains, more often found in males. The empathising brain seeks to identify with another's emotions and thoughts and respond to them with an appropriate emotional response. The systematising brain, however, is more concerned to analyse, explore and predict system outcomes. Baron-Cohen argues that those of whatever gender possessed of more empathising brains tend to be attracted to the caring professions, including teaching. It is perhaps possible that there is a higher concentration to be found in schools facing challenging circumstances. However, in spite of their highly developed language, communication and listening skills, it might be felt that such transformational leaders may lack the 'ruthless edge' to survive and prosper in a target-driven accountability culture. Conversely, it has been argued (Allix 2000) that even 'soft-edged' transformational leadership has the power to become despotic because of its strong, heroic and charismatic features. Such features may raise moral qualms about its appropriateness for democratic organisations. It remains highly arguable, however, whether schools can ever fully be regarded as falling within the descriptive category of a 'democratic organisation'.

Nevertheless, *participative leadership*, an approach concerned with the concept of shared or distributed leadership within a collegiate structure, can form a useful corrective to a heroic interpretation of transformational leadership by being seen "to locate power with the many and not just the few" (Harris 2002b, 11). Even within this style of leadership, however, whilst there may be improved outcomes through greater perceived ownership and commitment to the implementation of shared decisions, there remains the necessity for the leader to hold in balance the individual goals and pictures of the future within the envelope of the shared vision with its shared purposes and values. This requires of the leader, fuelled by "a vision of possibilities" (Starratt 1993, 57), a degree of overarching systems thinking: the capacity to recognise patterns and understand the connectedness of individual human actions and reactions. This capacity for systems thinking has been called 'the fifth discipline' of the learning organisation (Senge 1990), which integrates the other four identified disciplines of building a shared vision, creating mental models, promoting team learning and achieving personal mastery. Without the maintenance of such an underpinning cohesive vision for the system within a *post-modernist leadership* context in which career trajectories are increasingly lateral, non-linear and time-limited, a variety of skill sets are offered and deployed, and portfolio perspectives to career development applied, the diversity of subjective interpretations, multiplicity of experiences and variety of mind-sets of individual stakeholders can lead to fragmentation, dissonance and lack of direction which outweigh the inclusive benefits of wider participation in decision making.

1.2. Moral leadership

Moral leadership is rooted in the *values* and ethics of the leaders themselves. Sullivan (1997) argues that the articulation, promotion, defence and reconciliation of such values are at the very heart of the headteacher's work. Bass and Steidlmeier (1999) assert that to be truly transformational, leadership must be grounded in such moral foundations. The moral character of the leader is displayed in their attitude towards self and others, the awareness of the ethical values that underpin the vision and their articulation of it, and the analysis of the morality of the actions that stem from it. Such characteristics have been described as higher-order perspectives (West-Burnham 1997), demanding of the leader a basis of self-awareness which is revealed in moral confidence: the capacity to act, in extent and over time, often instinctively, in a way which is consistent with an underlying ethical system. West-Burnham asserts that inter-personal intelligence, "the authentic range of intuitive behaviours derived from sophisticated self-awareness, which facilitate effective engagement with others" (West-Burnham 2001, 2), is the vital medium which permeates all models of leadership, and that its application is a moral issue as much as a means of efficient communication. Behaviours and actions arising from such inter-personal intelligence become manifestations of the moral perspective underpinning it, and reveal the personal authenticity of the individual leader through congruence with a coherent personal philosophy.

1.3. A spiritual dimension to moral leadership

Bush and Glover (2003, 17), in their survey and extension of the Leithwood typography, indicate that "moral leadership is based in the values and beliefs of leaders. The approach is similar to the transformational model but with a stronger values base that *may be spiritual*" (emphasis added). Whilst accepting that leaders may adopt and adapt different leadership styles showing a *contingent leadership* response to the particular organisational circumstances they face, it is argued in this present study that 'spiritual', albeit defined in a wide-ranging and all-encompassing secular sense, is indeed an essential component of such a moral approach to school leadership.

If personal morality is encapsulated in the underpinning ethical principles which guide leadership actions, and which have become personally valid and meaningful for the individual leader as they lead the organisation in their charge, then moral leadership can be defined as leadership behaviour which is consistent with those personal and organisational values, which are then in turn derived from a coherent ethical system (West-Burnham 2000, 4). As such, however, this ethical system might be viewed at worst as a static set of parameters which provide a moral template within which leadership actions can validly take place, but from which no new learning, growth or development ensues. A spiritual dimension to moral leadership, however, locates it within the dynamic search for meaning in life, as we journey through it seeking personal growth, wholeness and fulfilment. It is shaped by experiences of suffering and struggle, and enhanced by celebrations of joy and success, and refined by space to reflect on history and relationships, within self-experience and in the stories of others.

Moral leadership infused with this spiritual dimension then becomes the ability to rise above the functional mode of leadership with its time-framed focus on control and delivery, to a transcendent mode of leadership with time for reflection, listening and consolidation, which will deepen an awareness of the authentic self and provide a greater sense of self-fulfilment (Neylan 2005). The challenge of spiritual-infused leadership is to reconcile the insistent demands of functional leadership with the finding of time and space to operate in the transcendent mode or, as Sergiovanni (1991, 329) has put it, "to make peace with two conflicting imperatives: the managerial and the moral". Duignan (2003) argues that it is necessary for a leader first to influence the self through a habit of (transcendent) reflexive practice in order to become a 'capable human being' rather than a competent (functional) administrator. Starratt (2003, 243) also focuses on the importance of leaders taking account of themselves 'on the inside' in questioning their deepest convictions and truest values, so that this 'inner work of leadership' can positively affect their outer work when faced with challenging external pressures (Moxley 2000).

Such reflection opportunities can provide a stability within the turbulence of events and pressures of demands but can also give the inner confidence to recognise strengths, weaknesses and developmental needs, thus facilitating the possibility of personal change, development and growth. In addition, however, such reflection also provides an opportunity to discern the gifts of others, and through a model of distributed leadership underpinned by mutually supportive relationships, can enable the gifting of opportunities to colleagues not only to further their own spiritual development but also to contribute more fully to the collective endeavour to secure the corporate vision, and by so doing enhance also the possibility of organisational change, development and growth.

Whilst the primary task of the school must be learning-centred, such learning can only be achieved within the context of relationships. For Duignan (2003, 14) "relationship is an organisational dynamic that is at the very heart of leadership". The school leader therefore needs to be skilled in leadership approaches that are both learning-centred (through instructional leadership) and inter-personal (through transformational leadership). It has been suggested (Williams 2001, 1) that these are in fact "two sides of the same coin: good relationships without a focus on the core business of teaching and learning will achieve little; a determined emphasis on pedagogy is unlikely to succeed without quality relationships". However, it can further be argued that spiritual and moral leadership is 'the edge of the coin', the binding force that holds together the learning-centred and inter-personal facets, without which vision is fragmented, values sacrificed and development hindered.

Before considering further such spiritual and moral leadership and how it is evident in the experience and practice of serving school leaders, however, it is necessary to consider definitions of spirituality that may underpin it.

2. Spirituality

2.1. Problems of definition

Establishing an agreed and workable definition of spiritual and moral leadership requires a consideration of the underpinning concept of spirituality. This is in turn as handicapped by the difficulty in finding agreement over the meaning of this term in the context of a largely post-modernist, non-professing pluralist culture as was the attempt to synthesise a working definition of the term 'leadership'.

Milacci (2006, 213) traces the etymological surfacing of the term from its historical and theological roots in the word 'spirit' (from the Greek word *pneumatikos*, expounded by Schweizer 1968) with its connotations of invisibility and power (Vine 1966, 64) and its intrinsic distinction yet at the same time indivisibility from that which is physical, secular and material. He recognises, however, a recent trend to construct a vaguer notion of spirituality designed to be more palatable to a wider readership by its decontextualisation from religion, which, whilst making the concept more accessible, has actually served in his view "to evacuate the term, leaving it with no real meaning" or to make it much easier for the term "to be co-opted, commodified [sic] and misused" (Milacci 2006, 214).

Sheldrake (1992, 32) also agrees that, "spirituality is one of those subjects whose meaning everyone claims to know until they have to define it". Wakefield (2000, 685) agrees that:

> Spirituality is a term much in vogue: it sounds significant, with a touch of mystery, seeming to allow escape from the intellectual quest and wearisome wrestling with mental problems. We turn with relief from theology to spirituality, but may find ourselves enmeshed in a bewildering variety of techniques, or excitedly following a trail leading nowhere.

For Wakefield (2000, 686) "in the end, spirituality is not a technique but a lived faith". As such it is not amenable to precise formal definition, but is rather recognised in its outworkings. Spiritual and moral leadership may thus be considered as 'a lived faith in action', the operational definition that will be used throughout this book. For Cottingham (2005) also far more important is the 'primacy of praxis', the embarking on a path of practical self-transformation rather than engaging in intellectual debate or philosophical analysis around definitions.

2.2. The concept of 'secular spirituality'

In spite of Milacci's expressed concerns about the decoupling of spirituality from religion, it is important to stress that the concept of individual spirituality used within this study is not necessarily tied to a particular theological perspective or grounded in a specific religious belief or faith community. As Byers (1992, 6) has cogently put it: "religions are particular answers to the universal human questions about the meaning of life. Spirituality refers to the universal personal concern for the questions". Equally for Tisdall (2000, 309, cited in Milacci 2006, 228), spirituality is not the same as religion: "religion is an organised community of faith that has written codes of regulatory behaviour whereas spirituality is more about one's personal belief and experience of a higher power or purpose". However, for Milacci (2006, 229), whilst the terms 'spirituality' and 'religion' are not identical, they are closely connected in that they both focus on foundations, fundamentals and foundational core beliefs. The danger perceived by Halstead (2003) is, however, that if the concept of spirituality becomes too closely associated with religion and its public or private practices, it may then exclude those who feel themselves to be outside that particular religious belief system. Given the aim of examining spiritual and moral leadership across all sections of the headteacher community, this is a powerful point to be borne in mind.

The decoupling of spirituality from organised religion is seen within a national picture of 'self-defined spirituality', a situation which has been memorably termed 'believing not belonging' (Davie 1994), where spirituality is accepted as a common human phenomenon which can include, but is not limited by, organised religion. Surveys repeatedly reveal that whilst less than 9% of the population are active churchgoers, 71% would still nevertheless identify themselves as 'Christian', with only 15.5% declaring themselves as being of 'no religious belief' (2001 Census). Equally, whereas 63% would not describe themselves as 'religious', with 43% saying they never attend religious services (*The Guardian*/ICM survey, December 2006), only 12% are willing to be put into the category 'not a spiritual person' (Opinion Research Business Survey December 1999).

For many, whilst the practices and language of the faith communities have no meaning, spirituality is still captured through moments of insight in nature, art or human love (Harries 2002). For others, whilst a motivational connection between religion and an ethical value system may have been broken, the ethical system still remains, albeit divorced from any concept of the commandments of a higher being in what has been termed a 'godless morality' (Holloway 1999). Some continue to hold to a 'religiously untethered spirituality' (McLaughlin 2003) as a subscription to a spiritual ideology without the avocation of a particular religious framework. Overall, therefore, it should be noted that even for those who do not espouse a religious faith or actively practise it, or have even a concept of a higher sacred being, there still remains possible an underpinning inclusive spirituality, that has been termed 'secular spirituality' (West-Burnham 2001, echoing a term possibly first used by Robinson in *Honest to God* (1963, 94) and further chronicled by Crossman (2003, 505) as "a shorthand for non-denominational faith or non-partisan spirituality") which can nevertheless espouse a system of beliefs and code of moral *values* which provide a personal paradigm for living, a moral prism through which the world is experienced and an implicit underpinning philosophy of ensuing praxis. Mohler (2005, 42) agrees that, "every individual is a person of *some* faith, even if that faith is secular. All persons operate out of some basic framework of beliefs and understanding of reality".

2.3. Metaphors of spirituality

In the absence of a universally accepted definition of spirituality other than a generic 'lived faith in action', most attempts to capture those diverse frameworks of belief therefore take refuge in the realm of active metaphor. Such metaphors are based around words such as searching, striving, journeying and withdrawing.

Zohar and Marshall (2000), following Frankel (1959, reprinted 2004), talk of the *search* for meaning that makes us the spiritual creatures we are and determines our subsequent behaviours. Haldane (2003) asserts that the spiritual is essentially concerned with how individuals experience the world and how they make sense of that experience by searching for meaning within it. Spirituality then becomes searching for the ultimate truth about the human condition and cultivating an appropriate mode of 'being' or 'doing' in response to the discovery of that truth.

Murray and Zentner (1988, 259), coming from a medical perspective, focus on critical life-changing moments where there is a similar *striving* for understanding. They state that:

> Spirituality is a quality that goes beyond religious affiliation...striving for inspiration, reverence, awe, meaning and purpose, even in those who do not believe in any good. The spiritual dimension tries to be in harmony with the universe, strives for understanding about the infinite and comes into focus when the person faces emotional stress, physical illness and death.

West-Burnham (2002, 3) describes spirituality in terms of the *journey* to find an understanding of the self which can thus inform future actions: "spirituality is the journey to find a sustainable authentic and profound understanding of the existential self which informs personal and social action". He argues that spirituality is the ultimate human journey, the means by which we develop selfhood and the realisation of our potential to be human. He tracks the significant stages of that journey, marked by the pivotal movement from the external to the internal, and with growth in personal authenticity developed through reflection, ethical purpose, wisdom and ultimately transcendence.

Moran (2002) develops further the concept of journeying by reflecting on the individual journey that school leaders make 'from shadow to light' in leading their schools. Both he and West-Burnham argue that the various facets of the journey require the opportunity for *withdrawing* from the activity of journeying to engage in the 'inner work of self-discovery' (Ackerman and Maslin-Ostrowski 2002), creating time and space for reflection and internal sustenance in a rhythm of withdrawal and renewal: "time on the balcony as well as time on the dance floor" (Munby 2005, after Heifetz and Linksy 2002), which can then emanate in personal development and social engagement. Lee (2005) has described this withdrawal into a reflective space as "strategic sanctuary...far from the madding crowd" which may be found in the 'safe space' of a particular school where it is safe to be vulnerable and explore (Terry 2005, 2), or in "the sacred spaces of everyday life" (Crouch 2005). These spaces, unique to each individual, be they riverbank or garden shed, headteacher's study or off-site location, can thus facilitate the translation of 'being' into 'becoming', 'longing' into 'belonging', 'landscape' into 'inscape' and 'authority' into 'authenticity'.

2.4. A working definition of spirituality

The School Curriculum and Assessment Authority (1995, 3, cited in Smith 1999), in discussing spiritual and moral development, does, however, attempt to go beyond metaphor, and usefully maps the territory by asserting that:

> The term [spirituality] needs to be seen as applying to something fundamental in the human condition which is not necessarily experienced through the physical senses and/or expressed through everyday language. It has to do with *relationships* with other people and for believers, with God. It has to do with the universal search for individual identity—with our responses to *challenging experiences* such as death, suffering, beauty, and encounters with good and evil. It has to do with the *search for meaning* and purpose in life and for *values by which to live*. (emphasis added)

The emphasised terms resonate with a definition of spirituality as 'a lived faith', and thus spiritual and moral leadership as '*a lived faith in action*', with living being predicated on relationships, faith being seen in the individual search for meaning, and both emanating in appropriate actions and behaviours when faced with diverse experiences. There is also congruence with the previously outlined concept (West-Burnham 2001) of inter-personal intelligence, as shown in moral leadership which is concerned with effective engagement with others (*relationships*), is based on a firm foundation of sophisticated self-awareness (in a concern for individual identity and the search for *meaning*) and is underpinned by a moral confidence to act in accordance with an underlying ethical system (a set of values by which to live) when faced with critical incidents (challenging *experiences*) and day-to day pressures.

Meaning, experiences and relationships may be seen to interact to generate a concept of *personal authenticity*: what it is to be a person, to be human. The search for meaning informs the values by which one lives, the experiences one has informs the stories which one tells and through which one strives to make sense of the world, and the building of relationships, underpinned by language both verbal and non-verbal, generates a nexus of interdependent mutual support. The *gestalt* of these factors is personal authenticity, as shown in Figure 2.1 (developed from West-Burnham and Ireson 2005, 17):

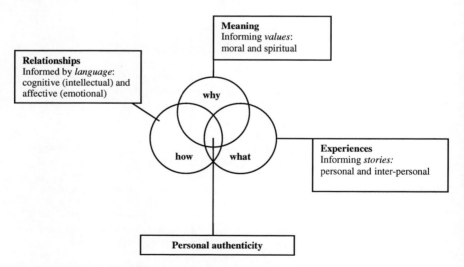

Fig. 2-1. Conceptual framework applied to personal authenticity

Each of these factors: meaning (the 'why', informing values), relationships (the 'how', informed by language) and experiences (the 'what' of leadership actions expressed in leadership stories) and how together they contribute to the development of personal authenticity, are now considered in turn.

Meaning, informing our values

Fundamental to a spiritual approach to leadership, and indeed to life, is therefore not only a concern with the means of living (the 'how') but also with the *meaning* of living (the 'why'), as we seek to locate our lives within some larger, meaning-giving context. Such an approach allows us to aspire beyond ourselves and the present moment in order to give our actions a sense of ultimate worth (Zohar and Marshall 2000), and allows us to transcend physical constraints and external pressures. In Nietzsche's words: "He who has a 'why' to live for can bear with almost any 'how'" (cited in Frankel 1959, reprinted 2004, 84).

Man's search for meaning has therefore been described (Frankel 1959, reprinted 2004, 104) as the primary motivation in life. This meaning is unique and specific to the individual, in that it must and can be fulfilled by him or her alone; only then can it achieve a significance that will satisfy his or her own 'will' to meaning. The search for meaning may be towards a deeper awareness of self, or it may be towards something higher than ourselves, so that spirituality becomes living out not only a set of deeply held personal values, but of honouring a presence greater than ourselves (Block 1993). Wherever that meaning is found for the individual, it provides 'foundations of faith' which permit the translation of their moral and spiritual paradigm into a coherent and meaningful set of personal constructs as values to inform future action.

Schneiders (1990) distinguishes between two referents of spirituality: as a fundamental dimension of 'being', and as the lived experience that actualises that dimension. Underpinning this is the belief that all human beings are capable of transcendence, a call to some higher value or meaning. That transcendence may then be felt through the experience of "self-surrender" (Evans 1993, 3) to a higher being in a theistic spirituality, or through 'self-separation' in an aesthetic experience of "super-sensible realities" (Wakefield 1983, 361) such as beauty, love and joy found in creation, relationships, art and music, within a framework of naturalistic spirituality, leading to a more unified and deeper awareness of the self through having gone out of oneself and beyond oneself, in what Macquarrie (1992, 45) has called "exience". The spiritual then becomes that dimension of life which underpins and complements its physical and psychological facets to provide that inner meaning, and to motivate a yearning towards a higher self, be it a deeper realisation of one's inner self or a search for communion with a higher being, in what has been termed "the self-transcendence of human existence" (Frankel 1959, reprinted 2004, 115).

And that self-transcendence may then impact on our attitudes towards others in our networks of interdependence with them. It may be revealed in a spirit of self-effacement, self-giving and self-emptying (kenosis) in a model of 'servant leadership' (Greenleaf 1977) which eschews a hierarchical approach in favour of an emphasis on collaboration, trust, and empathy (Spears 1998) and a move as "the servant leader from hero to host" (Wheatley 2002) to meet the mutuality of need, even if that means displaying one's own vulnerability, apparent weakness and 'woundedness' in the process (Nouwen 1994). It is also equally revealed in the community (koinonia) displayed through our relationships. The theological concepts of kenosis and koinonia are explored further in Chapter Six.

Relationships, informed by our language

Personal authenticity, or 'being true to oneself' (Taylor 1991) requires the symbiotic interaction of those same two contributory factors identified as components of moral leadership: an awareness of *self* as one of the 15 essential marks of a person (Fletcher 1979) and a capacity to reciprocate in *relationships* with *others* (Dennett 1988). Thus intra-personal self-awareness through a capacity to know yourself from the inside as no-one else will ever know you (Crosby 1996) needs to be balanced by confidence in inter-personal relationships, shown not only in a capacity to communicate and to relate to others, but to be motivated also by an empathic concern for them, shown through a display of emotional intelligence in understanding and responding to their needs (Goleman 1996) in "a tender network of interdependence" (Tutu 1999, 21), which is underpinned by a moral and ethical intention to produce a beneficial outcome (Arnold 2005, 25).

That concern becomes evident in how we communicate both verbally and non-verbally in those relationships with those who are seen as 'significant others', those who really matter to us:

> We become full human agents, capable of understanding ourselves and hence defining an identity through our acquisition of rich human languages of expression. No one acquires the languages needed for self-definition on their own; we are introduced to them through exchanges with others who matter to us. (Taylor 1991, 33)

To express ourselves in those relationships requires us to develop a personal *language* which allows the expression of both the affective (the emotions) and the cognitive (the intellectual) and which permits the capacity not only to communicate and converse in appropriately meaningful and empathetic dialogue with others, but also to have a language which facilitates an engagement in productive reflective internal dialogue with ourselves. And that language then permits effective reflection both on our experiences and the underpinning meaning of them by providing a vehicle for their expression through the medium of story.

Experiences, expressed in our stories

Such reflection on our underlying values and the acquisition of the language to permit the articulation of them to ourselves and others then influences our behaviours: the 'what' of leadership actions when faced with *challenging experiences*, be they high-level critical incidents or lower-level day-to-day pressures which reveal our values, so that 'what we believe and what we say influences what we do'.

Our language and our behaviours interact to create what Guignon has termed "our story-shaped selves", which in turn influence our articulation of our challenging experiences, not as mere anecdote or narrative but as 'story' in which the process of articulation can reveal our core values and inner meanings.

> As we impart meaning to events by telling them to ourselves and others, so we are constantly imparting cohesiveness and coherence to our lives by enacting a life story in our actions...we are not just tellers of a story, we are something told, we are a telling. (Guignon 2004, 126)

The development of personal authenticity thus becomes an unfolding *story*: a project (according to Guignon, 2004, 146) which requires both internal self-reflection and external expression, an inward turning of getting in touch with one's inner feelings, desires and beliefs and then expressing them in the external events and relationships in which one engages, and by so doing defining and realising one's own identity as a person. For Savage (2005, 45), "story is probably the biggest form of security we have as humans. It is very powerful in giving you identity", and for Gardner (1995, 42), stories are "uniquely powerful currency in human relationships". Thus *personal authenticity* has both a personal dimension in its concern for inner integrity and also a social dimension in its sense of relational belonging and indebtedness to the wider social context that makes it possible. In essence, we define ourselves and our inner integrities through our relationships and the telling of the stories of the experiences that have formed us.

Stories give coherence to the confusion of our experience and enable us to seek meaning within it (Armstrong 2006). For Faulks (2006), consciousness is the ability to tell our story to ourselves; for Bakewell (2005) it is in the nature of consciousness to explain itself in stories to others. Claxton (2005, 2) considers that "the telling of stories is the survival strategy that perhaps more than any other distinguishes our species". It is the contention of this present study that the telling of leadership stories not only to ourselves but to others, using a common professional language synthesised from shared backgrounds and experiences, and the mutual reflection on the relationships and values which underpin them, is not only a cathartic 'survival strategy' for school leaders but also allows the acquisition of 'leadership consciousness' alongside the development of personal authenticity through self-knowledge.

The telling of such stories and their analysis, interpretation and utilisation can provide effective vehicles of communication, learning and leadership in organisational life (Gabriel 2000). They may also be valuable in the development of future leaders by connecting theory with actual experience and practice (Danzig 1999). Sergiovanni (2001) applies a reflective practice perspective to draw out the stories of 'successful principals' to create an in-depth understanding of the roles and images of leadership. Loader (1997, 3), in a revealing narrative reflection on his own inner journey as principal, is concerned with the personal emotional burden of principalship and would support Beatty in calling for more narrative reflection "to break the silence about the emotional realities of leadership" (Beatty 2000, 335).

As personal authenticity is a synthesis between the two dimensions of internal integrity and social responsibility, between 'being' and 'doing' (Nouwen 1994), so authentic leadership (after Duignan and Bhindi 1997) then becomes the ability to develop relationships based on those inner ontological values of respect, care and compassion developed through the habit of reflexive practice, and to elevate human interactions based on them to new and higher levels of motivation and morality. Such leaders earn the allegiance of their followers through authentic actions and interactions in trusting relationships and through the shaping of organisational structures, processes and practices that enshrine those core values and ethical standards, so that authenticity in leadership can elevate the actions of the leader above mere pragmatics or expediency (Duignan 2003) to imbue them with a moral and ethical dimension. Authentic leadership may then be conceived (Begley 2001, 353) as "a metaphor for professionally effective, ethically sound and consciously reflective practice".

3. Spiritual and moral leadership

3.1. The value of metaphor in promoting reflection on leadership story

Capturing the essence of spiritual and moral leadership in schools from the reflective experiences of their leaders can best be done through the medium of *metaphor* and *story*. To find an acceptable metaphor with resonance for hard-worked professionals and to facilitate reflection on leadership stories which will bring out their nexus of relationships and underpinning value system requires a shared professional language and a foundation of mutual experience and empathy: a commonality of both the language of leadership story and the landscape of leadership experience.

Whilst it has been argued (Halstead 2003) that metaphors provide an essential tool for conceptualising spirituality by providing scope for exploring abstract spiritual ideas through stimulation of the imagination, metaphors of spirituality conceived as a search for meaning or a journey towards identity are felt by many school leaders to be couched in abstract language somewhat remote from the day-to-day exigencies of school life. What is felt to be more valuable would be a more accessible metaphor which can be readily called to mind and can focus on the spiritual and moral aspects of school leadership to permit both a reflective understanding of the external implications of that leadership and its impact on the internal wellbeing of the leader.

Beare (2004) has surveyed the management metaphors that leaders use to describe their schools. He argues that an image or metaphor is valuable in revealing how we can understand the working of an organisation by making comparisons to something found in nature that can be readily visualised. Such a metaphor, used recurrently, can then enter the language of leadership, and provide a way of thinking and a way of seeing to exert a formative influence on what we plan and do (Morgan 1986). It can permit reflection and provide a ready framework for the retelling of leadership story.

Sullivan (2002) has argued that, as for a commercial company a logo provides an easily recognised visual image which acts as a 'compressed meaning bearer' to symbolise the essentials of the organisation and its products, so also school leaders may be seen as 'living logos', providing an embodied form of communication of what the school stands for and the significance of its work. Hence the metaphor used to capture the essence of the leader as 'living logo' can provide, in parallel with its commercial counterpart a ready encapsulation of the school's vision and goals, its raison d'être and its modes of operation.

Day et al (2000) invited respondents from multiple perspectives to characterise the leadership style of the headteacher of their particular school by means of such metaphors. The emerging self-generated metaphors sought (following Beck and Murphy 1993) to capture the abstract nature of school leadership within a more concrete and more readily understood image. Self-generated metaphors from headteachers themselves included such terms as 'multi-faceted diamonds', 'captains of the ship' (although one governor interviewed in triangulation preferred the term 'admiral of the fleet'!), 'film director' and 'servant leader'. It is significant that the terms so generated are couched in terms of role rather than visual image. Difficulty was also found, particularly when triangulation was sought from other members of a school community, in encapsulating the complex functions of headteacher leadership into a single agreed descriptor. The provision of a unifying visually grounded metaphor would potentially ease these difficulties and strengthen the coherence of individual and collective reflection.

3.2. The metaphor 'reservoirs of hope'

The metaphor 'reservoir of hope' to describe spiritual and moral leadership of headteachers seeks to discharge the above functions. A phrase which was first coined by West-Burnham (2002) as a more direct definition of spirituality, it is extended in this study to encompass the concept that when critical incidents hit a school, colleagues look to the headteacher to be the *'external reservoir of hope'* for the institution, because 'hope' is what continues to drive the school forward towards the delivery of its vision in the face of external pressures, whilst allowing it to remain true to its fundamental values. In a post-modernist society characterised by a tendency to escape from perceived hopelessness through a concentration on the present moment (Moltmann 2002), colleagues in such circumstances look to the headteacher to provide the coherence of ongoing vision and the integrity of communal values, to project a spirit of hope rather than a spirit of despair (Palmer 1998), and to act as the wellspring of institutional self-belief when faced with critical incidents which threaten to drive the school off its course.

Walker (2005) sees the inspiring of such hope within the organisation as the major task of the leader, arguing that in building capacity for learning, 'hope-giving leadership' is a pivotal part of the process. Halpin (2003) argues the importance of maintaining 'optimistic illusions' or, as he prefers to term it, 'utopian thinking', and similarly argues that leaders must adopt "a militant optimism of the will" through which "hopefulness" can be brought to bear, and the utopian nature of the collective vision preserved and its fundamental values maintained. In outlining a theory of hope with implications for the practice of education, he argues for the primacy of three key ideas (Halpin 2003, 30):

> ...that teaching is premised on hope—that is, on the possibility that it will realise improvement of one kind or another; that being hopeful as a teacher facilitates innovation and an earnestness to do well in one's work; and that hope is a relational construct which in the education context requires teachers to look for and build up the 'Good' in their students.

These three key ideas can also be seen to provide the motivation for school leadership: a vision of the possibility of a better future; the motivation to engender change in order to bring it about; and the maintenance of a value system which is based on promotion of 'the common good' in so doing, no matter what the contextual pressures.

The preservation of this coherence of vision and integrity of values may be termed 'spiritual and moral leadership', not necessarily in a religious sense but in that sense of the concept of 'secular spirituality' as previously defined, where actions are based implicitly or explicitly on foundations of moral and ethical belief. To be required to act as the spiritual and moral leader of the school in this way demands of the leader an *'internal reservoir of hope'*, the calm centre at the heart of the individual leader from which their values and vision flows. This personal reservoir of hope has to be periodically refilled by a variety of replenishment and sustainability strategies, without which the leader will either burn out by being unable to sustain hope and energy levels in the face of relentless pressures for change, or drop out and withdraw from the change arena. Boyatzis and McKee (2005) identify this as 'the cycle of sacrifice and renewal', where the personal sacrifice incurred by the necessity for the leader to maintain 'resonance' within the organisation in the face of the pressures of external events, at the potential cost of his or her own internal wellbeing, is restored through 'mindfulness, hope and compassion': 'mindfulness' by developing the capacity for deep self-awareness, 'hope' through the preservation of belief in a vision of a feasible and attainable future and 'compassion' in understanding and responding to the needs of self and others engaged in the mutual continuing journeying towards that future.

School leaders therefore need to secure and maintain their value systems in the face of such external pressures by standing firm on their formative foundations, drawing support from personal reflection strategies to maintain self-awareness, affirmation of hope through participation in communities of like-minded belief and engaging in networks of support from both within and beyond the world of education. The sustained and replenished internal reservoir of hope, secured by what Gardner (1983) has called intra-personal intelligence, a sophisticated level of self-awareness which allows the creation of personal meaning, confidence in purpose and integrity of values, then in turn liberates the individual to engage in effective and compassionate inter-personal engagement and thus sustain institutional self-belief in the face of external pressures and crises.

3.3. Outworking in relationships

Bell (2002) defines spiritual and moral leadership in terms of relationships: *relationship with self*, which can be seen as the operation of intra-personal intelligence, which can be seen as equivalent to drawing from the personal internal reservoir of hope, and *relationship with others*, that is inter-personal intelligence, which can be seen to come to the fore in relationships when the leader is called on to be the external reservoir of hope for the institution. Fullan (2001, 5) also focuses on the paramount importance of relationships: "spiritual and moral leaders must therefore be consummate relationship builders with diverse people and groups, especially with people different than themselves".

Leadership standing on this foundation is thus more than technical management virtuosity. It is a moral activity in which the leader enters into what has been termed 'a covenantal relationship' with members of the organisation (Sergiovanni 1992, developing de Pree 1989), a relationship which rests on a shared commitment to ideas, to issues, to values and which provides, in de Pree's view (1989, 12), "expressions of the sacred nature of the relationships". Indeed, Sergiovanni goes so far as to argue that "the heart of the school as a moral community is its covenant of shared values" (Sergiovanni 1992, 108), and Bridger (2003, 16) has asserted that this doctrine of the covenant represents the wellspring from which a theology of professional responsibility can flow. The theological implications of this are considered further in Chapter Six.

The distinction is drawn between the 'secular' model of professional relationship based on the *contract*, and a 'sacred' model based on the *covenant* (Gula 1996, 15). In the former, there is specific definition of the contractual relationship and the precise rights and duties that flow from it. The contract, implicit or explicit, circumscribes the amount of service being sought and offered. In the latter, the covenant partners are bound together not by a set of legal, contractual requirements but by what has been called (Bridger 2003, 16) "a relational nexus of gracious initiative followed by thankful response", often displayed in a willingness 'to go the extra mile' as necessary.

Such covenantal relationships underpin effective spiritual and moral leadership. They are evidenced in a degree of relational open-endedness that is based on mutual caring relationships rather than formal institutional hierarchies. These relationships are particularly effective in maintaining a sense of community when the institution is under threat from critical incidents and day-to-day pressures. Equally, however, they permit the constant renewal of a collective understanding of the central meaning and values of the organisation, which then allows the 'routinisation' (Starratt 1993) of its values and mission in organisational structures and procedures and by so doing "changes the root metaphor for schools from organisation to community" (Sergiovanni 1997, 238). The embedding of routinisation thus moves the focus away from the charisma of the leader himself or herself, with his or her strong self-confident sense of his or her own moral values and desire to elicit high levels of commitment and performance by inculcating those values in his or her followers (Conger and Kanungo 1998), towards the institutionalisation of collectively agreed and mutually subscribed values: from charismatic leadership which internalises the vision towards transformational leadership which synthesises and embeds it.

Thus the spiritual and moral leadership of such a *community* may be seen to be rooted in its connectivity, in the richness and complexity of social relationships, in the development of supportive networks and through service to others, within a culture of shared community values based on reciprocity and mutual esteem, and the creation of 'communities of connectivity' to advance the collective cause.

3.4. The value of reflection on critical incident experience

How such communities of connectivity stand firm against the pressures of challenging experiences, be they high-level personal tragedies such as pupil death or lower-level organisational difficulties and day-to-day pressures, can be revealed through the recounting of the leadership stories of headteachers. Facilitating reflection on such experiences can best be done through the use of the 'critical incident technique', a well-established method (Flanagan 1954) used for evaluating systems in functioning work environments. This uses recollections of 'critical incidents' captured through semi-structured reflective interviews with participants, to generate learning about the behaviour of systems and communities under stress, even though those recollections may be considered to be of incidents of relatively low-level operational significance, and may be personalised in focus, distorted in remembrance and non-triangulated against the recollections of others who were involved.

Such personal recollections, no matter how apparently low level in terms of their operational significance, can be used not only to reveal the underlying value system which has informed the actions taken but can also give an indication of the strategies, support networks and webs of relationships from which the leader draws personal sustainability. Fullan (2005), in linking systems thinking with sustainability, defines the latter as the capacity of a system as a whole to engage in the complexities of continuous improvement, consistent with deep values of human purpose. Hargreaves and Fink (2005), however, adopt a more person-focused approach. They argue that leaders develop sustainability not just by how they approach, commit to and protect deep learning in their schools, and sustain others in promoting and supporting that learning within the 'eco-system' of the school, but also how they sustain *themselves* in so doing, so that they can persist in their vision and avoid burning out. In other words, sustainable leadership should be concerned not only with the sustainability of initiatives but also with the sustainability of the leaders themselves.

The capturing and codification of such sustainability strategies through the articulation and recording of leadership stories, rooted as they are in vivid and topical professional experiences of critical incidents and described in contextual detail and professional vernacular with which many school leaders can readily identify, not only offers compelling micro-narratives from which learning can be drawn and disseminated, but can do so through an authentic rendering of practitioner voice which makes that learning more readily accessible to fellow practitioners and those charged with their ongoing professional development and support.

Conclusion

This chapter has surveyed a range of available literature on school leadership and also on spirituality. It has located spiritual and moral leadership within a typography of school leadership styles by developing a concept of moral leadership that is infused with a spiritual dimension rooted in the values and ethics of the leaders themselves. It has developed an operational definition, a concept of spiritual and moral leadership as 'a lived faith in action'. It has argued that all leaders from whatever faith perspective, be it sacred or profane, may be seen to display a 'secular spirituality' arising out of their personal value system and its ethical base, which governs leadership behaviours and actions, whether or not that spirituality is tethered to a particular religious tradition or untethered from it.

The chapter has considered various ways of describing spirituality through the use of metaphor, before synthesising a working definition in terms of meaning, relationships and experiences, which can be seen to reinforce one another to determine personal authenticity. It has explored how practitioner reflection on challenging experiences can be facilitated through both the medium of metaphor and story. It has outlined how the metaphor 'reservoirs of hope' can assist such reflection and how critical incident analysis can be of value in revealing the underlying values base, support structures and nexus of relationships which school leaders rely on to sustain themselves in such challenging circumstances. Subsequent chapters will now capture practitioner reflection on critical incidents within the leadership stories of a range of school leaders drawn from a variety of school contexts.

CHAPTER THREE

RESERVOIRS OF HOPE

This chapter draws on and develops further *Reservoirs of Hope: Sustaining Passion in Leadership*, first published as chapter 3 of B. Davies and T. Brighouse, eds. 2008. *Passionate Leadership in Education*. London: Sage Publications.

Having synthesised in previous chapters a concept of 'secular spirituality' as 'a lived faith' from whatever source, leading to an operational definition of *spiritual and moral leadership as 'a lived faith in action'* within the professional sphere of school headship, and having explored a suitable methodology for engaging with headteachers in this area, this chapter now turns to an exploration of the metaphor 'reservoirs of hope' as an aid to such engagement. An introductory section that forms the first part of the chapter outlines the metaphor and considers its perceived value in promoting reflection on spiritual and moral leadership with defined samples of headteachers in both England and Australia.

The second part applies the conceptual framework, which posits that spiritual and moral leadership as 'a lived faith in action' lies at the confluence of the 'why', 'how' and 'what' of school headship, to the data gained from interviews with headteachers. First, it codifies the underpinning systems of beliefs and values identified by school leaders as the reason *why* they remain in the role, informing its meaning and purpose, maintaining vision and motivation, and providing the foundations of a personal reservoir of hope. Second, it focuses on *how* headteachers act as the spiritual and moral leaders of their schools, when having to live with the pressures of challenging circumstances and critical incidents. It shows how headteachers are prepared to empty themselves in the service of sustaining others, as they deploy their empathetic leadership skills to maintain effective inter-personal engagement and caring relationships in the testing times which threaten to drain the collective reservoir of hope. It identifies how for certain categories of early-leaving headteachers, the pressure becomes unsustainable and they choose or are forced to leave headship in advance of the normal retirement age 'when reservoirs run dry', and how for others the emergence of a 'plateau effect' reduces their operational effectiveness. Finally, it concludes by identifying *what* are the leadership actions and sustaining strategies deployed by headteachers to replenish and refill their personal reservoir of hope, to ensure that the effectiveness of spiritual and moral leadership is maintained.

To do this, the chapter develops research originally conducted under the auspices of the National College research associate scheme, initially involving interviews with 25 serving headteachers of varying length of experience from a cross-sectional sample of schools in England (Flintham 2003a), and then extended to encompass discussions with 15 headteachers who left their headship in advance of the normal retirement age (Flintham 2003b). It is supplemented with data from a further 10 Australian secular school leaders interviewed as part of a Winston Churchill Travelling Fellowship (Flintham 2006a). It draws substantially on and develops further a codification of this work (Flintham 2008b). Overall findings are therefore based on a total of 50 reflective interviews with headteachers of a wide range of expertise and experience, background and context, triangulated with the more general views of some 20 supporting educationists. Full details of the sample composition can be found in the Appendix.

These interviews have provided a non-judgemental opportunity for school leaders to draw on their expertise and experience in reflecting on critical incidents in their leadership stories. Such incidents are 'critical', not necessarily in the high level sense of creating a significant turning point, epiphany or life-changing moment, but rather they are incidents which are "indicative of underlying trends, motives and structures" and which "are rendered critical through analysis" (Tripp 1993, 25). Headteachers welcome the opportunity to relate what Tripp (1993, 103) has memorably termed their 'war stories'—the battlegrounds where moral dilemmas are confronted and moral issues played out—and to articulate what had sustained their spiritual and moral leadership in the face of such challenging pressures. They validate the usefulness of the metaphor 'reservoirs of hope' in promoting such reflection and drawing conclusions from it in terms of what underpins and sustains their leadership, even when that leadership is severely tested by external pressures. Interviews have also enabled the capture, as shown in subsequent italicised quotations from serving school leaders, of an authentic rendering of practitioner voice.

Introduction: the metaphor 'reservoirs of hope'

In one of the early 'Superman' films, Lois Lane, thrown from a skyscraper to apparently certain death, is rescued by the eponymous flying hero who zooms up and catches her in mid-fall with the immortal words "Don't worry, I've got you". To which she replies in stunned disbelief, "*Yes, but who's got you?*". In similar fashion, when critical incidents hit schools, colleagues look to their leaders to be the calm centre at the heart of the storm, to catch those in danger of falling. But to do this requires inner reserves in the school leader, which have to be replenished and sustained if effective spiritual and moral leadership is to be maintained in such circumstances. So leaders have to have sustainability strategies to preserve their own inner self-belief and emotional reserves to sustain them in the testing times when staying aloft in leadership becomes problematical.

In this chapter, it is argued that the successful leader acts as the '*external reservoir of hope*' for the institution, as the positive and public representative face both within and beyond the school, because 'hope' is what drives the school forward towards the delivery of the collective vision of the gathered community in the face of external pressures, whilst allowing the retention of agreed fundamental values. The school community looks to the headteacher, both as leader, representative and protector, to represent and maintain that coherence of vision and integrity of values, to preserve a sense of hope against the temptation to despair, and to lead them through and protect them as far as possible from the challenging circumstances which threaten to blow the school off course.

To be able to act in this way demands within the leader a personal and individual '*internal reservoir of hope*', the calm centre at the heart of the individual leader, "at the still point of the turning world" (Eliot 1936, 15) from which their own values and vision flows and which continues to allow effective inter-personal engagement and sustainability of personal and institutional self-belief in the face of draining external pressures and challenging critical incidents in the life of the school, when the danger is that "things fall apart; the centre cannot hold" (Yeats 1921, 158). This personal 'reservoir of hope' at the centre of leadership has therefore to be periodically refilled by a variety of replenishment and sustainability strategies, without which the result will be burn out or drop out as leaders withdraw from the change arena, and as one primary headteacher put it: "*collapse into frozen inactivity like a rabbit caught in the headlights*", or as one secondary headteacher confessed: "*take refuge in the illusion of action through low-grade displacement activities such as stapling and filing*".

In feedback from both headteachers interviewed and other serving school leaders participating in conferences on the topic, it is clear that the 'reservoirs of hope' metaphor has value in promoting personal reflection on approaches to spiritual and moral leadership. One English primary headteacher enthusiastically indicated: *"It's singing true for me. I was so excited by it I went home and talked to my wife about it, and to my deputies the next day"*. One Australian secondary school principal also testified: *"It resonates with me and the colleagues I've shared it with. It sums up the difference between people who stay and people who don't"*. Indeed some colleagues were anxious to refine and develop the metaphor further. A female primary head reflected that: *"Reservoirs store water. I had to learn the hard way not to give it all out at once, to pace myself or I'd get emotionally drained"*, and a male secondary head valued the dynamic nature of the metaphor:

> *"Reservoirs always have movement; they are always filling up and emptying, so it's a good metaphor because headship is dynamic. Reservoirs are open to the elements and gather rainwater, they are fed by a variety of springs, as heads need to be open to external influences and opportunities...and reservoirs unfilled lead to drought."*

Wittgenstein (1922), in his picture theory of language, argued that human beings gain their awareness of the world through picturing the way things are within it. For any community to develop, there consequently needs to be a shared language of expression to facilitate that collective picturing. However, Wittgenstein's concept of 'language games' suggests we should also strive to get outside the 'picture' that may hold us captive within a monolingual environment in order to provide multilingual appeal to a wider constituency. Visual metaphor is one way of providing that shared collective awareness. Thus the metaphor 'reservoirs of hope' was felt by respondents to give *"a shared language to describe and aid reflection"* and to provide a powerful visual image to support leadership when confronted with critical incidents such as pupil deaths, aggressive parents and the consequences of external events such as terrorist outrages, all of which *"gut-churning critical incidents threaten to drain the reservoir of hope"*. As one Australian principal who had faced such latter circumstances, movingly put it:

> *"Hope is fundamental when you are walking in the valley of tears and your reservoir running dry is a constant fear. You have to see the wider picture framed by hope."*

It should be noted therefore that the metaphor relies for its resonance with those who have experienced school leadership not only on the visual image of the reservoir, but on its linkage with the concept of hope as the essential component of spiritual and moral leadership. A clear conceptual distinction needs to be made between 'hope' in school leadership and 'optimism' (Watts 2002, 138-9). Optimism as a confident expectation that 'it will all come out right in the end' is easy in positive leadership situations; hope characteristically is what is required in the darkness of community tragedies, acute personnel problems and organisational crises when leadership is put to the test and there is no guarantee of a successful outcome.

This distinction between 'hope' and 'optimism' is the first of the four 'rules of hope' formulated in a 'grammar of hope' (Averil et al 1990, cited in Watts 2002). The remaining rules have resonance with the definition of spiritual and moral leadership as 'a lived faith in action' that is used throughout this book. The second rule postulates that hope is circumscribed by and intertwined with moral values ('faith') in a way which optimism is not. Third, hope is constrained by an assessment of what is really important in a 'lived' situation, not what is actually trivial or just appears to be important. And finally, hope carries with it a commitment to action. This action must be based not simply on administering and enforcing 'rules' which are the minimum set of shared values which need to be collectively applied and adhered to in order to maintain co-existence, nor in simply displaying a value system concerned solely with 'instrumental' values such as competence and honesty as the means by which goals are to be achieved and delivered (Rokeach 1973) through the application of effective leadership competencies in a skills-based model of leadership (Sullivan 2003). Rather the concern must be for 'terminal' virtues (Himmelfarb 1995) such as wisdom, justice or freedom, related to the desired ends: 'not just doing the thing right, but doing the right thing'. This, in the face of the immediacy of pressures in a critical incident situation, can in itself be further draining of emotion and energy from the internal reservoir of hope.

Halpin (2003, 16-17, following Godfrey 1987) draws a distinction between 'ultimate hope' which is 'an aimed hope' with an orientation towards a better specific state of affairs to be worked for in the present, and 'absolute hope' which is displayed more in a positive general orientation to the world: "an openness or readiness of spirit towards the future", where such hoping sets no conditions or limits but rests on a faith that "all shall be well, all manner of things shall be well" (Julian of Norwich 1373). Hence to sustain hope for the organisation in the face of critical incidents requires both the sustaining of absolute hope in the individual headteacher by the maintenance of their own internal reservoir of hope as a positive antidote to the negativity of despair of others around them, as well as a commitment to ultimate hope through directed positive action in a belief that it is possible to improve the immediate situation, no matter what its challenges and obstacles.

The 'internal reservoir of hope' metaphor was felt by those interviewed to be of particular value in visualising, promoting and legitimising the need to preserve that calm internal centre of absolute hope against the external pressures on leadership, so that: *"If you feel OK inside, it gives you the courage so as not to compromise on your values when the going gets tough"*. The need was recognised consistently to present that sense of absolute hope against the vicissitudes of the world: *"it's the Boy Scout motto: smiling and whistling under all difficulties. You have to resist the martyrdom model of headship"*, avowed one practitioner, with resonances of the example of Goldsmith's village schoolmaster: "full well the busy whisper circling round, convey'd the dismal tidings when he frown'd" (Goldsmith 1770, 230). But this inner calmness does not have to reveal itself in exterior remoteness, Olympian distance or even superman tendencies. As one headteacher confessed: *"I allow my humanity to show...I can get quite emotional, perhaps it's the internal reservoir overflowing"*.

Indeed the process of reflection and discussion with a fellow practitioner in the research interview was in itself of sustaining benefit to the internal reservoir. As Adey (2007) has commented, the function of the interviewer is to facilitate the telling of the story by the person with the real lived experience, for out of that relived and retold story comes the authentic voice of experience to inform, re-energise and root the story in its external and internal reality not only for the hearer but for the teller also. As one head of a socially challenging secondary school who was interviewed for the research was moved to testify:

> *"How helpful I actually found the [interview] session with you...it has really helped me to internalise things. It made me realise how rewarding I find the job [of headship] and it has made me realise that I can and do make a difference, and I know I would not like to do anything else."*

Reflective practice does not travel distances, it "just makes a great deal more sense of where we *are*" (Bolton 2000, 201; emphasis added), and allows us (after Eliot 1936, 59) "to arrive where we started and to know the place for the first time". The opportunity to engage in such guided self-reflection by means of articulation of leadership story, and the erstwhile experience of the interviewer as a fellow head with a commonality of experience base, facilitated the interview process. Bolton (2000, 1) has commented that "stories are the mode we use to make sense of ourselves and our world...we tell and retell episodes...to our colleagues, to our loved ones, to therapists and priests", to which list also could be added the category of fellow practitioners. However, as one male secondary headteacher of long experience was rather sadly moved to comment at the end of his interview: *"14 years in headship and I haven't had the opportunity to talk like this before".*

1. The foundations of the 'reservoir of hope'

The 'foundations of the reservoir of hope', the spiritual, moral and ethical bases on which individual leadership stands and which provide the wellspring which motivates, replenishes and renews the capacity for spiritual and moral leadership, are provided by a clearly articulated value system which explicitly or implicitly underpins leadership actions by providing the reason *why*. Such value systems, the internal structure of ethical beliefs and ideological concepts which govern leadership behaviours, provide a paradigm which shapes, informs, motivates and empowers individual and collective action when confronted with a situation of moral choice (Breton and Largent 1996). "A paradigm is our map of reality, and it is a blueprint for the way we see the world and make sense of it" (Duignan 2003, 5). Paradigms "give us the mental tools to make sense out of life and to survive in it" (Breton and Largent 1996, 6, cited in Duignan 2003, 6). In addition to giving meaning and purpose to existence, in the exposition of a theory of meaning which strives to answer the question 'why are we here?', they provide a set of directions and goals in a theory of values (axiology) related to 'what then are we here for?', and stimulate leadership practice, often instinctive, consistent with those espoused values, in a theory of action (praxiology) which reveals 'therefore how should we behave in this situation?'.

Varieties of value systems

In the totality of interviews conducted with 150 school leaders in both the UK and Australasia, not one headteacher was unable to articulate, instantly and often passionately, the value system that inspires and motivates their leadership. Although these value systems derive from a variety of faith perspectives and belief frameworks, and it is accepted that the clustering of values of individual headteachers often resists simplistic categorisation, they may be codified as either *generational, faith-based* or *egalitarian value systems*, or a combination of these. Generational values may have been inculcated by formal and informal teaching in the formative years or from the influence of modelling by 'significant others' (Tripp 1993, 107), both positively from mentors or negatively from 'tormentors'. Faith-based values may have been clarified through the intellectual critiquing of or emotional engagement with an established belief tradition, evoking a spectrum of possible responses ranging from enthusiastic embrace to total rejection. Egalitarian values may have been synthesised by reflection and analysis of personal experience. Whilst clearly accepting that such categorisations into generational, faith-based and egalitarian value systems are not mutually exclusive, they do provide a useful approach to studying the value systems of the headteachers interviewed, and how they were laid down. Each will now be considered in turn.

1.1. Generational value systems

The generational imperative of leadership stems from a value system laid down by early upbringing. As Parker (2002, 3) has put it: "How we work and how we lead depends to a significant extent on who we are, which in turn is a product of what we have been". Many headteachers interviewed were first-generation entrants to higher education. Many indicated that their foundational values were laid down in often working-class upbringings *"which laid down core values of inclusivity"*. That value system, coupled with a vision of education as *"a passport out of deprivation"*, had led to a consequent *"ethic of obligation"* fuelled by a *"passion to make a difference"* to the life chances of future generations. As one male secondary head put it:

> *"I'm here because someone made a difference for me, and that has led to a sense of duty to give something back, to make a difference for others like it made a difference for me."*

This influence of family upbringing on present leadership actions was highlighted succinctly and movingly by a female primary headteacher working in an area of significant social deprivation:

> *"I'm here as a way of saying thank you to my Dad for what he did for me...and my actions are determined by the acid test of what would my Dad think of this?"*

1.2. Faith-based value systems

Faith-based value systems were cited by a number of headteachers as influencing their professional practice, creating a faith-based imperative for leadership actions. It is significant that this was not restricted to those serving in schools of a specific religious character, nor to participants engaged in active religious practice. For some, the guiding overtly religious value system was underpinned and supported by membership of a faith community *"which feeds me through its worship and empowers me in service"* and results in a perceived *"call to live out the message of the gospel to love one another"*. For others, whilst the original motivational connection between the religious beliefs laid down in childhood and the present adult ethical value system had long since been broken, the erstwhile bedrock of values still remains, a residue albeit divorced from any belief in the concept of a higher being, in what has been termed "a godless morality" (Holloway 1999, 4). Whilst there had been 'a moving on' from the original faith perspective, there was a retention of what was termed *"the universal values, the common thread of all religions"* which had left *"a deep inner spirituality based on love and care for my neighbour as myself"*. For all headteachers, however, there remained the responsibility of ensuring that leadership actions could be validly judged against the articulated value system: the need to ensure that 'the talk is walked', especially in the testing times of coping with critical incidents, when a value system which hitherto may have been implicit in day-to-day practice becomes explicitly visible in the harsh glare of leadership challenge. In such circumstances, headteachers reveal their personal authenticity, and any lack of fit between what one officially espouses to believe and what is displayed in moral reaction to events is mercilessly exposed (Taylor 1991, 9). As one interviewed headteacher of a church school put it: *"Every leadership decision has to stand the test of comparison against your publicly avowed principles"*.

1.3. Egalitarian value systems

For many, irrespective of faith perspective, there was an egalitarian imperative which underpinned their leadership: a commitment to fairness and social justice, a belief in social inclusion and equality of opportunity, summed up pithily in the Australian concept of the 'fair go'. This engendered a sense that *"everyone has the potential to lead a good life...the school's job is to realise that potential"*, a motivation pithily summed up in one school's mission statement: *"Everybody here can be somebody"*. That egalitarian approach, inspired by a 'transference imperative' which tested professional leadership decisions against the personal yardstick of *"would I be happy if this were being done to my own children and if not, why I am I doing it to someone else's children"*, is, however, often tinged with a realistic recognition of its potential costs, as articulated by a headteacher leading a large secondary school:

> *"I want to make a difference, although I know it will mean going the extra mile. You've got to have the courage to take risks, to risk that it may all go wrong, and not to compromise just to meet the expectations of others or the system. If you feel OK inside about it, that it is true to your values, then you know you are right."*

The *"passion to make a difference"* no matter what the professional cost is particularly but not exclusively exemplified by those leading schools facing challenging circumstances (Flintham 2006b). In being asked specifically 'what's good about leading a school in challenging circumstances', headteachers of such schools report being energised by the challenge and feeling secure in their capacity to make a difference both to their schools and also the communities in which they are set. They are motivated by the search for 'excellence', going beyond an acceptance of the status quo or the simply 'ordinary' achievement. They have a passionate belief in the potential for the success of their schools, even if that might be 'success against the odds'. Particularly in such schools facing challenging circumstances, it is felt that an impact can be made straightaway, with the opportunity to make rapid changes and see significant fast improvement, making the ratio of effort to progress seem more advantageous: *"there is so far to go that it is easier to move forward"*. And that movement forward provides in itself both motivation and catalyst for further development towards 'excellence': *"you can have small tastes of success...and they taste good, so you want more"*.

Headteachers in whatever context are driven by core values that are people-centred and founded on effective relationships. They combine moral purpose with a high respect for others and a strong belief in the capacity of all to succeed within an inclusive environment. These core values thus provide not only a 'moral compass' which determines the direction of leadership actions when faced with moral dilemmas arising out of critical incidents, they also provide a 'moral anchor' which holds those actions and their underpinning motivational values within consistent and established ethical systems. Adherence to such well-defined ethical systems may not be explicitly articulated by headteachers. However, in the application of their core values as evidenced in daily practice, headteachers implicitly display the Aristotelian virtues codified by Aquinas in Part II of the *Summa Theologica* (1997, 466) into the four cardinal virtues of prudence, justice, courage and temperance (at least in the sense of self-restraint!), in striving to achieve through balance and moderation *"a culture of excellence"* leading to *"happiness"* resulting from the fulfilment of personal goals. Such 'happiness' is not to be construed in a hedonistic sense of present pleasure, but in the Aristotelian sense (2004, 16) of the ultimate goal of life being achieved through a lifetime of virtuous action in striving for, and encouraging others so to strive for, the fulfilment of one's full potential: *"being all that you could be"*. It is significant that these emphases are all terms used by the headteachers interviewed, revealing their greater concern for longer-term virtue ethics than the more short-term dilemma-based ethics applied in the immediate aftermath of the critical incident situation.

Virtue ethics is concerned less with the focus of dilemma-based ethics on 'what should I do', but rather with 'who should I become' (Keenan 1998). It sees the fundamental task of the moral life as the development of a vision of 'who we ought to become', and then striving to attain it. All headteachers interviewed could articulate a vision of what they wanted their schools and pupils to become. Without such a vision, inspired by the hope of a potentially better future, and clearly articulated and collectively supported, schools remain static in their development at best or at worst regress. Virtue ethics, proactively applied and concerned with the ordinary and all-encompassing pressures of school life, has surely therefore more to offer the hard-pressed headteacher in delivering progress towards the long-term vision than what has memorably been called (Keenan 1998, 90) the "emergency room" reactive application of dilemma-based ethics in the immediacy of the critical incident situation, being "caught up in a world of fast-paced educational triage" (Stebbins 2002, 2).

Aquinas, in *Summa Theologica* (1997, 332), argued that every action is a moral action in that it affects us as moral people, and offers us the potential for growth towards what we might become. Such a virtues-driven philosophy is, however, tinged in the day-to-day operational practice of headteachers with a teleological utilitarianism, asking 'what is the result of a proposed action', in a recognition (after J.S. Mill) that an essential criterion in judging the rightness or otherwise of an action lies in its consequences. School leaders therefore consider their ethical decisions not only in the light of continued striving towards the collective developmental vision, but also in the costs and benefits for each participant in the event: the pupil, the parent, the staff, the wider community of the school and beyond. They seek to balance the often conflicting views and pressures that each constituent group brings to bear, even if such balancing requires a pragmatic application of the philosophy that 'the end justifies the means' and 'a bending of the rules' to achieve it. Casey (1990, 146) has called this capacity "moral imagination", an ability to see "what is at stake where the application of rules may not be at all obvious, and to know how to respond". As one experienced school leader trenchantly described this operational hard-headedness: *"I want my kids to get the best deal possible. I will rise above my principles and break the rules in order to get them that deal"*.

Nevertheless, there are times when a 'duty-based' Kantian deontology, which focuses on the rightness or wrongness of the actions themselves rather than on the rightness or wrongness of the consequences of those actions, has to be brought to bear, in the recognition that there remain certain universal moral obligations and categorical imperatives: *"lines in the sand"* which cannot be crossed. Headteachers accept there are times when their core values may be buffeted by the pressures of external events and it is necessary to remain firm. For example, in respect of schools facing challenging pupil behaviour and pressures militating against inclusion, one headteacher was prepared to explicitly state that *"it is sometimes necessary to remind your staff that these are your lines in the sand...to state that these are my values [on pupil inclusion]; you need to stand with me on this"*, even though there might be an operational price to be paid in staff recruitment or retention as a result of the moral stand being taken.

However, some moral philosophers such as MacIntyre (1981) have argued that moral issues should be seen in the social and historical context of the tradition in which they are located, rather than seeking directly to apply abstract, generalised moral systems such as utilitarianism or Kantian ethics. It is suggested that within any cultural tradition, certain virtues are identified as particularly representing prevailing community values within the specific context, which varies in time and place as "Aristotle's Athens differs considerably from Jane Austen's Hampshire [and] what allows us to decide what is virtuous is an adequate grasp of the values which are embedded in those communities and the practice of life which is in accord with them" (Goodliff 1998, 78-9). For example, McLeod (1998, 274) indicates that, "in many counselling circles, authenticity is regarded as a primary virtue. In the academic community, by contrast, the key virtue is intellectual rigour or rationality", although surely these perspectives can never be mutually exclusive. Within the education tradition, what could be seen as a primary virtue is a sense of moral purpose amongst headteachers, which sustains them in difficult times and provides a moral compass and an anchor for their work (NCSL 2007, 7).

McLeod (1998, 274) also raises an interesting point regarding the tension between generalised moral systems and the tradition-based approach to moral enquiry in relation to perceived gender differences in the modes of moral decision making applied. Citing the feminist writer Chodorow (1978), McLeod (1998, 274) suggests that "men aspire to make moral decisions on the basis of abstract *principles*, whereas women's moral decision making is grounded in consideration of the impact different decisions would have on the network of *relationships* within which the woman lives her life" (emphasis added). In interviews conducted for the present research study, however, no such gender polarisation in expressed value systems was detected. This finding resonates with the arguments of Baron-Cohen (2003), as previously indicated in Chapter Two, that irrespective of biological gender, possessors of 'empathising brains', albeit found more on average amongst women than systematising brains, are attracted to the caring professions, including teaching, where the maintenance and development of effective inter-personal relationships are surely the *sine qua non* of successful leadership, both at classroom and whole-school level.

A concern for the maintenance of effective inter-personal engagement and the sustaining of both personal and collective self-belief when confronted by external pressures results in a pragmatic contextual application of an internal guiding ethical compass founded on moral purpose. This may either be instinctively followed or deliberately and carefully decided; it may have as an overriding priority the preservation of relationships or the integrity of a moral system, but it nevertheless remains firmly ethically anchored, even if a knowledge and articulation of the precise theoretical underpinning in terms of theories of moral philosophy may never be formalised nor made explicit. In essence, headteachers feel it necessary, as one put it: *"to stick with your convictions, to make clear what you believe in and stick with it...or you will not survive"*. And often the experience of having to do so was a personally developing one for headteachers. As one headteacher testified:

"The experience [of a critical incident] shook my belief system about what I stand for, but then paradoxically led to a reaffirmation and strengthening of what my core values actually are."

2. Draining the 'reservoir of hope'

Serving headteachers not only face an extensive range, frequency and depth of day-to-day pressures, but also unexpected and challenging critical incidents. Such pressures call on them to display sustained high-level leadership skills and maintain their passion for the role, yet threaten to drain their personal reservoir of hope as they empty themselves in the service of others to maintain effective inter-personal engagement and caring and mutually supportive relationships against the fragmenting pressures of external events. Such self-emptying leadership actions constitute the *how* of spiritual and moral leadership. Headteachers are able to offer compelling micro-narratives of situations they have been called on to face where they felt such draining pressures, and have valued the opportunity to reflect on how they had been sustained through them.

The opportunity to recount such experiences in a non-judgemental and supportive forum has proved to be a cathartic and liberating experience, and equally the opportunity to hear such leadership stories from colleagues in similar circumstances has provided a powerful support mechanism in itself to combat the isolation of leadership. As one headteacher put it: *"Wrapping it up in a story makes it more powerful and memorable. It gives you self-confidence and an awareness that you are not alone in having had to face such circumstances"*. However, the recounting of such critical incident stories requires careful guidance, monitoring and assessment by the interviewer. Whilst of significant potential value to participants in connecting specific leadership behaviours to a wider network of meaning, and linking particular circumstances to more general leadership realities, it is important that anecdote, narrative and description and the potential temptation to be 'economical with the truth' in the telling of 'a good story' are sensitively probed and interrogated to access deeper meanings and implicit purposes. As a result, on several occasions in the interview process, respondents were led to identify and articulate learning points of significance for them, were able to release long pent-up emotions, and many were prepared to indicate: *"I have never talked to anybody like this before"*.

2.1. Confronting critical incidents

Whilst confidentiality issues make it inappropriate to engage in contextual detail, critical incidents described by headteachers interviewed can be classified as *community tragedies*, *personnel problems* and *organisational crises*.

Community tragedies

As regards the tragedies which can afflict school communities, schools and their leaders are long used to dealing with anticipated death through the loss of pupils, staff and parents from long-term illness, and having to keep the school on emotional track through the process of loss, bereavement and beyond. Much more difficult to deal with are the unexpected deaths, often sudden, violent or self-inflicted. Schools and their leaders in such circumstances find themselves in the eye of the storm, with the school being seen as *"the community space in which to grieve and reflect in mutual sympathy and support"*. An inner confidence in one's ability to cope with the situation, a personal reservoir of hope that progress through it can be maintained, and an empathetic concern for the strength of relationships with all who are caught up in it, whilst articulated in different ways, provide the essential characteristics which enable school leaders to deal with the aftermath of such tragedies. They are required to call on high levels of personal emotional resilience and empathetic leadership skills in order to deal with the community implications of such loss, not simply within the school itself but also within the wider community that the school serves. Headteachers dealing with such events find themselves in the front line of maintaining community relationships often fractured by anger and grief. In responding to such circumstances, the school provides *"an oasis of calm in a troubled community"*, an oasis which is clearly watered by the wellspring of values of the leaders themselves as they act not only as external reservoirs of hope for their schools but also for the communities in which they are set.

Personnel problems

Equally draining if somewhat less overt are the personnel problems which are part of the day-to-day lot of the school leader, be they child protection issues, allegations of assault or staff redundancies, wherein much work needs to be done unobtrusively at a personal level to maintain morale when the full details of the situation, or what is being done behind the scenes to resolve it, cannot be made public, and ill-informed criticism of leadership actions becomes endemic. In such circumstances the head's primary aim must be *"restoring the community and leading it on"* whilst recognising the draining effect on their own personal internal reservoir and the consequent need not only to maintain an inner equilibrium and faith in the rightness of one's actions when measured against the greater good. It is necessary also to supplement that inner self-belief by consciously engaging in compensatory post hoc replenishment strategies, particularly by seeking out restorative personal space to reflect on and make sense of the experience, and to benefit from networks of support from families, friends and colleagues.

Organisational crises

Organisational and management issues to do with the running of the school, and operational decisions taken in matters such as dress code, pupil exclusion or external inspection, all have the potential to turn a 'drama into a crisis', with all the ensuing potential publicity implications which can result. This also tests leaders' 'reservoir of hope', with the dual need both to retain continuing internal self-confidence and integrity and to ensure the retention of agreed institutional values in the face of such pressures. There is the necessity to remain the perceived centre of calm for the school community, even at some inner personal cost in unseen emotional turbulence: what could be described as the 'swan syndrome', apparently calm and serene on the surface whilst paddling like mad underneath! One headteacher described the personal hidden emotional cost of such behaviour:

> *"I didn't let go until a week later [after a difficult Ofsted inspection], after I was sure that everyone else was alright. Then I went home that weekend and cracked up. It took me the weekend to re-establish my values base, but by Monday morning I was OK."*

This gives a further example of the capacity of the successful school leader to continue to act as the 'external reservoir of hope' for colleagues and the community as the first priority, and then to return thereafter to rebuild and refill the personal internal sustaining reservoir that makes the continuance of such self-emptying behaviour possible.

With hindsight, however, many school leaders found that such testing through critical incidents was in itself a learning and developmental experience in terms of growth in emotional resilience and leadership confidence. This engendered a feeling that *"if I can deal with that, I can deal with anything"* and a concomitant sense that the school becomes collectively stronger too. It was felt that: *"Nothing succeeds like success against the odds in building inner confidence and in building hope in the school"*. Many heads, however, were thankful that such unsought learning experiences had not come earlier in their leadership careers, recognising the growth in confidence, self-awareness and willingness to use more creative and adventurous solutions whilst remaining true to their value system that experience had given them and that they could now display. Many identified with a perceived 'sea-change' in headship as their experience had deepened, with a move from 'doing headship' into 'being the head'. This not only gave more confidence in dealing with the mechanics of headship, it also allowed a shift in focus towards being more concerned with reflecting on and articulating the values governing leadership actions and the development of the relationships which facilitated their effective implementation. As one experienced secondary head summed it up:

> *"I now know how to be a head as opposed to doing the headship job. It's the difference between knowing the words and knowing the tune."*

This in turn impacted on how she was able to relate to her staff. She described how her growing experience of headship and surmounting its pressures had given a sense of *"now being able to 'feel' the tune when you are dealing with people"* even when the pressures of unexpected events threaten to turn leadership into *"more of a rap than an aria!"*.

2.2. When reservoirs run dry

For some headteachers, however, the pressures of unexpected events prove excessively draining or even unsustainable, and they face the prospect of withdrawing from the leadership arena through choice or necessity, 'when reservoirs run dry'. A cross-sectional sample of 15 such early-leaving headteachers cited reasons for their premature departure which spanned the full spectrum from successful heads with a planned and career-driven exit strategy, who had sought to capitalise on their experience in the wider educational arena, to those who felt burnt out and had suffered high levels of psychological stress which had made it impossible to continue in headship or even in gainful employment. They can be clustered into three distinct categories, termed as 'striding', 'strolling' or 'stumbling' headteachers.

'Striders'

'Strider' headteachers were those whose exit was based on a clear career plan. They recognised that there was a finite time limit to successful headship, both for the school and for themselves. A male secondary headteacher aged 51 and now in local authority project work, indicated:

> *"I knew that I had reached the 're-ploughing the same furrow' point and that new blood was needed for the good of the school... I had done it successfully for a long time and could have happily continued, but I was ready for new stimulation and a new challenge to put my expertise and experience to use in a new context."*

Such heads wanted to have sufficient energy and enthusiasm left to maintain and develop an ongoing contribution to education. They had clearly defined exit strategies for such moving on, which had often been planned well ahead, sometimes as the result of having experienced the revitalisation of alternative professional development opportunities such as short-term advisory, training or consultancy work which had offered a taste of a wider sphere of influence beyond their schools.

'Strollers'

'Stroller' headteachers were those who wanted to walk away from headship in a controlled manner, often at a high spot in the school's fortunes, knowing that it would be difficult to sustain this: *"I made a conscious decision to leave on a high. I knew I couldn't keep going at that high"*, said a female primary head aged 58, now in part-time governor training work. Others chose to exit from headship as a result of taking stock of the quality of their personal lives, catalysed by *"the tension between becoming a grandad and the demands of a 70-hour working week"*, as experienced by a male secondary head aged 54, now in part-time education consultancy work. Some developed a lack of sympathy with the burgeoning national or local change agenda, when clashes occurred between "the oppressive burden of targets, tests and tables [and] the clutches of the curriculum accountants and assessment auditors" (Brookes 2008, 9) and their own personal value system based on the needs of the individual and their social and emotional development. Although some were energised by what was termed 'the roller coaster of headship' and the challenge of how to cope with or even subvert each fresh wave of change, others suffered from a crushing sense of déjà vu as problems they had experienced and resolved earlier in headship came round again in a new guise. All, however, recognised the beginnings of failure in the capacity of their sustainability and support systems to continue to cope, and were anxious to depart, difficult though the personal process of 'walking away' might be, before burn out became a damaging reality. As one, a female primary headteacher aged 54 now in local authority project work, trenchantly indicated:

> *"It [the decision to leave headship early] didn't seem like strolling to me. It was damned difficult to walk away from a school I had known and loved for so many years, but I knew if I didn't do so, I would not survive."*

'Stumblers'

'Stumbler' headteachers were those to whom the realisation of burn out came suddenly and unexpectedly (the metaphor of the frog not appreciating the increasing temperature of the water until it was too late was cited more than once), with stress-related or psychosomatic physical symptoms resulting in early retirement often on health grounds. Amongst such 'stumbler' heads, there was a commonality of symptoms: a sense of powerlessness and a questioning of personal competence in feeling unable to affect the situation, and a consequent loss of hope, a physical impact such as the disruption of sleep patterns or frozen inactivity that are the classic symptoms of stress, and a perceived draining of the emotional reservoir: *"The water was running out faster than it came in. School was overtaking me...I had no time to think about myself or look after myself"*, said one such headteacher, a female secondary headteacher aged 56 now in part-time education consultancy work. For those such as her whose departure was thrust on them, be it by illness or increasing inability to cope with events, there had been no chance to plan a proactive exit strategy, and consequently no immediate positive outcome. In time, however, she was adamant that hope could be restored:

> *"Giving the job up [through ill health] was like a bereavement. I had nine months grieving the loss, but now I can't imagine going back. The fact I had to finish, now looking back, was a good thing, although at the time it was like jumping into the abyss. I now have a lifetime of new opportunities, bolstered by time for myself that I never had as a head."*

However, in respondent validation of the 'strider', 'stroller', 'stumbler' categorisation, several participants drew attention to the fact that the difference between these categories could be very slight, and heavily dependent on the pressure of prevailing circumstances and the personal repertoire of leadership skills available on which to draw. As one male 'stroller' headteacher aged 54, with 14 years of apparently successful headship experience in two schools but now in full-time consultancy work put it:

"How great or small are the steps between striding, strolling and stumbling? Very few steps are needed I suspect, if the circumstances are such, to move you from one gait to another very quickly. I may have been a strider at one time, and I certainly recognise elements of the stumbler. Taking control [in respect of the decision to leave headship early], being proactive and 'doing' rather than being done to, have helped me to retain my professional dignity and to leave physically and mentally intact."

Indeed, it can be argued that 'survival' in headship is not simply a function of the robustness of an individual's sustainability strategies, and of their own personal strengths and weaknesses, but also of the particular contextual circumstances they are called on to face, in that the more demanding the circumstances, the faster the internal reservoir becomes empty and the greater the need for its robust and rapid refilling. Consequently headteachers who have the capacity to be 'striders' in one context may find themselves as potential 'stumblers' in another. However, whilst accepting the need to be attuned to specific contextual circumstances and to fine-tune leadership actions accordingly, this could not be at the expense of compromising one's fundamental values. It would be a step too far to embrace the view of a self-confessed cynical 'stumbler' headteacher that *"the less idealistic a head is, the greater the chance of survival in post"*.

In fact, there was found to be no difference in the range or robustness of value systems described by the former heads compared to those still in headship, nor indeed between the categories of early-leaving heads. Some expressed foundational Christian beliefs, even though in some cases active faith had lapsed; some cited the influence of upbringing, particularly when that had involved first-generation higher education experience; and many had strong egalitarian imperatives underpinned by a strong sense of moral purpose to provide for others less fortunate something of what they themselves had enjoyed. Leaving headship early created therefore a particular sense of loss, especially amongst 'stumbler' heads. The cynical 'stumbler' headteacher cited above, a male secondary head aged 48 who had felt obliged to resign his post after only two years experience, and who was now in freelance Ofsted inspection work, had felt that sense of loss most keenly:

"I wanted to make a contribution to society, to work with and support those who can't look after themselves. I now feel frustrated [since leaving headship]. I'm now doing a job rather than a vocation."

Equally, such early-leaving headteachers had faced similar levels of leadership pressures to their serving colleagues. Faced then with critical incidents similar in severity to those experienced by serving heads in testing the capacity of the 'internal reservoir of hope' to withstand, it is the absence or adequacy of their sustainability strategies that constitutes the essential difference between 'strider', 'stroller' or 'stumbler' heads. 'Strider' heads had robust and enhancing sustaining mechanisms and appeared more able to compartmentalise the problems of school from their own personal concerns and self-image. They were prepared to admit their own vulnerability and to be proactive in seeking out support. 'Stumbling' heads found this more difficult. For example, the previously cited 'stumbler' head, significantly the youngest in the sample both in terms of age and headship experience and facing a severe breakdown in headteacher–staff relationships, felt too personally isolated and wounded to carry on. He felt his self-image had been fatally compromised and recognised the absence of sustainability, 'switching off' and particularly support strategies as a major factor in this:

> *"If I'd had sustainability strategies I'd have seen a way forward. The only one I had was more of the same: I enjoyed innovating which gave me satisfaction but ironically caused me to work even longer hours. I had no one professionally to turn to. My self-belief was undermined. I felt a good head would have solved this, and I had no one to convince me otherwise."*

In order to continue to act as spiritual and moral leader when faced with critical incidents, it is necessary to maintain motivation and enthusiasm for the leadership role, to remain true to an espoused value system no matter what the pressure to seek an easier more pragmatic course, and to sustain self-belief in one's capacity to cope with the challenge of the circumstances. Above all, the leader is required to 'empty himself or herself' in the service of others, often sublimating personal wellbeing, position and self-interest, in order to maintain effective inter-personal engagement to ensure the synthesis of productive solutions which can be collectively discharged. To do this, however, is draining of the personal emotional reservoir. When replenishment strategies are insufficiently robust, or motivation weakened, operational effectiveness is diminished as internal equilibrium is disturbed.

2.3. Pharaoh's dream: confronting the 'plateau effect'

Whilst for some school leaders it is the unexpected additional pressure of facing an unanticipated critical incident situation which makes compartmentalisation of emotions difficult, disturbs internal equilibrium and threatens to overwhelm the defences of the reservoir or cause it to run dry, for others it is the long-term relentless repeated pressure of the continual waves of change over time, and an accompanying sense of déjà vu in having to revisit circumstances already previously experienced, that wears down the reservoir's retaining wall. If there is an acceptance of the sea-change in leadership around the four to five year mark with the transition from 'doing' to 'being', then equally there is also a recognition amongst experienced headteachers of the emergence of the well-documented 'plateau effect' around seven to ten years in post, which threatens slowly and imperceptibly to drain the reservoir of hope and cause a potential decline in effectiveness as leadership becomes "a chore not a challenge" (Earley 2006, 15). Headteachers would recognise the Pharaoh's dream scenario (Genesis 41) where *"7 years of plenty"* with *"plenty to do"* and the enthusiasm and motivation to do it, can be replaced by *"7 years of drought"* with the draining of enthusiasm through *"having been round the block too many times"*.

To confront the plateau effect and to preserve motivation against the jaundice of excessive repeated experience requires re-energising professional refreshment and renewal activities to be provided or sought out. As a male secondary 'stroller' headteacher aged 55 with 12 years of experience in a socially deprived inner-city area put it:

> *"I had a window round about the seven year mark to bring about change. Thereafter I felt I was marking time. I should have cashed in my experience and moved on. I needed something different, even for a year, to re-energise me."*

One headteacher with over 10 years experience consequently argued for the need to *"develop an area of interest and expertise outside your school and fertilise it. It benefits you and it benefits the school"*. She also showed an appreciation of the benefit to other senior leaders in the school:

> *"Seek professional time away from headship. You renew your reservoir away from the school and there is a development of the others who are left behind managing the school in your absence."*

There was, however, a sage recognition of the need to preserve a balance between personal fulfilment and the organisational needs of the school, and the danger of 'the absentee landlord syndrome', as perceived by members of staff.

For some, however, confronting the potential draining of the plateau effect is best done by ensuring that it never arrives in the first place. An emerging post-modernist generation of school leaders can be identified with a world-view based more on primacy and immediacy of choice and context and with less of a sense of linear career progression, who view their careers as a series of professional personas constructed as appropriate to the multitude of settings in which they expect to find themselves. Such colleagues do not see headship as being for life nor as being the summit and endpoint of a professional career, but rather as part of a 'portfolio' of professional development which will encompass advisory, consultancy and school improvement work to build on that concentrated headship experience and allow it to be generalised into wider contexts. They see their headship contribution more in the fulfilment of short- to medium-term objectives over a three to five-year period than as a long-term 'marathon' commitment. In line with the previous categorisation of 'strider', 'stroller' and 'stumbler' heads they might be described as '*sprinter*' headteachers.

Such 'post-modernist portfolio principals' (Flintham 2004) recognise that the required role of the headteacher will vary at different stages of the school's development as well as of their own, with a change of requirement from perhaps being the 'heroic head' at one stage to acting as the 'consolidator head' at another, with consequently different clusters of professional strengths being necessary. A school in a particular phase of its life might well look to appoint a head with a particular set of skills that match those identified needs and who recognises a fixed-term objective to see the school through to its next phase of development. Potential headteacher appointees might then say to an interview panel: "this is my particular skill set and this is how it matches the present needs of the school within my time framework". Appointing panels would then need to be honest in their objective evaluation of the school and its present needs and then select from a menu of headship types depending on those identified needs, as follows:

- the '*heroic*' head who moves into a school to 'rescue' it perhaps from special measures or persistent underachievement
- the '*consolidator*' head as the steady hand on the tiller to see the changes through and embedded in day-to-day practice
- the '*nurturer*' head who rebuilds fractured relationships and bruised professional morale in schools that have been through crisis or tragedy
- the '*shaper*' head who cuts away some of the previous developments which have outlived their usefulness in order to make room for new growth

- the *'visionary'* head who sees the long-term development potential of the school and has an extended plan for its achievement.

To change the metaphor to a gardening one, it would be possible to categorise these headteacher styles as 'planters' and 'rooters', 'growers', 'pruners' and 'garden designers'.

This post-modernist viewpoint is not an argument for fixed-term contracts in headship, such as occurs in the Australian school context (although even here, principals testify that the time-limited nature of tenure provides a paradoxically liberating sense that *"the job is not forever, and that can be quite liberating in having a life outside it"*). In British school circumstances, heads may need to be prepared and have the capacity, in the words of one secondary head who had been in post in the same school for over 20 years, *"to reinvent their headship at various stages as the school has developed and as the needs of the school have changed"*, or as one primary headteacher now in her third headship put it even *"to recognise when it is right for the head to move on"*. That moving on may not necessarily be to another school in a different phase of development, but may be to a completely new facet of professional life as another card in the professional portfolio.

All of this is underpinned, however, by a clearly expressed belief in the time-limited nature of a particular headship style within a particular context and the need to address the short-term sustainability and long-term succession issues that arise from this. Consequently such 'portfolio' headteachers have a proactive exit strategy planned in order to move on into other facts of educational life before the plateau effect kicks in, or a conversion strategy to acquire and develop a new set of leadership skills as required by changing school circumstances. They are characterised by having robust short-term sustainability strategies coupled with the ability to compartmentalise their feelings, be proactive in their responses to external pressures, and the capacity to recognise when it is appropriate to disengage from school leadership once they feel their task is complete and *"before the fruit begins to rot on the vine"*.

Interview data from such portfolio headteachers, coupled with that of their early-departing colleagues, indicates that acting as the external reservoir of hope for the school when faced with critical incidents and systemic pressures requires a 'self-emptying' by the leader in the service of others, as he or she seeks to maintain effective inter-personal engagement and mutually supportive relationships against the pressures of events. However, only if the emotionally draining consequences of that self-emptying can be protectively compartmentalised and the internal reservoir of hope refilled by robust sustainability strategies can effective spiritual and moral leadership in such circumstances be maintained.

Having explored the 'why' of spiritual and moral leadership in the value systems of headteachers and the message of hope that they convey, and 'how' they exercise such leadership by being prepared to empty themselves emotionally, it is now necessary to turn to consider 'what' are the sustaining mechanisms used by headteachers to refill and replenish their internal reservoir of hope.

3. Refilling the reservoir of hope

The personal reservoir of hope of headteachers has to be periodically refilled against the draining effect of external pressures, by a variety of replenishing and sustaining strategies, without which the implementation of the espoused value system will fail, the intensity of motivation fade, and withdrawal from the task of leading change occur. Interviews with headteachers revealed *what* of the self-termed 'survival strategies' they used to replenish their internal reservoirs. Headteachers utilise a range of personal and corporate sustaining strategies to provide *reflection* opportunities, *reinforcement* of self-belief and *relaxation* strategies. These may be provided through *belief networks*, *support networks* and *external networks*.

Belief networks

Reflection time, *"often in the middle of the night"* or in a special quiet place with *"just me and my God"*, provided essential breathing space. The reinforcement of that reflection on values was enhanced by feedback from *belief networks* of like-minded colleagues imbued with similar value systems, whose affirmative support is to be captured at all costs: *"You jockey for position as to who to sit next to at heads' conferences. You need to be alongside someone on the same wavelength as you are"*. Such affirmative support comes not only from colleagues but from parents, governors and from what is felt to be the core of the job, the pupils: *"children are a touchstone; I walk round [the school] and draw strength from their reactions"*, said one inner-city secondary headteacher, and Woods (2002, 14), in his seminal study of 'enchanted heads' who remain committed and enthusiastic after many years of service, reports on "a passionate outpouring of anecdotes" from such primary colleagues as to the joy of being with children and seeing them thrive, especially in demanding social circumstances.

Support networks

Reinforcement also comes from *support networks* of families, particularly long-suffering partners, and friends also sustain the inner reservoir of hope. Some colleagues are able to 'compartmentalise' the problems of the day so that they do not leak across into home life; others value the existence of 'a sounding board' at home as a catharsis to verbalise and off-load the events of the day; others are adamant that they would not do this but know nevertheless that the support is there. One was prepared to go as far as to state that: *"I don't see how you can go home on your own at night and come back the next day sane"*. Others, however, paid testimony to the value of *"talking it through with the dog (who always seems to agree!) on early morning walks"* or valued the opportunities of *"conversations with yourself"* on the long drive home.

Many heads recognise the need to create the capacity for strategic reflection opportunities where it is possible to re-examine and renew a personal value system through the challenge and support of a fellow practitioner, who can act as *"a detached sounding board, with similar experience, who is a good listener but who can also plant the key questions to aid formative reflection"*. They thus valued the opportunity for a peer support relationship with a colleague headteacher acting as *"a professional listening and learning partner"*. This was deemed to be more valuable than mentoring or coaching, with its implications of a more senior experienced colleague supporting a more junior one, but rather envisaged a more symbiotic and mutually beneficial relationship, providing the cathartic spiritual support of a 'soul friend'.

It was felt that it should not be necessary for a school leader to have to be proactive in seeking out such peer support, and potentially feeling guilty for accessing it. Rather it should be provided as part of an entitlement within a leadership support package for those who wish to avail themselves of it. An example of this philosophy translated into action is to be found in operation within Nottinghamshire Local Authority in England, where a peer support scheme known as 'Heads Count' offers to serving school leaders of whatever length of experience the opportunity of participating in a paired professional relationship with a colleague headteacher trained in listening and emotional intelligence skills, in a mutually beneficial scheme free at the point of delivery (Flintham 2007b). There is also some parallel with the 'Principals First' scheme operating in Melbourne, Australia, which provides both professional mentoring and counselling support on health and wellbeing issues from a team of recently retired principals, albeit on a costed subscription basis. However, in the

'Heads Count' scheme, there is an additional symbiosis of benefit both to peer supporters, who value *"the opportunity to step out of one's own school and reflect on headship and what it means to you"* through *"the sharing of joys as well as concerns"* in deep and empathetic mutual reflection sessions in which *"the nurturing of one's own humility and admitting one's own vulnerability makes one more effective as a leader"*, as well as to those being peer supported, who value *"the unconstrained non-judgemental nature of the relationship"*.

Such personal support was not seen to be drawn just from other headteachers, nor indeed senior leadership colleagues within the school. Several heads would also identify with the benefit of *"the day-to-day support of the office staff in providing tea, sympathy and laughter"* as a welcome antidote to the pressures of the day. Similarly, the opportunity to engage in corporate networks of colleagues is valued, especially if they are of a similar mind-set: *"a supportive network of like-minded colleagues from schools in similar circumstances and facing similar issues, where you can have an open honest relationship based more on support than challenge"*. Such networks, often self-generated rather than externally imposed, develop *"an ad hoc networked learning community"* which provide not only cathartic personal nurturing support, mutual reflection opportunities and information flow, but also a bulwark against a perceived sense of isolation in headship, particularly when working in pressurised or challenging circumstances. It is interesting that such networking is not confined simply to local colleagues, but through the power of the internet can take on an international dimension. As one Australian secondary principal was able to testify: *"There are some schools half a world away that I have more in common with than schools two kilometres away!"*.

External networks

In addition to affirmation drawn from such belief networks and support networks of colleagues, *relaxation* strategies for heads are provided by *external networks* of engagement with interests and experiences beyond education, giving what could be called the 'hinterland of headship', following Denis Healey, who was accused of having "too much hinterland for a politician" (Healey 1990, 564). It is ironic, however, that in order to create a reservoir in the first place, vast tracts of hinterland have to be submerged, external interests lost, relationships strained and friendships forsaken, in order to create the single-mindedness of vision thought necessary to aspire to and succeed in headship. Then, somewhat paradoxically, it is such interests and relationships that have to be reacquired or regenerated in order to provide the sustaining strategies needed for continuing survival of its pressures. Freed from the habitat of professional context, that external 'landscape' in which the 'doing' of leadership is performed, into a hinterland of different opportunities and interests, the individual nevertheless continues to display his or her habitus or 'way of being', that 'system of lasting transposable dispositions' (Bourdieu 1977, 82) or (after Gerard Manley Hopkins) 'inscape', which determines instinctive behaviours irrespective of contextual circumstance. However, the non-professional hinterland of interests needs to remain congruent with the espoused and declared value system if the personal authenticity of the leader is to be maintained in the eyes of colleagues and inner integrity of self secured.

Experienced headteachers therefore strive to preserve at all costs their hinterland, valuing a capacity to *"get away from it all by disappearing into something else"*. That 'something else' often involves participation in relaxation and renewal opportunities far removed from the professional role. Some valued *"the precious 38 minutes [the effective capacity of an oxygen tank] out of communication whilst scuba diving"* or the *"masochistic satisfaction"* of supporting the local football team. Such external pursuits may for some be seen as 'escapism' to *"a world where life is different, selfish, non-serious, even trivial"*. Others, however, in spite of working a self-confessed "60- to 70-hour week" found satisfaction in the opportunity of participating in the local soup run to the disadvantaged and homeless, to ground them and root them in a different reality. All, however, appreciated the chance to refocus on *"a world elsewhere"*, far removed from the particular pressures of the school situation, in order to return to it with fresh ideas, no longer dulled with over-familiarity or dogged by exhaustion. Such participation reinforced a firm belief in the importance of 'compartmentalisation' as a sustaining strategy in preserving both personal integrity and the passion for leadership. As one Australian school principal trenchantly put it: *"You cannot be a successful school leader if you are only involved in school life. Don't live to work...work to live!"*

Conclusion

An Australian study of school principals' workload and its impact on health and wellbeing (Saulwick and Muller 2004) was aptly named *The Privilege and the Price*. It found that principals almost universally 'love their job' and think of themselves as having the 'privilege' of caring for and developing young people and their families. A number of respondents in the survey indicated that a commitment to the people in their care will usually take precedence over everything else, be it demands from outside the caring relationship, monetary reward or personal preferment. The 'price', however, is an inherent leadership tension between this caring imperative and the managerial demands of the role: what is termed "the carer versus manager tension" (Saulwick and Muller 2004, 22).

A study conducted by ACU National, the Australian Catholic University, (Duignan et al 2005) into socially responsible indicators for policy, practice and benchmarking for human service organisations, also identified similar potential tensions between economic and social imperatives. The study contrasts a managerial economic efficiency orientation, driven by a concern for competencies, targets and measurable outcomes, with a caring socially responsible imperative, with indicators of service, care, stewardship and trust. The chief investigator in this study, writing in another context, argues that authentic leaders do not earn the respect of their colleagues through performance compliance: "Leaders *earn* their allegiance through authentic actions and interactions in trusting relationships" (Duignan 2003, 2).

In no circumstances is that trust called on more fully than when critical incidents hit a school community. In terms of the metaphor 'reservoirs of hope' as applied to school leadership, the *'privilege of principalship'* in such circumstances is to be trusted as the external reservoir of hope for the school. The *'price of principalship'* is the potential draining of the personal internal reservoir of hope by being called on to do so. Investing in the support and sustainability of principals regarding the leadership they are called on to exercise in such circumstances is a sound investment when compared to the potential human cost of burn out or under-functioning. And such investment would not only reinforce the privilege of principalship and enhance the ease of recruitment to it, and redeem the price of it paid in terms of human commitment, it would also retain amongst its adherents the passion for leadership which drew them into the role in the first place and which is needed to sustain their continuance in it.

This chapter has explored practitioner perceptions of the value of the 'reservoirs of hope' metaphor in promoting and facilitating headteacher reflection on spiritual and moral leadership and its capacity to withstand the personally draining pressures of critical incidents such as community tragedies, personnel problems and organisational crises. It has codified the foundational values that underpin such leadership, in terms of the generational, faith-based and egalitarian imperatives that provide the fundamental motivations for school leaders. Fundamental to these value systems is the message of hope on which they are predicated, a vision of a better future and a passion to make a difference in the present circumstance in order to move towards it. Chapter Six returns to this notion of motivational vision to link it with the theological concept of kerygma.

It has been argued that when faced with critical incidents and day-to-day pressures, headteachers display their spiritual and moral leadership in their capacity to empty themselves in the service of others, being prepared to drain their internal reservoir in order to sustain the quality of inter-personal engagement and mutually supportive relationships. This self-emptying may be linked to the concept of kenosis, as will again be shown in Chapter Six. This chapter has considered how for some colleagues the pressures of such kenotic leadership prove unsupportable, resulting in early departure from headship, 'when reservoirs run dry'. In contrasting different types of early-leaving headteachers, from 'striders' who have robust sustainability strategies and a capacity proactively to compartmentalise emerging problems, to 'stumblers' who do not, it has been possible to identify a new type of 'sprinter' headteacher who adopts a short-term, post-modernist portfolio approach to school leadership.

This chapter has also postulated a sea-change in headship as experience progresses, from 'doing headship' to 'being the head', but has also considered the emergence of a 'plateau effect' later in headship, which requires re-energising professional development opportunities to overcome it. It has codified the replenishment strategies used by headteachers to refill their internal reservoirs and to allow them to continue to function as the external reservoirs of hope for the schools they lead. Such sustainability strategies encompass reflection opportunities, reinforcement of self-belief and relaxation strategies, and are supported by belief networks, support networks and external networks of engagement. As will be discussed in Chapter Six, such networks form a koinonia, a 'fellowship in community', to sustain the 'internal reservoir of hope' of the headteacher in order that the 'privilege of principalship' may be maintained against the 'price' of its pressures.

The next two subsequent chapters move on to consider how the concept of 'reservoirs of hope' may be applied to further specific groups of headteachers, both those coming from specific faith perspectives whose 'foundations of faith' underpin their approach to leadership, and those who have chosen to lead schools facing particularly challenging circumstances as 'labours of love'.

CHAPTER FOUR

FOUNDATIONS OF FAITH

This chapter, and the succeeding one, applies to specific groups of headteachers the central concept of the 'reservoirs of hope' metaphor, which is that when acting as the external reservoir of hope for the school when critical incidents hit it, the school leader must call on individual reserves of self-belief and sustainability drawn from a personal inner reservoir of hope, in order to maintain effective spiritual and moral leadership in such circumstances. Thus, the headteacher acts as the bellwether in leading the school through the turbulent times of critical incidents and day-to-day pressures whilst maintaining a personal 'internal reservoir' of self-belief and clarity of purpose, replenished through robust sustainability strategies and supported by a vision of a better future illuminated by hope.

A school cannot take action to move forward without a clear vision of where it wishes to reach. Without such a vision, clearly articulated and collectively supported, it remains static at best, or at worst regresses under stress, when confronted with unexpected incidents or challenging circumstances. In the event, colleagues look to the headteacher to demonstrate spiritual and moral leadership, to act as the wellspring of its values and to provide the necessary coherence and unity of corporate vision. That vision needs to be underpinned by a readily articulated and firmly adhered-to value system or 'spirituality' which governs the leader's professional and personal actions and which delineates the acceptable means to be deployed in reaching the desired ends. Headteachers base their actions either implicitly or explicitly on that value system as their own personal foundational basis of belief, which may be termed a 'foundation of faith', even though that faith may in some cases have no religious connotation whatsoever.

In this chapter, the validity of this concept is tested against the structured reflections of groups of headteachers who lead their schools from specific personal faith perspectives. These may be termed collectively 'school leaders of faith', who may or may not also be 'faith school leaders'. All, however, lead their schools from a 'foundation of faith'. In the following chapter this analysis will be extended to leaders of schools facing particularly challenging circumstances, where such leadership can be described as 'labours of love'. Both chapters explore the development and professional implications of the value systems of such headteachers from data gained from semi-structured interviews that allowed reflection on the spiritual and moral foundations of their leadership and how it affects their professional work, using a similar methodological approach to that adopted in Chapter Three that studied school leaders operating in predominantly secular contexts.

This chapter, after describing the composition of the research sample and how it was formed, continues to apply the conceptual framework by examining the 'why', 'how' and 'what' of the leadership of these headteachers of faith. The first part of this chapter investigates the call to leadership service in particular contexts and the foundational bases of belief on which such leadership stands, and how these were laid down to provide the reasons 'why' that call was fulfilled. The second part of the chapter identifies 'how' that school leadership is displayed in action, codifying the specific leadership attributes that are felt to be required. Third, the chapter considers 'what' are the support strategies that are valued by such school leaders, and how they may also enhance the identification and recruitment of succeeding generations of headteachers. Finally, it concludes by arguing that the essential difference between school leaders of faith and their secular counterparts is in the motivation drawn from the individual faith perspective and the fluency with which it is expressed in the language of faith.

Introduction: research samples

The research sample totalling 60 headteachers and 10 educationists used for this chapter was formed in two parts. The first group to be interviewed consisted of headteachers representing a wide range of individual personal faith perspectives from Anglican to Atheist, Jewish to Muslim, Hindu to Humanist, working in either faith schools or secular schools in England, in order to explore issues of commonality and difference between their 'foundations of faith'. The sample was further extended using data from an additional 10 Australasian faith school principals interviewed as part of a Winston Churchill Travelling Fellowship (Flintham 2006a). It then proved possible to develop the study using funding from the Roman Catholic Diocese of Parramatta in Australia, the East Midlands Leadership Centre (ELMC) in the UK, and Liverpool Hope University, in order to investigate a second group of Roman Catholic school principals in 12 dioceses in

England and Australia, to investigate their spiritual formation, development and sustainability, 'grounded in faith' (Flintham 2007a). Full details of the samples can be found in the Appendix.

The original 'foundations of faith' sample was selected to reflect different categories of foundational faith perspective worked out in the professional environment. Some 36 headteachers were interviewed, garnered as an opportunity sample drawn in the first instance from delegates to an NCSL Leading Practice Seminar on leading schools of a religious character in 2004 and supplemented by personal knowledge and recommendation to ensure representation from a cross-section of schools in different social and geographical contexts and phases across England, and in Australia . Their individual personal faith perspectives drew from the Roman Catholic, Anglican, Methodist, Charismatic Christian, Christian Scientist, Muslim, Jewish, Hindu, Sikh, Buddhist, Humanist and Atheist faith traditions.

Some were leaders of schools of the particular religious tradition that was congruent with their own personal faith perspective (including one Evangelical Christian family who had set up a faith-based 'home school' for their own children). Some exercised leadership roles in schools of a different religious character to their own faith perspective (for example, a Roman Catholic headteacher of a Jewish secondary school, an Anglican headteacher of a Muslim girls secondary school and an Anglican headteacher of a Methodist primary school, together with two headteachers of joint Roman Catholic-Anglican secondary schools). Some operated purely within the secular school environment. All, however, were content to be described as 'school leaders of faith' even though that faith perspective varied considerably.

This original sample was then extended by interviews with some 24 Roman Catholic school principals and 10 national and diocesan educationists in England and Australia. The original research intention was to explore issues of formation, development and support through a comparative study in two Roman Catholic dioceses, Nottingham in England and Parramatta in Australia. In the event, burgeoning interest from principals and diocesan educationists, itself an indicator of a desire for reflection opportunities on this issue, caused an expansion of the scope of the research to encompass interviews with principals in a total of nine English Roman Catholic dioceses together with three in Australia.

The conflation of these two samples thus gives a database of some 60 headteachers leading their schools from a personal faith perspective. For some of the headteachers interviewed, the guiding value system is an overtly religious one, underpinned by active religious practice as a member of a faith community. For others it is one in which, whilst the original motivational connection between religious belief and an ethical value system may have long since been broken, the erstwhile ethical system still remains, albeit divorced from any concept of the commandments of a higher being, in what has been termed 'godless morality' (Holloway 1999). For still others, who whilst still believing in a higher being, sit more loosely to the religious practices of any specific faith community, there holds the concept of an 'untethered spirituality' (McLaughlin 2003) with a subscription to a spiritual ideology without a linkage to a particular religious framework.

This chapter explores such foundations of faith, be they tethered to a particular religious tradition and worked out within an *intra-faith* context of leadership in a school reflecting the religious character of that tradition, or are more 'untethered' through exercising leadership in an *inter-faith* context in a school of a different religious tradition to that subscribed to personally. It also considers the experience of those who serve in the *extra-faith* context of the secular school environment, where they operate at least ostensibly (in spite of the theoretical Christian parameters of the 1944 Education Act) within more of a 'godless morality' milieu. Such latter headteachers may well still be active within faith communities but feel called to work out their faith through leadership in a secular environment. Alternatively some may no longer be active in the profession of faith or even subscribe to the basic tenets of a belief laid down in childhood upbringing, but still retain the essence of its value system, being content to be described as 'crypto-Christians'. For others, espousing a thought-through humanist or atheist framework of belief which does not accept the concept of moral commandment from a higher being, nevertheless admit to having moderated and developed the tenets of a formative Christian value system (often laid down in childhood) through a process of syncretism into a non-theistic morality.

Individual interviews with these school leaders, supplemented in the case of the Roman Catholic headteacher sample by discussions with national and diocesan educationists, explored the career development paths which had led to the present leadership role and context in order to reveal the call to service and the bases of spiritual belief on which that leadership stands and the attributes which are drawn on in exercising it, and how those attributes withstand the test of critical incidents when rhetoric is required to become reality and leadership skills are pushed to the limit. The value of headteacher sustainability strategies and corporate support mechanisms were explored together with the perceived preparation needs of aspirant and newly appointed school principals and the generation of leaders that are to follow. The findings of these interviews may be codified in terms of *bases of belief*, that is, the call to service and the foundations of faith on which it stands; the application of leadership attributes in practice, of *rhetoric into reality*; and the *scaffolds of support* which provide sustainability and succour to school leaders of faith as they exercise their leadership role: the 'why', 'how' and 'what' of leadership.

1. Bases of belief

When asked *why* they had been drawn into the school leadership role in the first place and in particular to the present type of school and the bases of belief which sustained them in it, the headteachers interviewed, irrespective of their personal faith perspective, were all characterised by a strong sense of calling to service, and were able to articulate firm foundations of personal faith which underpinned it. This perceived call to service and underpinning foundations of faith will now be examined in turn.

1.1. Call to service

Headteachers testified to an original firm sense of a call into teaching, although not necessarily at first into school leadership. There was a concomitant strong sense of a calling to service in a specific context, be it to a particular faith tradition, type of school or social area. Those who felt called to exercise a leadership role in an intra-faith context in a school linked to their own faith perspective expressed the view that *"here I can live out my faith...and fulfil a duty to make that faith accessible to others"* in a place where it was felt that there was *"no cognitive dissonance"* between a personal belief system and the espoused values of the school. For some, however, a cognitive dissonance could arise even in such circumstances, for example in tension between a personal philosophy that *"all are of infinite worth as children of God"* and the application of the pupil admission criteria of an oversubscribed church school.

For those operating in the inter-faith environment, there was a sense of *"being in the right place for self and school"* and of fulfilment arising from surmounting the challenges that such circumstances brought, be it in what was seen as the *"creative tension"* rather than "cognitive dissonance" of two faiths working together in joint provision, where the different perspectives of others' *"disturbed comfortableness"* caused re-evaluation of essentials and honed *"a faith capable of jumping out into the unknown"*, or the opportunity to 'make a difference' in a community which, whilst different to one's own perspective, nevertheless was founded on faith. It was felt to be *"easier to understand people of faith if you are a person of faith (even a different one) yourself"*. For such leaders operating 'beyond the comfort zone' there was a need for an explicitly declared framework of faith-based values within the school. As one such inter-faith head put it:

> *"I couldn't be headteacher of this school if it didn't have a faith background (even if it is different to my own). I need an explicit morality, not morality behind a mask."*

Those working in secular environments as 'extra-faith' leaders also felt that this was where they were 'called' or 'meant' to be. Such feelings might be expressed in the language of faith—*"God's call to me to be a servant leader"*, in a challenging comprehensive school—or described in secular terms as the opportunity of service to a local area long known and loved. For some with a particular faith perspective, there was a realistic recognition that headship in a school linked to that tradition would have brought about unsustainable tensions between a personal 'liberal' faith perspective sitting somewhat loosely to the tenets of the tradition, and the expectations of the authority structures of the faith community. Better then, it was felt, to accept the challenges of the secular role, whilst remaining *"comfortable in yourself"* in the belief that it was still *"God's purpose"* that this challenge was accepted.

For a large majority of the sample, irrespective of faith perspective or context of role, the sense of call was to service in areas of social deprivation, be they the disadvantaged communities of the inner city, the 'forgotten' areas of rural hardship or to those 'damaged' by personal circumstance even in apparently affluent surroundings, a sense of *"call to the hard places to be"* wherever they might be found. Again that sense of call might be expressed in the vocabulary of the language of faith, referring to a *"call to ministry"* as a teacher and to a 'mission' to work in a deprived area although tempered by the realism that, as one headteacher admitted:

> *"I might have romanticised this when I look at the good I could actually do (when I got here) with what I thought I could do (before I went)."*

For some, the call was described in the language of faith as *"the hand of God"* which had *"prescribed, ordained and destined"* service to such communities, and a confirming heartfelt sense that a particular course of action was "right". For others who *"cannot believe that God moves us around like puppets"*, there was nevertheless a feeling that *"part of the jigsaw had fallen into place"*. For those serving in the secular environment, the sense of 'rightness' of place was expressed in the robust language of professional confidence: *"my strengths were right, the school was right for me, I made it right"*, or, as another put it: *"I had the single-minded, bloody-minded skills to do it"*. The same sentiment, albeit couched in the language of faith, was expressed by a leader of a school associated with a specific religious tradition: *"I was a tool prepared by God to do a difficult job"*.

For many, irrespective of faith perspective, there was a feeling of a call to social justice, to offer *"care at the margins of society in standing alongside and on the side of those in need"* which provided a sense of fulfilment because *"you are making a real difference to the lives of disadvantaged children"*. This gave a powerful drive to confront societal challenges, as one inner-city headteacher active in community engagement and advancement declared:

> *"You know how people talk negatively about schools in challenging circumstances like this. Well we decided that not only would we do something about improving the school's situation, we would also challenge the circumstances."*

Some faiths were very explicit about this: one ethnic community educator spoke of education being *"the escape route from deprivation"* for such communities, and a Jewish headteacher spoke of education as *"a form of Holocaust protection"* where a good educational foundation is seen as one of the best defences against prejudice, discrimination and abuse, for it is perceived as giving a firm foundation of confidence from which to fight off the pressures of the world.

Of the Catholic school principals interviewed in both England and Australia, over half were serving in areas of some significant social deprivation, not always fully recognised by proxy indicators. One principal averred that, *"this is where a Catholic school should be, in the middle of challenging circumstances"*. Some principals were explicit about *"a sense of calling to this sort of school and its difficulties"* and felt that this was working out the gospel call to the marginalised and dispossessed. As one put it: *"God was calling me to broken people who needed to be helped, and He wasn't going to go away"*. Some schools in the sample were oversubscribed with pupils from Catholic backgrounds, causing potential tensions over rigidity of admissions policy, whereas others had significant proportions of pupils from minority ethnic groups, and adopted an explicit philosophy of *"welcoming the stranger in our midst"* and *"celebrating the diversity"* that this brought.

In the vast majority of cases, the career experience of these principals had been exclusively in the Catholic sector. Those who had started their teaching career in secular schools had either been 'headhunted' or 'drawn back' into Catholic education, but had nevertheless valued the experience of teaching elsewhere. There was a strong sense of calling into specifically Catholic teaching, although not necessarily at first into Catholic principalship. The Catholic system was felt to provide *"a ready-made purpose"* of service and community and working in it gave not only *"a way of putting something back into the faith"* but also the opportunity *"to live out one's faith in a community of consistency between personal values and school values"*. As one principal succinctly put it: *"you can be yourself here"*. However, the opportunity to 'be yourself here', echoed by many in the intra- and inter-faith environments, was more readily accessible to such leaders of schools of a religious character than those serving in secular environments, where a degree of greater circumspection in revealing and openly discussing matters of faith was felt to be necessary, for fear of being falsely perceived as having a "hidden agenda of evangelisation" (Sullivan 2008b).

For school leaders of faith, from whatever perspective, in common with their secular colleagues, a passion was displayed 'to make a difference' in socially disadvantaged communities, a motivation *to "broaden horizons beyond the poverty of aspiration and deprivation"* and a relishing of *"the power to make it happen"* by the application of *"a can-do philosophy"* based on quality of relationships, care for the underprivileged and shared values. This provided a powerful leadership driving force to make progress no matter what the countervailing pressures. As one headteacher of a school serving a community of significant social deprivation was moved trenchantly to assert: *"I don't do maintenance"*.

1.2. Foundations of faith

When asked to describe the foundations of their faith, that is, the spiritual, ethical and moral bases on which they stood, which sustained them in times of trial and which informed explicitly or implicitly their professional actions by providing the reason why a particular course of action was to be favoured, headteacher responses focused around the themes of *respect*, *redemption* and *revelation*.

Respect

There was a strong, unifying philosophy of inclusion based on the need for respect. This encompassed all faith perspectives, albeit expressed in different ways. For some from the intra-faith perspective, it was specifically couched in the language of faith: *"Every person is of infinite worth in the eyes of God"* and so *"as we are all God's children, this should show in the way we treat each other"*. From others representing the inter- and extra-faith contexts, there were more generic responses. It was felt that *"there is not much difference between religions in terms of the universal verities of respect, tolerance and looking for the good in everyone"*. These *"universal verities of honesty, truth and empathy with the underdog"* were thus linked to an imperative to espouse the cause of equal opportunity, respect and responsibility towards others and *"standing up as an advocate for the weak"*. This imperative for social justice for all is in fact little different from that expressed by the generality of colleagues working in the secular sector. For example, Day and Schmidt, reporting on a research project exploring successful and sustainable leadership in UK schools, found that:

> Despite pressures from multiple policy implementation accountabilities, social disadvantage and changing expectations, successful headteachers who demonstrate resilient leadership are those whose values cause them to place as much emphasis upon people and processes as they do on product. These heads demonstrated a clear and abiding concern for learning, care and justice. (Day and Schmidt 2007, 82)

However, what is different for school leaders of faith is the manner in which these imperatives are expressed. For headteachers of Christian faith, it is couched in terms of *"a call to live out gospel values"* in the way that people and processes are treated, to operate in the light of *"what would Jesus do, with every decision being taken in the light of this?"*. For others it is seen as an imperative to fulfil what was seen as the universal commandment to 'love your neighbour as yourself'. For heads operating in the secular environment, it is expressed in the conviction that *"we are all 'gifted and talented', so it is a question of developing the potential in all of us"*, by an inclusive philosophy of equal opportunity.

Redemption

And so if *"no-one is of lesser worth"*, this opens up the possibility of redemption for all, be that expressed in Christian theological terms as the requirement *"to operate as a Christ-like figure in the school"* in striving to emulate the compassionate forgiveness of an ever-loving God who forgives sins of omission and commission, or (as spontaneously translated into secular language by the same respondent as an interesting example of the professional bilingualism which will be discussed in Chapter Six) in the need to grant *"an entitlement to make mistakes and then to have the opportunity of buying into a fresh start"*. For some, this possibility of personal redemption leading to the possibility of *renewal* through a fresh start being offered was one of the irreducible core beliefs to be protected at all costs: *"It is non-negotiable. I would break the rules if necessary to preserve it for the good of the children"*, with an interesting resonance with the secular headteacher cited in the previous chapter who avowed he would rise above his principles for the sake of getting a better deal for his students. For others, the belief in renewal operated not only at an individual but also at a community level, in the call *"to challenge prevailing circumstances and to make a real difference"*, and *"to broaden horizons beyond the poverty of aspiration and deprivation"*, so that *"reconciliation, forgiveness and hope can triumph over dark and difficult things"*, so that that blighted communities could be offered the prospect of renewal and growth.

In common with many of the secular headteachers described in Chapter Three, for almost all the school leaders of faith interviewed, the foundations of their present faith had been laid down in childhood upbringing within a strong familial faith system. For example, virtually the totality of the Catholic school principals interviewed were prepared to describe themselves as 'cradle Catholics', born and brought up in active Catholic homes which had given for many *"an early experience of gospel values at home"*. Almost all had come through an experience of Catholic education. For some the influence of Catholic teachers who modelled the faith had *"bridged the gap between words and practice"*; for others, however, the experience of a Catholic education had been a less than positive one, which had provided an adult motivation now to improve the situation for pupils in their leadership charge, *"to do unto others as one would have wished to have been done by"*. Nevertheless there was a strong sense of *"belonging to the big Catholic family of faith"*, and a sense of a call to minister to those within that family no matter where they are set; this was a frequently and powerfully expressed motivational factor in both entering teaching in a Catholic school and subsequently exercising leadership roles in it.

For some associated with other faith traditions and still active within those faith systems, the powerful influence of parents had 'enveloped' them within the faith and created an enduring call to emulate their example of practice. For others, there had been dramatic charismatic conversion experiences that had galvanised childhood faith into higher levels of commitment or into different consequential courses. For still others, it had been more the 'slow burn' of a spiritual journey of occasional revelation and ongoing acceptance, a contemplative yet enquiring journey of faith seeking understanding and love seeking intelligent action. However, in some cases, that questioning enquiry had led to the rejection of the superstructure of childhood faith but nevertheless the retention of its value system in the belief that *"a godless world is not a valueless world"*.

> *"Whilst the values of my parents have been highly significant in developing my own values, even though we used a different vocabulary, I am no longer driven by a belief system in a deity, but by belief in humanity. I have faith in humanity."*

Some were able to trace the growth of their foundational imperative of respect for all to childhood school experiences of social justice and equality of opportunity, or from recollection of experiences of racial segregation out of which had come a belief that it was still possible *"to celebrate the difference whilst valuing everyone from the position of strength of knowing your own identity"*. Some had found the possibility of personal redemption and renewal through the experiences of 11+ examination failure or marriage breakdown in which they had been supported by the care of others, which had laid down an imperative to reciprocate: *"I gained so much from people who cared for me, I now feel called to put something back"*.

Revelation

For Catholic school leaders in particular, when asked to describe the foundations of their faith, the spiritual bases on which their school leadership stood and how these were revealed in their schools, three words summed up the responses from principals: *inclusion, invitation* and *imperative*. There was a sense that as *"all are called uniquely by God"* and are *"included in His love"*, then so there is a calling to school leaders to include and value equally everyone as a child of God with equal dignity and worth. As one principal put it: *"God's selfless sacrificial love displayed in Jesus shows not only God's love for me, but how I must invite, welcome and care for others"*. And that invitational care for others must display the gospel values of love, justice and forgiveness, embedded in day-to-day actions within *"a servant ministry as "an agent of agape"*.

To stand on these inclusive and invitational foundations as a school leader creates an *imperative of inclusion* even to the so-called 'grey revolutionaries of headship' *"to challenge and to change the existing social order to bring about social justice and the advancement of the Kingdom"*, in *"making real the rhetoric"* of inclusive forgiveness, compassion and reconciliation. This imperative was particularly valid when faced with pressures for pupil permanent exclusion. As Grace (1995, 167) has pointed out, there is an inherent tension between the "prodigal son imperative" with its implications of forgiveness and reconciliation for the individual, and the leader's responsibility for the collective wellbeing of the whole community, of which he or she is often stridently reminded by staff. Consequently, because of the publicly expressed value system based on love, compassion and care, "the act of exclusion has powerful symbolic and cultural meanings within Catholic schooling" (Grace 1995, 167). This tension was seen in the example of one secondary Catholic principal (who had only been driven to resort to permanent exclusion on four occasions in 20 years of principalship) who spoke of having to reconcile the tensions between staff pressure to exclude a child against his fundamental belief that *"all are God's children; our mission is to help them succeed and so we have to try, try and try again"*. Indeed he queried whether permanent exclusion could ever be considered an acceptable solution *"in a Christian school motivated by the gospel of the second chance"* which is continually striving *"to provide a bridge to come back over"* for those who have strayed. The redemptive gospel imperative of inclusion was to value and include every child, no matter how difficult, even in an accountability culture: *"being brave enough to be prepared to lose out a little on [academic] results for their sake"*. As one primary principal put it: *"we don't have naughty children here, only naughty behaviours"*, an echo of the old adage 'hate the sin, love the sinner'.

Equally there was felt to be an *imperative of invitation*, in either explicitly 'reaching out' to diverse communities even if this required *"standing against those who fear that this is in some way diluting the Catholic faith of our school"*, or allowing the values and vision of the school to 'seep out' into the community in a gospel of infiltration which welcomed and promulgated diversity. This was felt to be particularly important when confronting the intense social problems of some communities, the necessity *"to recognise the good somewhere in everyone and to bring it out, for nobody is outside His love"*, or in resisting the temptations of hidden selection in recruitment to a more affluent and oversubscribed school.

School leaders of faith expressed that faith in different vocabulary and drew on different tenets of belief from within their respective faith communities. All, however, were able readily to articulate the value system that underpinned their leadership actions. They saw that value system not as a stand-alone theoretical fixed construct, but one which had been tested, refined and renewed by the pressures of events, and which governed day-to-day leadership actions and continued motivation. Irrespective, however, of specific faith perspective, all the school leaders of faith were imbued with a passion to progress the lives of the individuals and communities in their care, and a sense of call to apply the power of polemic and practice to turn the rhetoric into reality.

2. Rhetoric into reality

The implications of faith expressed in practice were considered by seeking headteacher views on *how* it had influenced their leadership style, approaches to learning and the nurturing of staff and pupils in their school. In other words, they were challenged to respond to the question: 'if you were accused of being a school leader of faith, where would be the evidence to convict you?'. That evidence was adduced in a concern for *"people more than paperwork"*, *"a consultative and collegiate leadership style"* which *"walked the talk and set the example in relationships, listening and caring"*, compassion shown towards personal problems, much valued by staff, and a constant encouragement to staff to be similarly person-centred in their dealings with others, which was felt to have borne fruit in an ethos of *"fairness, equality and upholding of respect for the individual"*, and the possibility of redemption and renewal through *"forgiveness of mistakes, so we can put them right together and move forward"*.

This was particularly seen in the imperative of inclusion articulated by Catholic leaders but displayed across all faith perspectives. This 'passion for inclusion' was evident both in terms of a resistance to using the sanction of permanent exclusion—*"we don't give up on any child"*—and in admission policies, for example the ready inclusion of traveller children into a school serving an affluent suburban area. Equally, there was a willingness to challenge the prevailing orthodoxies in approaches to learning to meet individual pupil need, maintaining that inclusive philosophy in practice so that all could have the best opportunity to succeed. As one headteacher put it:

> *"We are not a SATS-obsessed school; for us education is a long-term investment. We are not concerned with SATS but with citizens."*

It is readily accepted that such egalitarian values are also common across schools in the secular environment, in that school leaders in the secular sector equally have such secure ethical and moral bases and the capacity and courage to articulate them as a vision for their school. Indeed an international review of research on teaching and leading (University of Western Sydney 2007) covering studies published in the last five years, reported that high-quality school leaders of whatever background were found to have the following attributes, not dissimilar to those reported above:

- setting direction by articulating a clear vision
- developing people by offering intellectual stimulation
- establishing collaborative processes and leadership opportunities
- understanding and forging community partnerships
- valuing and empowering students

all of which were also identified in some form by the headteachers in the sample. *"Wouldn't any good school do this?"*, reflected one colleague leading a school associated with a specific religious tradition, but then, having responded in the affirmative, they went on to say: *"Yes, but it is why we are doing it that is important"*. And as another headteacher operating in a faith-based environment indicated: *"the 'plus factor' here, however, is the naturalness of the expression of such values in the language of faith"*.

The difference, then, is in the overt expression of the primary motivation that shapes these values and attributes: *"the explicit commitment to a theocentric and christocentric view of life...a commitment to the reign of God in making meaning and in building the common good"*, as one Catholic school leader put it. Faith therefore provides 'the reason why' in that making of meaning, and it is *"this faith element frame that makes the difference in ensuring the congruence of values and practice"* across the whole school community. It is therefore not the values themselves that are intrinsic to many schools across the whole faith-secular spectrum, but rather the underlying motivation and language of articulation of those values that provides the distinguishing characteristic. Leaders of intra-faith schools feel able to talk overtly and comfortably in the language of faith to staff and pupils, and to articulate a motivational theocentric vision of development: *"We have the example of the way Christ lived his life. I can say to them [the pupils], you have a right and a duty to follow that example"*, said one Catholic school leader. However, those leading schools of a different faith perspective to their own, or indeed operating in a purely secular milieu, believe that it is as much the covert actions of faith as its expression in theological language that can offer students an additional perspective and can carry the message of 'love in practice'. As one such headteacher put it: *"You come to faith by seeing faith in actions, day by day"*.

It was felt that demonstrating that such foundations of faith in action demands of the school leader of faith the following attributes, expressed in the words of the leaders themselves:

- *Courage: "to challenge and not be conformed to prevailing social mores, to stand up and be counted for the faith and its values"*; *"to be prepared to go beyond the comfort zone"*; *"to walk the extra mile for pupil and community, often for not very much in return"*.
- *Vision: "to have a clear sense of where we are going, to articulate what we do and hence in particular why we do it"*; *"to follow however imperfectly, Christ's example explicitly as well as implicitly"*; *"to offer the possibility of redemptive forgiveness to all in our care"*.
- *Capacity: "to articulate the language of faith fluently confidently and comfortably, with the capacity to translate it to make it accessible"*; *"to walk the talk of gospel values in the way one deals with others"*; *"to demonstrate faith in action, in humility and humanity, even if it exposes principal vulnerability"*.

The implications of these leadership attributes in action may be seen in the day-to-day pressures of principalship and the ongoing requirement constantly to test pressures for change against the articulated needs of a value system and vision which connects faith and life and results in social justice in action. They are seen in *"the way we do things and express things round here"*, which gives an implicit sense of the prevailing ethos of the school, and *"in the way we model respectful relationships"*. Indeed, relationships were seen to be the key: as one principal put it (in a deliberate echo of a British Prime Minister's phrase "education, education, education"): *"it's all about relationships, relationships, relationships"*. This *"majoring on relationships, even the difficult ones where I can't hide that I love these people"* was evidenced in *"celebrating the personal rites of passage and handling the human stories"* of staff, in knowing and nurturing them in the context of their personal circumstances, in applying a compassionate and flexible interpretation of the rules depending on those circumstances, and *"taking time to talk and care"*, and in *"random acts of kindness and in the way we speak to and of each other here"* between students, *"modelling behaviours in putting into practice my values, so that what you think and do and say reveals your faith in action"*. Such attributes may be seen not only in the apparently little things of a primary principal having dinner with the children every day to the bigger issues of staff responsibility restructuring to promote distributed leadership: *"remodelling on a principle of service compared to hierarchy, to produce a flatter management structure in a climate of trust, empowerment and encouragement"*.

Attributes of faith in action may also be seen in the testing times when critical incidents hit a school. In common with their colleagues in predominantly secular schools previously described in Chapter Three, many school leaders of faith had faced the trauma of pupil or parent death, often sudden, violent or self-inflicted. They had found themselves in the eye of the storm, with the school being seen as the community space in which to grieve and reflect in mutual strengthening and support: *"the community looked to me...we had to gather, we couldn't not gather. I had to invite them in [the parents at the gate], for I was* meant *to be here for this situation"*.

In these and more prosaic situations, such leaders, although having to admit both privately and publicly their *"own humanity, vulnerability and lack of answers"*, drew inner strength from *"falling back humbly and questioningly onto the bedrock of faith"*, with *"prayer as the life-support machine"* that brought them through, and a conviction that *"God would not put me to the test beyond that which I could bear"*. They drew sustenance from an inner self-belief that *"goodness will always win"* and that what they were doing was "right", and so felt able *"to put your feet in the right place and have the courage to stand firm"*. They drew further strength from the opportunity for post hoc reflection, or structured "mindfulness" as one termed it, in order to be able to recognise after the event that *"it's OK to work with something that's not perfect...I did what I could and I did it as well as I could"*.

As with their secular colleagues, all headteachers interviewed described a wide range of testing times, from high-level critical incidents such as the murder of a pupil, the threat of school closure and inter-racial community tensions, to the so-called "piffling minutiae" of day-to-day pressures which nevertheless threatened to be overwhelming *"when every day is a critical day in a challenging school"*. As one headteacher described it:

> *"Ironically it was the piffling minutiae [of pressure from relentlessly confrontational parents] which came closest to breaking me as the straw that broke the camel's back. There were times in the middle of ad libbing an assembly on tolerance and compassion when I felt: Why don't I just walk off the stage and not come back?"*

Support, however, had been drawn from professional networks, a connectedness of like-minded supportive colleagues described movingly as *"a bit like the disciples together"*, and *"the empathetic care of a fellow-sufferer head"*, coupled with the strong internal self-belief that *"I have been put here by God to sort this out, not to cut and run, and He will sustain me and renew me"*.

Thus the sense of the possibility of personal renewal, earlier identified as one of the all-pervading core values when dealing with pupils, was also felt to be equally applicable to school leaders themselves. For it is out of such experiences of being 'pushed to the edge' of leadership capacity that personal as well as professional renewal can come. For one head of an intra-faith school, a similar experience, exacerbated by a lack of support from the faith community, had actually been a liberating and developmental experience:

> *"...the critical incident [of sustained pressure from aggressive parents over pupil behaviour] changed the way I practice my faith. It liberated me from the pressure to conform to the model of a 'religious' headteacher and gave me the freedom to express my faith in my own way. So the experience was worth the pain...but it doesn't mean I want to repeat it!"*

In this case, support was drawn from inner faith reserves, from a conviction that *"God will care for me through the process"* and that *"if I stick with my values it will work out in the end"*. This was complemented by an expressed belief (after Nouwen 1994) that the leader is called to leave themselves vulnerable as fellow human beings with the same wounds and sufferings as those they seek to serve, so that as 'wounded healers' in their own woundedness, they may become a source of healing for others. Indeed, one principal argued it is essential to be prepared to display that vulnerability: *"God knows we are not perfect, so it is sinful to pretend otherwise. I am only human"*, which provides a refreshing antidote to the 'superman' approach to school leadership.

There was a particular tension when personal beliefs about *respect* for the individual and their needs came into conflict with community expectations. For one leader of a school of a specific religious character that was exemplified in a mismatch between personal liberal values of dietary tolerance as applied to specific individual needs, and the more rigid cultural demands of faith practice expressed by representatives of the faith community. A parallel situation was described from the secular environment in a clash of value systems between a pupil-focused learning agenda and a more rigid behavioural expectation, where the failure to impose harsh disciplinary sanctions was perceived as a sign of weakness by the wider staff and school community. In both cases, it proved necessary for the headteachers to stand firm on the non-negotiable foundations of their own beliefs and ultimately to be prepared to challenge those in opposition to that standpoint: *"Tolerance is what we believe in here"*, so *"if you can't go along with these values, should you really be here?"*.

For many headteachers in schools 'living on the edge' serving difficult socio-economic areas, pressures arise not only from external community tensions but from associated behavioural problems spilling into the school, where pressures for the removal of 'difficult' pupils come into conflict with personal leadership values based on the possibility of *redemption* through retention. In one school of a religious character, parental pressure involving an "over-rigid" definition of alleged bullying and a demand, supported by senior staff, for the removal of the perpetrator, had obliged the head "to set out the ground rules" of inclusion and to draw a line over which they were not personally prepared to go. Although tempted to walk away, *"my faith held me there. I could not truthfully answer the question: 'Have I achieved the goals and objectives God has put me here to do?'"*.

For another headteacher, new to headship in an intra-faith school, her compassionate understanding of behavioural problems in a particular year group had led to conflict with the more 'hard-line' view expressed vociferously by staff with a demand for permanent exclusion and the possibility of a vote of no confidence in leadership decisions from them:

> *"I had to stand firm on the principles of my faith: my belief in redemption, renewal and reconciliation. I had to bare my soul about this, which was a frightening thing to do, but I gained respect by so doing, and eventually for my decision, especially from the children. They feel I care."*

Although the memory of the situation still remained painful, the testing experience was "a maturing point": *"I had to grow up quickly as a head, but it was also a turning point for the school"*, in showing that espoused values would actually be delivered in action "when the going gets tough".

Such challenges could, however, prove personally draining. Being 'on the edge' can be a lonely experience in exercising values-driven leadership in such circumstances. Colleagues of all faith perspectives drew support and succour, when facing such critical incidents and their aftermath, not only from an inner conviction of the 'rightness' of the stance they had adopted and feedback from those whose opinions they valued (including the pupils), coupled with the buttressing power of personal faith and a clearly thought-through value system, but also from the 'seamless structures of support' provided by colleagues, families and friends, summed up as "strength in faith, strength in community". Irrespective of specific faith perspective, the experience of 'being' on the edge as opposed to what is done there, can provide opportunities for personal learning, development and growth, and thereby bring about ontological change. It can allow a recognition that however painful an experience, it has been a formative one, that *"you are what you are because you have come through the pain"*. It can enhance community cohesion *"that having been through the pain together, and having been given the strength to survive it, we can still have hope"*. It can open up *"an awareness of new possibilities for service"*. It can ensure that the passion and power of spiritual and moral leadership exercised in such circumstances, and its underpinning foundational values of respect, redemption and renewal, can continue to be imbued with that essential ingredient of leadership, a sense of hope in a better future.

3. Scaffolds of support

Headteachers were asked *what* were the sustaining strategies which replenished and renewed their personal reservoir of hope and which provided a scaffold of support to enable them to continue effectively to discharge their leadership role in the face of critical incidents and external pressures. They were also asked what in their opinion should be done to identify, grow, develop and support the next generation of school leaders who were to succeed them, and what was the role of the existing school leader of faith in contributing to this. These aspects will now be considered in turn.

3.1. Sustaining existing principals

In sustaining themselves through challenging circumstances, headteachers drew on a range of personal and corporate sustainability strategies. These can be codified as *reinforcement, renewal* and *refreshment* strategies.

Reinforcement

Reinforcement of the rightness of their leadership actions came from a variety of sources. The shared faith of senior staff and the governing body *"walking alongside with me"* provided feedback, affirmation and encouragement in self-belief. Strength was also drawn from the pupils: *"teaching them, interacting with them and getting honest feedback from them"*. As one secondary principal put it: *"If I want to reinvigorate myself, I go for a trip in the playground"*.

Networks of peer support from colleagues in similar contexts or facing similar circumstances were not restricted to the specific faith sector but drew from the common context of the universal nature of school headship. However, such networks were often supplemented by a close relationship with a trusted colleague of similar faith perspective, who was able to act as more than a mentor, more than a professional listening partner, in providing the cathartic spiritual support of a 'soul friend'. The parish or its equivalent provided for some *"quiet support and affirmation"* as well as *"spiritual sustenance in my practice of faith"*. It offered an affirming knowledge that *"people who know me are praying for me and my work"* and some felt that the connection with a local parish had *"strengthened me in the tough times of school leadership"*. Others, however, sought *"the need for anonymity so I can pray and be myself"* and so appreciated worship opportunities away from the immediate locality and role expectations of the school, where the ever-present requirement to be on display as 'the moral icon' within the community was felt to be reduced.

Renewal

Some described experiences of personal renewal through experience of 'periods of turbulence' where no matter how bleak the personal and professional situation appeared to be and no matter how hard-pressed and defeated they might have felt, they had been supported by *"Elijah moments in the struggle, with sustenance from unlikely sources"*, which had caused them to reflect anew on their fundamental values and purposes and had given them courage, strength and refreshment to allow the struggle to continue to a successful conclusion.

Renewal also came from opportunities for further professional study *"opening windows to a more thinking allegiance to the faith"*. Seen as more important even than the content of such study was the opportunity for 'time-out' reflective space in the presence of like-minded colleagues, *"giving an away-day experience of spiritual discussion at an adult level"* and the opportunity for overt discussion of issues in the language of faith. There was a *cri de coeur* for the provision of such *"events with a spiritual heart"* with *"the opportunity to talk about the role of principalship in the context of the distinctive nature of a faith school"*. In this, the opportunity for structured retreats and sabbaticals, such as those described in the subsequent section on support structures, was highly valued, particularly in creating space *"to set the problems of school in the perspective of eternity"*.

Refreshment

Refreshment came from the opportunity to 'switch off' from the immediate demands of principalship, to become immersed in worship, meditation and reflection activities, and in the daily lives of families, friends and other interests. As with headteachers in the secular environment, this 'capacity to compartmentalise', to switch off from immediate professional problems and thus prevent 'cross-contamination' between work and home, was felt to be an important sustaining strategy.

Corporate support provision, as well as offering release from the immediate pressures and tensions of principalship, also provided the opportunity for continuing adult spiritual formation and development. However, this was felt by many to be largely ad hoc, with the necessity to be proactive in *"working out one's own salvation"*. This had been done in a variety of ways by principals, through accessing support from the diocese both at a personal and corporate level in conferences and meetings, engaging in further study of spiritual matters, participating in retreat and sabbatical opportunities, discussions of faith in networks of like-minded colleagues both within and beyond the school and through generating oases of personal reflective space. Particularly valued was access to the opportunity for retreat and sabbatical experiences. Chapter Six considers further the reinvigorating power of such sabbatical and secondment opportunities for those leading schools in particularly challenging circumstances.

In the Roman Catholic Diocese of Parramatta, the ELIM Leadership Programme for Experienced Catholic Principals is named after the oasis in the desert where the Israelites rested on their way through the wilderness

(Exodus 15, 27). Provided by the diocese in association with ACU National, the Australian Catholic University, it is billed as "something different...something more" than is ordinarily available through conferences or post-graduate study, in "providing an opportunity for experienced principals to integrate the theory and practice of Catholic school leadership and personal spirituality...in a community experience over a sustained period of time", was said by many participating principals "to do the business". The ELIM opportunity, symbolising "an oasis experience" for busy principals, was affirmed for "its focus on being instead of doing" and its capacity to enrich and further develop a personal culture of reflective space, providing "time for reflection and grounding yourself". Equally valued by Parramatta school principals was the present proactive access to three personal spiritual development days available in term time during the course of the school year. It was felt that it would be a retrograde step if this perceived valuable opportunity were to be removed or transferred into school holiday periods, and that it provided a model of good practice which could be equally beneficially applied to school leaders in other contexts.

Indeed, so highly valued were these sorts of experiences that one colleague who felt that *"the system doesn't do much unless you are prepared to be proactive"* wished to set targets for all principals for participation in such activities *"to develop the spirit of the Catholic principal in all"*. Another principal, whilst applauding ELIM as a valuable experience, bemoaned the perceived lack of regular strategic planning in principal spiritual development compared to professional development, and called for the provision of more structured, targeted, protected and even mandated opportunities for principal spiritual formation and growth. One diocesan educationist, an erstwhile principal of two schools, recognised, however, the inherent tension that such mandated participation would cause with the "intimacy of dynamic" required to create a safe forum to articulate, question and affirm issues of faith, and wondered whether the necessary setting-aside of role and ego could occur in such a directive situation. There needs to be *"a recognition that faith is a growing organism which may suffer periods of drought"*, even among faith school principals. Better therefore perhaps to reach the non-participating school leaders through what was memorably described by an English educationist as "seduction and wiles", through "positive stroking and encouragement", offering entitlement to "spiritual headspace" no matter where it is to be found and "hard-edged pragmatism", with discussions on specific delivery responsibilities subtly infiltrated by spiritual perspectives as "the pill in the jam".

Such 'hard-edged pragmatism' may also be secured in the translating and reinterpreting, contextualising and personalising, directing and focusing of mandatory national programmes such as the National Professional Qualification for Headship (NPQH) in England into 'the language of faith' for those who are being prepared as potential principals for the leadership of schools of a religious character. Such preparatory programmes for aspiring church school headteachers have already been piloted by the Roman Catholic Archdiocese of Birmingham, the Roman Catholic Diocese of Salford and the Church of England Diocese of Coventry.

3.2. Supporting potential principals

Identifying and growing the next generation of school leaders is a crucial priority for all education systems, because sustaining the flow of high-quality school leaders is critical to achieving the best outcomes for all children and young people. However, faith schools in both England and Australia face more than most the problem of principal recruitment. The demographic challenges of the age profile of current school leaders, the difficulty in overcoming negative perceptions of the pressures of principalship, the added perceived requirement to be not only the professional and spiritual leader of the school community but also a faith leader within the local community, have highlighted the need to make leadership succession a collective responsibility for such schools and their stakeholders.

The National College in England has as one of its four corporate goals the identification and growth of tomorrow's leaders (NCSL 2006a). Through the provision of supporting consultants, it has worked with schools, local authorities and dioceses in 10 pilot areas to help develop systematic strategies to replace the school leaders due to retire in the next five years. It is felt the solution lies not in a 'one-size fits all' national initiative but in the generation of local solutions, which will encompass programmes, events and conferences as well as coaching, mentoring, secondment and professional development opportunities. Such diocesan initiatives have parallels in Australia, for example in the Leaders for the Future Programme for Teachers under 30 (Canavan 2006). Two English Roman Catholic dioceses, namely Hexham and Newcastle, and Hallam, are participating in the NCSL pilot scheme, and from these dioceses, both representative school principals, diocesan officers and the assigned NCSL leadership consultant were interviewed as part of this present study. Participants interviewed were asked to address the issue of mechanisms that were or should be provided to address the spiritual formation and development needs of aspirant and potential Catholic school principals. The main collective message was clear, and equally applicable to leaders of schools of differing faith traditions: the imperative to:

> *"...spot and grow your own future leaders; invite and identify, nurture and affirm them; see potential and provide appropriate developmental opportunities for them."*

'Growing your own' requires leadership to be seen as a continuum, beginning at first appointment as a teacher. Emergent leaders need to be identified at an early stage, 'talent spotted' by principals (indeed one colleague felt that it should be mandatory for existing principals to talent spot potential successors), told in specific terms that they have been spotted ("you'll be a head one day") and given opportunities for early responsibility and the 'psychological air' to discharge it within a system of distributed leadership. This may require innovative approaches to traditional staff responsibility structures. Young leaders should be inducted into 'a community of belonging' in a leadership cadre, supported and mentored by a nominated member of the senior leadership team and nurtured and affirmed so that they know their contributions are valued. 'Give them a taste of success' should be the early watchword. For existing middle leaders with perhaps a more post-modernist mind-set, it was felt that a more structured programme of spiritual formation should form a mandatory gateway to the role to develop them not only as professional leaders but also as religious leaders within the school, and that the discharge of this role should be formally evaluated within the appraisal process.

For aspirant and potential principals, there was felt to be a need for specific staged succession preparation programmes for Catholic schools, and the need to 'translate' national programmes into the language and vocabulary of faith, *"so that people of faith can talk about faith together"*. Such programmes should aim to give aspirant principals a deeper embedded personal spirituality before appointment to principalship, aiming to articulate the culture of Catholic education through the capturing and transmission of leadership stories. It was recognised particularly in the Australian context that there was a potentially shallower pool of faith awareness and practice from which to draw future principals, with a decline in active practice founded in 'cradle Catholicism' and its replacement by greater numbers of what have been termed 'CnE Catholics' (Christmas and Easter), who sit more lightly with the teachings of the Catholic Church and suffer from 'Catholic amnesia' regarding its worship practices and religious meta-narratives. It was argued that it might be necessary to offer 'remedial intervention' to remedy this, one colleague going so far as to propose a three-month pre-principalship retreat and induction programme of spiritual preparation as a formational and incubational experience. This would parallel and complement the existing corporate and personal enrichment opportunities for experienced principals. Whilst recognising the financial implications of this, it was argued that these should be seen in the context of the long-term salary costs of the totality of principalship.

There was an imperative to contemplate *"a future that will be different: it won't be the same, even if we stay the same, and we need to prepare for that difference"*. The importance of acknowledging that changed situation requires offering 'total honesty' about the demands of the Catholic principal's role, especially in its 'added layers' of community expectations. It was accepted that Catholic school leaders require "an enthusiasm for the things of God", with "a fluency in a Catholic world view, Catholic morality and a deep lived faith, with a capacity to promote a Catholic identity and an enthusiasm for the things of God, in the face of secularism", but this must be linked with the ability "to integrate the language of faith and the secular language of school improvement" (Bracken 2006). Diocesan educationists echoed these sentiments. For the Bishop of Parramatta, the perceived 'crisis' is not one of faith but of the transmission of faith, and here it is felt that Catholic schools and their leaders have a vital role to play in the education of the whole person, with Christ at the centre, the maintenance of an ecclesiastical unity through linkage with the pastoral mission of the Church and the involvement of students in a wider mission of social justice (Manning 2007). However, diocesan educationists were even more explicit than their school principal colleagues in articulating 'the difference of the job' in terms of it "being done in the name of and in partnership with the Catholic Church". School leaders are therefore called to be resolute in fulfilling these demands, but there was realistic recognition of the need to 'manage' the partnership and in particular to deal with possible tensions between personal and ecclesiastical belief. The need to publicly 'uphold the code' not only in the immediate school community and its Catholic environs, but also in a bridge-building role within the pluralist and secular world, could create the perceived added burden of 'being the moral icon' and 'modelling the community's expectations', which requires additional 'reserves of resilience' in Catholic school leaders over and above their secular school counterparts. The capacity of existing school leaders to confront and resolve these additional tensions and their enthusiasm to do so should be harnessed and transmitted by greater use in mentoring and 'training principal' roles.

Equally there is a need to draw on and develop the expertise of other senior leaders. For example, for experienced Catholic senior leaders who do not presently aspire to be principals, there exist Established Leaders programmes (EMLC 2006) containing 'values-driven faith-based content', supplemented by shadowing and taster opportunities when the substantive principal is on short-term secondment, and supported by a diocesan 'toolkit pack' for acting principals. There is also a need to explore through further research the reasons why Catholic teachers move out of the Catholic sector (more prevalent in England than in Australia where state and faith sectors are more structurally distinct), and particularly why experienced deputy principals either move out of the Catholic sector into secular school leadership positions or decline to apply for principalships at all.

One factor may be the perceived rigidity of selection procedures. It was argued by headteachers interviewed that there is a need for *"a paradigm shift"* in the selection process, away from competition between candidates to *"the offering of who you are"* as a candidate as well as what you have in terms of a skill set, *"offering insight into your being in addition to what you are capable of "doing"*, to those who are 'letting' the role and a concomitant obligation on selection panels to exercise discernment of *"the what else: not just the hoops of headship capability but its heart"*.

To facilitate such discernment, it is useful to draw on the work of Duignan (2006), who distinguishes between 'narrow and simplistic' models of leadership competencies, with their concern for checklists of performance indicators and their encouragement of black-and-white thinking, and leadership capabilities, the knowledge, skills, attributes, qualities and wisdom needed to cope with and respond to the dynamic and unpredictable contexts which constitute the 'grey areas' of day-to-day school leadership decision making. He cites Stephenson, who distinguishes between competency and capability, and introduces the moral dimension of fitness *of* purpose as well as fitness *for* purpose in envisioning and implementing the leadership vision:

> Competency is about delivering the present based on past performance; capability is about imaging the future and bringing it about. Competency is about control; capability is about learning and development. Competency is about fitness for (usually other people's) purpose; capability is about judging the fitness of the purpose itself. (Stephenson 2000, 4)

And as de Pree (1989, 136) has suggested that leadership is "more an art, a belief, *a condition of the heart* than a set of things to do" (emphasis added), then the difference between competency and capability in leadership may be conceived as the difference between the 'head' and the 'heart' of headship.

Conclusion

The essential difference between school leaders of faith and their secular counterparts is seen in what might be termed the 'what else', a concentration not just on the hoops of headship capability but its heart. That 'heart' is to be found not only in the maintenance of a vision of hope in the prospect of a better future, as displayed by all the school leaders studied, but in the building and sustaining of a community of faith committed to work towards it. Chapter Six considers further how the belief in the transformational nature of hope makes it an important underlying philosophical theme for school leaders of whatever faith perspective, in providing a unifying 'theology of hope' for their work. Whilst that core message of hope stands on a firm and clearly articulated personal moral and ethical base, it is also clearly linked in many cases to the tenets of a particular faith tradition or has been substantially derived from it. That link with tradition provides for many school leaders of faith a sense of consistency and coherence, together with access to the support networks and teachings of the faith community: a 'sea of faith' which replenishes and renews the individual and collective 'reservoirs of hope' and provides 'the reason why' which underpins leadership motivations and actions.

The difference is also in the language that is used to articulate this motivational purpose. In those operating within the intra-faith and to some extent the inter-faith environments, faith and the explicit support of the faith community provide *"a mandate to integrate faith into the everyday lives of students"* so as to build up the common good. That mandate allows openness in discussing issues of faith and a rich heritage of story and teaching to support such discussions. It is particularly supported by *"a shorthand language in which to express such matters"*, for example for leaders operating from a Christian perspective within a Christian milieu, readily understood phrases such as 'gospel values' or stories such as that of the Good Samaritan and the Prodigal Son provide a ready platform from which to explore the spiritual dimensions of life. The capacity to articulate, fluently and without embarrassment, deeply personal attributes and values in the language of faith, within the work environment, and to seek out and draw succour from sustaining refreshment opportunities from the faith community where such language is a natural part of the *zeitgeist*, is a powerful supportive mechanism for such leaders. This commonality of language, and fluency in and ease with it, then helps to legitimise and de-privatise practice "so we become the 'we' rather than the 'I' and can build a collective community of faith, vision and praxis" (Gore 2007) in a unique way which is denied to those who do not have the spiritual and cultural capital which underpins such language, or who have to exercise their leadership in extra-faith circumstances, where somewhat more circumspection is required.

How that vision of hope is delivered is through relationships: a majoring on the primacy of them and being prepared to empty oneself in the service of others in order to sustain them. *"All leadership is about relationships"*, said one principal interviewed, and although because of the complexity of those relationships between staff, pupils, parents and the wider community beyond the school it is not possible to establish a direct link between high-quality school leadership and pupil outcomes, there is clear research evidence (summarised by the University of Western Sydney 2007) that principals do have a salient if indirect effect on pupil outcomes through the goals they establish and the quality of the learning environment they foster, and that effective school leadership must be responsive to context and adaptable in the face of change. Facing such change pressures requires from the school leader of faith attributes of courage, vision and capacity, supplemented by additional reserves of resilience necessary to meet often unrealistic community expectations to be the moral icon and a faith leader within that community. Such resilience is clearly linked to faith in that it is:

> ...closely aligned to a strong sense of moral purpose...fundamental to both an ethic of social justice and a concern for promoting achievement... Leaders with moral purposes are values led... These values are at the forefront of their decision-making processes, their perceptions of the purposes of schooling, their understanding of the concept of education and their choice of 'right' or 'good' actions. (Day and Schmidt 2007, 65, 67)

It can therefore be argued that a 'resilient' leader of whatever faith perspective is not simply a leader with the capacity to withstand a particular set of challenging circumstances or to adapt to a particular context, but rather a leader with a specific 'toolkit' of enduring attitudes: self-belief, humility, compassion, trust, which can continue to be applied no matter how lonely or critical the circumstances become, and a value system which can continue to provide a motivational personal and collective drive to withstand the pressures of those circumstances, and maintain effective inter-personal engagement throughout them.

Developing and supporting principals in their spiritual and moral leadership of schools is thus crucial in sustaining them in that task. One indication of a mature spirituality for school leaders of faith is an awareness of the presence of God in all aspects of experience, a discerning through reflection of God's activity within one's own life and in the lives of others, and the awareness of progression on a faith journey towards greater knowledge of God and oneself. As one headteacher put it:

> "The core of leadership is to understand people, but before that you have to understand yourself... We search for God within ourselves. As we discover ourselves, we discover more about God."

Reflection on the foundations of one's faith and how they were laid down and continue to be developed provides stability within the turbulence of events and pressures. It provides space to discern personal strengths and weaknesses. It gives the opportunity to discern the gifts of others, and through a model of distributed leadership to enable the gifting of opportunities to them not only to further their own spiritual development but also to be able to contribute fully to the collective endeavour to secure the corporate vision.

The voices of school leaders of faith recorded in this study, irrespective of whatever faith tradition they are associated with, reinforce the call from their secular colleagues for a continued recognition of the importance of personal sustainability and support strategies in principalship. However, in particular they cite the need for a leadership entitlement to reflective opportunities which are concerned with spiritual growth as well as professional competence, and which are equally fostered and legitimised through appropriate availability and funding. For the school leader with a personal faith centre, this would facilitate opportunities for individual reflection through a disciplined offering of protected time for continuing self-discovery, personal renewal and spiritual growth, together with access to participation in networks of like-minded colleagues, and support and understanding from the appropriate faith community. Above all, the vision must be of an alternative paradigm which places the development of leadership capabilities above competencies, 'heart' above 'head', 'being' above 'doing', relationships above results, and belief at the centre of all things, rooted and grounded in faith.

This chapter has explored the views of school leaders of faith who approach their task from a range of faith perspectives, be they overtly religious or non-religious, tethered or untethered, and exercised within faith-based or secular institutions. It has identified the common threads of passion, power and capacity for progress shown by such leaders, supported and sustained by their fundamental belief in relationships which are underpinned by resilience, respect and the possibility of redemption, and sustained by personal reinforcement, refreshment and renewal opportunities. It has highlighted the expressed need for there to be a concern for the capabilities of leaders as well as their competencies, a concern for the 'heart' as well as the 'head' in leadership, and the importance to be placed on the need to find time 'to be' as well as time 'to do', distinctions which surely epitomise the essential difference between leadership and management.

The next chapter turns to consider a further group of school leaders, those leading schools in particularly difficult contexts, for whom issues of sustaining passion and purpose, energy and enthusiasm, drive and determination, in the face of such challenging circumstances, are particularly pressing.

CHAPTER FIVE

LABOURS OF LOVE

As has been seen from the previous chapter, some school leaders feel called by their 'faith' to serve 'in the difficult places'. This, however, is not only true of those coming from a religious perspective, but also those of a more secular mien, who feel equally drawn to service in challenging circumstances. This chapter, the third and final chapter mining the data from the headteacher interviews, explores the interpretation and impact on practice of spiritual and moral leadership as understood by a group of 40 headteachers who have felt called to work predominantly in schools facing challenging circumstances as a 'labour of love'.

Although it can be argued that all schools face challenging circumstances of some sort, through exposure to critical incidents or systemic pressures, schools in challenging circumstances can be defined as those who either fail to meet defined outcome targets for pupil attainment, serve communities with significant social deprivation or face contextual challenges such as falling rolls, population mobility or severe pupil behavioural problems. This chapter draws substantially on data from interviews conducted with a small cross-phase sample of eight headteachers leading such schools, who addressed the question 'what's good about leading schools in challenging circumstances' (Flintham 2006b), and extends this with data from a further 22 interviews with those leading similar schools. This is then supplemented with the recorded views of a further 10 headteachers and 10 supporting educationists responsible for provision or evaluation, to investigate the perceived value of sabbaticals and secondments in providing opportunities for reflection and renewal particularly to headteachers in schools facing challenging circumstances.

The aim in this chapter is to supplement and extend the findings of the previous data chapters by not only considering the spiritual and moral leadership of a different group of school leaders, namely those leading schools facing challenging circumstances, but also by developing a small-scale quantitative approach to studying their professional and personal characteristics, to validate findings revealed through qualitative interview.

An introductory section considers what *defines* a school in challenging circumstances and reviews the extant literature regarding the type of leadership style that has been found to be prevalent in such contexts.

The conceptual framework is then applied to explore the 'why' 'how' and 'what' of spiritual and moral leadership across an interview data set of 30 headteachers leading schools in challenging circumstances. First, the chapter examines, through interviews held on a one-to-one basis, what *motivates* the headteachers of schools in challenging circumstances in terms of their core values and the sharing and implementation of their vision for the school, to provide the reason 'why' they feel called to leadership in such contexts.

Second, it considers what *characterises* such headteachers in terms of 'how' they lead their schools in such constantly challenging circumstances and the spirituality that underpins their actions. Goldsmith (1994) has linked spirituality with explorations of personality type and temperament (Goldsmith and Wharton 1993) as revealed through application of the Myers-Briggs Type Indicator (Briggs-Myers 1993), and Craig et al (2006) and Francis et al (2007) respectively have extended this into studies of the psychological profiles of Roman Catholic and Anglican clergy. However, preliminary enquiries by the author to seek possible similar engagement by headteachers revealed that this would probably be seen as a step too far. However, it has proved possible (Flintham 2009) to collect small-scale quantitative data on professional characteristics rather than the more threateningly perceived categories of personality type or psychological profile.

This was carried out through piloting the use of a self-reflective online analytical instrument with a small and geographically compact sub-set of 10 headteachers leading schools facing challenging circumstances predominantly within one local authority area, to explore whether there were particular clusters of professional characteristics and personal qualities which were common to the spiritual and moral leaders of such schools. This small-scale quantitative analysis sought to validate the qualitative findings derived from the interviews. It applied a quantitative rather than qualitative lens to test below the surface text of the leadership stories expounded in interview, to reveal patterns of leadership behaviour, moving from the retelling of leadership story to the analysis of leadership attributes, from a concern not only with 'doing' but also with 'being', and from the empirical to the ontological, in order to identify the prevalent clusters of professional characteristics that were displayed.

Third, the chapter considers 'what' *sustains* and supports such headteachers both personally and corporately in their work, particularly when confronted by critical incidents and additional external pressures. It explores the perceived value of secondment and sabbatical opportunities in providing reflective space so that personal refreshment and renewal may occur. It draws on the views of an additional 10 participating headteachers and a similar number of educationists with responsibility for enabling or evaluating such supportive provision. Finally, it concludes by summarising the particular characteristics of leaders of schools facing challenging circumstances in terms of the 'why', 'how' and 'what' of their spiritual and moral leadership, and compares them to the findings of previous chapters which have been based on leaders with specific faith perspectives or those operating predominantly in the secular sphere.

Introduction: defining schools in challenging circumstances

Keys et al (2003), in their review of the literature into leadership of schools in urban and challenging contexts, conclude that whilst there exists a body of literature on the subject, definitions of what constitutes such a school are rarely offered or agreed. One definition (Ofsted 2002) focuses on student performance, and defines challenging circumstances as when a school is failing to meet government 'floor targets' of 25% 5A*-C grades at GCSE or their primary SATS equivalents. As Keys et al point out, however (2003, 20), whilst such a definition has operational value in directing attention towards lower attaining schools, it has less value in considering the nature of the circumstances that they face, or indeed in recognising that there are some schools facing challenging circumstances that nevertheless have relatively high levels of pupil attainment. A second definition (Ofsted 2000) attempts to use a free school meal indicator of above 35% as a proxy indicator for social and economic deprivation, without recognition of the fact that in many communities, free school meal entitlement take-up may be depressed through cultural and social reasons. However, in spite of the absence of an agreed formal definition of 'challenging circumstances', there is a consensus amongst school leaders that such schools face a multitude of complex and socially related problems (Harris 2002b) with low levels of pupil attainment on entry, with limited parental education, expectation and support, and in some cases, high levels of pupil mobility. Such challenging features are not always fully reflected in the surrogate measure of free school meal entitlement, nor are they solely to be found in schools in urban or inner-city areas, but can equally be found in schools in rural environments (contrary to Keys et al 2003, who regrettably conflate challenging contexts and specifically urban areas). Such contextual challenges are often accompanied by a number of school-related issues such as falling rolls, unsatisfactory buildings, staff recruitment difficulties, low levels of parental involvement and pupil behaviour management problems, coupled with the ever-present accountability pressures of striving to meet the so-called 'floor targets' or facing the threat of potential takeover or closure as a consequence of failing to do so.

In the face of such contextual challenges, effective school leaders use a range of leadership and management approaches selected to meet the developmental stage of the school (Harris and Chapman 2002, 3). A memorable distinction has been drawn (Grint 2002, 248) between the concepts of leadership and management. The term 'management', deriving from the Latin word *manus* (meaning hand), and the subsequent Italian word *maneggiare* (meaning to control, often of horses), can conjure up an image of Ben Hur chariot races with their control of unruly beasts. The term 'leadership', however, from the Old German word *lidan* and its Old English derivation *lithan* (to travel, to show the way, to guide), offers an image of Moses parting the Red Sea and pointing the way to the Promised Land. In the face of challenging circumstances, it might be expected that leaders in such schools would operate in a Ben Hur control mode of seeking to harness and tame the 'unruly beasts' of contextual circumstance. Indeed early attempts to 'turn around' such allegedly 'failing' schools involved the drafting in of a so-called 'superhead', *"a hero on a horse"*, as one rather more conventional colleague described the breed. Such attempts, more often than not, ended in failure, burn out or withdrawal of the individual concerned, and their replacement by a calmer, less charismatic, organisational approach (Stark 1998): the replacement of the 'heroic headship' style with the consolidator and nurturer styles of leadership identified in Chapter Three. Interviews conducted for this present research study with a sample of present-day leaders of schools in challenging circumstances support the findings of Harris and Chapman (2002, 3) in showing an emphasis less on operational management and more on leadership that is people-oriented, transformational and empowering, operating more in 'guidance' rather than 'control' mode, with the leadership characteristics of Moses rather than Ben Hur.

It is important to reiterate that the concept of spiritual and moral leadership being used in the present research study does not have exclusively religious connotations nor linkage to a specific set of beliefs, but is rather based on a wider concept of 'secular spirituality': whatever it is that gives individual leaders their foundations of ethical behaviour and bases of belief that have been suggested as the fundamental motivation and purpose that distinguish leaders from efficient functionaries (West-Burnham 2001). Such spiritual and moral leadership, as so defined, is therefore concerned with the often intangible aspects of inter-personal engagement and quality of relationships, particularly when these are tested by the pressures of external events, and their preservation through a clearly articulated structure of moral and ethical values: a distinction between leadership and management in headship that can be neatly encapsulated as the difference between 'being' and 'doing'. When this concept is explored within the context of the leadership of schools in challenging circumstances, it will be seen that such leaders, whilst facing more than their share of critical incidents and external pressures, display spiritual and moral leadership by drawing on significant clusters of inter-personal skills. They prefer to operate at the 'enabling' end of a controlling-enabling continuum, whilst still being able to operate in control mode should the exigencies of circumstance dictate. They maintain high levels of enthusiasm, passion and motivation for service in schools of this type, having often consciously chosen to answer a perceived call to work in such communities as a 'labour of love'.

1. What motivates heads of schools in challenging circumstances

In common with their colleagues leading schools from a personal faith perspective or serving in the secular sector, as studied in previous chapters, headteachers leading schools in challenging circumstances are motivated by their core values, what can be termed "the irreducible… bottom line of non-negotiable beliefs" common to many called to public service (Hyman 2005, 80), which provide the reason 'why' service in such schools is preferred. Previous research into the leadership of schools in challenging circumstances (Harris and Chapman 2002, 2) has identified effective leaders of such schools as having "to cope with unpredictability, conflict and dissent on a daily basis without discarding core values". To do this their actions must be *"people-centred…*underpinned by a set of personal and professional values that placed human needs before organisational needs…" and which "combined *moral purpose* with a willingness to collaborate and to promote *collaboration* amongst colleagues" (Harris and Chapman 2002, 2; emphasis added). The 30 headteachers of schools facing challenging circumstances interviewed for this present study described foundational values and leadership approaches in sharing and promulgating those values that are consistent with this categorisation.

The underlying theme of the value systems articulated showed a moral base of core values which was people-centred and regarded all as equal and therefore worthy of equal respect. There was a strong sense of striving for *"inclusive individualism"* which was displayed in a recognition that *"everyone is important, everyone matters, everyone has a voice"*, be they adult or child, parent or staff. This *"respect for others and their beliefs"* was underpinned by a strong imperative based on the Golden Rule of *"doing as you would be done by"*, and measuring leadership actions against the yardstick of *"treating others as you would want your own children to be treated"*. As one headteacher summed it up: *"it's all down to how you treat people...how you are with people"*.

Leadership actions were thus imbued with a sense of moral purpose to ensure that all were given equality of opportunity to achieve their potential within an all-embracing inclusive philosophy. The firm belief that all are capable of achieving was not to be gainsaid by challenging circumstances being used as an excuse for low expectations: *"we strive for excellence...to be the best that we can be"*. The primacy of this moral purpose thus meant that negative expectations of pupils by staff, an undermining of the eternal hope of redemptive change even in the most challenging of behaviours or a dismissive writing off of potential with the words *"what else can you expect from children like these"* had to be vigorously challenged, *"even at the risk of losing the member of staff, which actually happened"*, as one headteacher testified.

In common with the headteachers studied in Chapters Three and Four, this sense of moral purpose had often been laid down in upbringing or was reinforced from an active faith perspective. Significantly, of the headteachers interviewed, whilst only one third were still active in the profession of a religious faith, a further third recognised that their value system had been laid down through the influence of an education in Christian values, either at home or at school: *"I am an agnostic humanist now, but I recognise that I still believe in Christian values, if not the rest of the Christian faith package"*, as one headteacher explained. The remaining third of respondents recognised that their moral code had been laid down by often working-class upbringings that had given them *"a passion for equal opportunities and social justice"* and *"a righteous anger to confront injustice and ensure fair play"*. There were times when in leadership these core values were buffeted by the pressures of events, and it was necessary to stand firm on the declared values of mutual respect, even if that sometimes exacted a heavy price: *"a price to be paid in staff recruitment and retention for the moral stance being taken. It's a risk strategy but one on which I'm not prepared to compromise"*, avowed one headteacher. In essence, it was *"necessary to stick to your convictions, to make clear what you believe in and stick to it...or you will not survive"*.

Not only is it necessary to maintain such personal conviction when faced with external pressures—*"to have the confidence to stand by your values and not to be pushed around by every wind of change, so that irrespective of the national agenda, if it is good for our children we will do it...and carry the can if necessary"*—it is equally important to ensure the collective sharing of such values through the promotion of collaboration. "Creating a common meaning" is a primary leadership function in schools in challenging circumstances (Muijs et al 2007, 3, drawing on Gardner 1995) with the headteacher as 'the meaning maker' creating a commonality of values, through a combination of imposition, staff changes, negotiation and discussion, and promoting collaboration to ensure the sharing and collective implementation of those values across the school community. Often a newly appointed headteacher is obliged to wrestle with entrenched countervailing attitudes in order to ensure a collective subscription to those core values:

> *"In the early months (of my new headship), my work was really about taking back control of the school climate... I set about making changes that would start to build a school that had collective energy for the challenge... We had to begin with losing some of the long-term staff who took retirement and excluding some of the pupils who were at the heart of the disruption. It felt drastic, but it needed to be done."*

But the outcome of such 'drastic' action was ultimately a positive one:

> *"I believe in offering our pupils the best start in life and I know my colleagues [now] believe the same. Sharing and working for a belief like that can have a powerful effect."* (cited in Ditch 2006, 26)

Such decisive and potentially draining leadership actions need to be underpinned for such headteachers by the collaboration and support of a strong staff team. Not only do such headteachers see it as their role to encourage and promote collaboration, they themselves draw sustaining strength from it. As one said:

> *"You need a supportive team...a team founded on trust and confidence where there can be mutual offloading of concerns and supporting of each other...you can't do it on your own."*

In such a supportive team environment, especially at senior leadership level, there is a symbiotic relationship: *"My strong supportive leadership* team *'watch my back'. In return, I give them space to grow"*, said one headteacher. But such teams have to be grown, nurtured and developed within a collaborative culture where leadership is delegated and distributed within a system of collective responsibility: *"I've grown and developed a lot of my own people...and made them* my *people".*

2. What characterises leaders facing challenging circumstances?

In considering *'how'* leadership in a school facing challenging circumstances is exercised, and in particular whether there are any specific professional characteristics and personal qualities deemed desirable if not essential in such a context, this section draws first on qualitative interview data and then compares and contrasts this with quantitative data revealed in a small-scale online survey of professional characteristics of a sub-set of those interviewed.

2.1. Qualitative findings from interviews

In describing and characterising their own spiritual and moral leadership and in particular how it was exercised when faced with critical incidents and external pressures, headteachers expressed views in interview which replicated larger-scale research findings drawn from a database of 1,800 serving headteachers who had engaged with the Leadership Programme for Serving Headteachers (LPSH) (NCSL 2006b) by focusing on personal conviction of moral purpose and reiterating the need for respect for others and the promotion of collaboration with them which had been featured in the core value systems previously described. The findings of this LPSH report indicated that *"strong visions* and strategies seem to be built 'one-on-one' through *developing individuals*, creating role clarity, *showing empathy* and *working together"* (NCSL 2006b, 2; emphasis added). Headteachers interviewed for this study felt it was important to demonstrate personal conviction in the ultimate strength of one's vision and in the rectitude of one's beliefs, tenacity in applying them, sometimes *"bordering on stubbornness"*, and a resilience *"to take the pain"* in standing by them. However, this is tempered by personal humility in being prepared to *"let your humanity show": "I haven't got all the answers"...* *"I project confidence whether I've got it or not, but I'm prepared to admit my mistakes when I get it wrong".* There was a perceived need for high levels of emotional intelligence to generate trust through building relationships and rebuilding battered and fractured ones, to show respect for others and to display integrity and honesty. Indeed, over half those interviewed specifically drew attention to the need for emotional intelligence and the ability not only to 'know yourself' but also to engage with empathy at a personal level with those around you: *"The quality of relationships is key. EI [emotional intelligence] is paramount: not just awareness of self but empathy for others"*, said one headteacher interviewed.

Running through all the responses was a leitmotif of expressed passion, a passion for the development of the pupils, for the school and for the role: *"A strong belief system and a passion to carry on making a difference...that's what makes me 'a serial offender' in schools in challenging circumstances"*, averred one headteacher, now on his fifth headship of schools in challenging urban circumstances. Such so-called 'serial offenders', in second or multiple headships in schools in challenging circumstances, recognise a development of capacity as their leadership experience has progressed and their repertoire of situation experience has developed, leading to greater confidence and less constraint in calculated or instinctive risk taking to drive the school forward. One experienced headteacher described this development of risk-taking capacity:

> *"I was a quiet risk taker at the beginning but I can now be more upfront as I have grown in confidence. I've become a calculated risk taker, but with an intuitive instinct: you know this is going to pay off."*

One area where such 'risk taking' is evident is in the development of staff. The NCSL report *Leading Under Pressure: Leadership for Social Inclusion* (Muijs et al 2007) suggests an emphasis on 'strong' directive 'top-down' leadership evident especially when heads first came into schools in difficulty, and linked this with the strong pressure 'to turn it around' felt by schools and leaders as a result of their challenging circumstances. The report suggests that moves towards a more distributed form of leadership, and hence the concomitant development of staff, occurred only belatedly if at all, and was more likely to happen "in less achievement-oriented schools" (Muijs et al 2007, 3). This is at variance with the findings of the present research study, where heads argued that they were certainly concerned with measurable achievement within an accountability culture, but felt able to draw on their considerable experience of school leadership in difficult circumstances to 'take the risk' of distributing leadership in order both to develop individuals and also to establish a collaborative team approach to school development. These heads were in turn energised by:

"...the buzz of seeing staff who were in danger of going under when you arrived, develop and grow to the point where paradoxically losing your staff to promotion becomes one of the achievements."

Significantly, however, triangulation of the views within the LPSH database of 1,800 headteachers (NCSL 2006b, 4) with those of their staff showed that whilst 'teambuilding' emerged as the perceived dominant strength of the headteacher, 'risk taking' was seen as the weakest characteristic. This may be a function of type of school (as the LPSH database covers all schools and not just those in challenging circumstances, where more 'risk taking' may be deemed necessary in order to engender rapid improvement) or a function of length of experience (in that LPSH is normally completed after around four to five years of first headship experience, whereas the average length of headship service of the present research sample was eight years, with half of the sample of 30 being in their second or multiple headship, a considerably more experienced data set on which to draw).

To sum up, the essential professional characteristics identified by the 30 headteachers of schools in challenging circumstances who were interviewed for the present research study focus around the capacity to maintain rectitude of moral purpose in recognising the essential worth of every individual and their capacity for redemptive change, to build effective relationships both on an individual and collaborative team level and to engage in calculated risk taking in order to move the school forward.

2.2. Quantitative findings from online analysis

The personal qualities and professional characteristics identified as required may be seen as 'the iceberg below the surface' that supports, sustains and characterises public leadership actions. A small-scale quantitative attempt was made as part of this present research study to investigate with 10 of the headteachers who had been interviewed whether it is possible to identify and quantify particular clusters of such personal qualities and professional characteristics held by headteachers of schools in challenging circumstances from an analysis of their self-reported leadership actions in a set of specified contextual situations, and then to match these against those described in the qualitative interview situation. The research instrument used was an internet-based professional development tool known as School Mentor (Verity 2005), part of a suite of self-evaluation tools commercially available as Mentus School Self-Evaluation.

Building on the work of Goleman, Boyatzis and Key (2003) on leadership competencies and using the National Standards for Headteachers (DfES 2004) to provide an overarching framework and commonality of professional language, the School Mentor personal qualities instrument (one of a trilogy of instruments which also analyse leadership performance and professional knowledge and understanding) considers the professional characteristics of headship across three global dimensions of 'thinking', 'energy' and 'people', and breaks these down into 20 specific personal attributes clustered around 'thinking skills', 'personal management skills', 'inter-personal skills' and 'leadership skills'. Extending this analysis using concepts from Tuohy (1998, 148), these clusters may be categorised as: intellectual skills, concerned with thinking and planning; intra-personal skills, concerned with purpose and meaning; inter-personal skills, concerned with the management of relationships; and extra-personal skills, concerned with qualities of leadership. These may be viewed as relating to the dimensions of 'awareness of self' and 'working with others', as shown below in Figure 5.1.

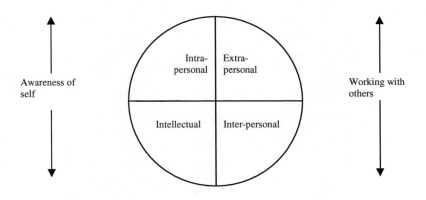

Fig. 5-1. Quadrants of leadership skills

Each cluster may then be broken down into related professional characteristics to be explored by the School Mentor reflective instrument, as shown in Table 5.1:

Global dimension	Cluster	Professional characteristic
Awareness of self	*Intellectual skills*	Information search
	concerned with thinking and planning	Analytical thinking
		Conceptual thinking
		Strategic thinking
		Decision making
	Intra-personal skills	Self-management
	concerned with purpose and meaning	Self-confidence
		Initiative and innovation
		Passion and motivation
		Continuous improvement
Work with others	*Inter-personal skills*	Communicating
	concern for relationship management	Teamworking
		Respect for others
		Building trust
		Empathy
	Extra-personal skills	Developing others
	concerned with leadership qualities	Holding others accountable
		Influencing skills
		Adaptability and flexibility
		Delivering results

Tab. 5-1. Clusters of professional characteristics

Users of the instrument are given a series of 140 reflective prompts of the type: 'when faced with situation X, I would show behaviour Y', grouped in accordance with the above framework, and are asked to respond 'intuitively' as to their normal or anticipated behaviours in such circumstances, on a scale ranging from 'never' to 'always'. Examples of such reflective responses are shown below, in Table 5.2.

Respect for others	Initiative and innovation
I always demonstrate respect for other people irrespective of their status and background	I often take calculated risks to stimulate improvement
In challenging situations, I assert myself in a way that demonstrates respect for the other person	I am often the first to go into new territory in the cause of improvement and new learning
I am aware of my subjectivity and take steps to manage it	I do not allow others 'to go through the motions'
Respect for others always underpins my approach and style in working with other people	I can cope with non-achievement of objectives if it is part of a learning process
I demonstrate that I listen to, understand and respect the views and opinions of others	I often lend energy to new initiatives
I am committed to the equality of provision for all; I am even-handed at all times	While benchmarks are useful, I strive to set new levels in professionalism and achievement

Tab. 5-2. Examples of reflective prompts

Responses are then transmitted online to be codified by computer analysis by a central School Mentor team to yield percentage indicators of perceived strength in particular professional characteristics areas. Although the instrument is self-administered and based on personal and hence potentially distorted reflection, the opportunity is provided for 360 degree triangulation against the anonymous views of up to five colleagues selected by the participant as 'reviewers', enabling comparisons to be made between respondent and reviewer responses to show whether self-assessment is validated by the views of colleagues.

Funding constraints in the present research study meant that access to the instrument was restricted to a small cross-phase sample of 10 volunteer headteachers, leading schools in challenging circumstances drawn almost exclusively from one local authority area, who were willing to contribute a small amount of their Leadership Incentive Grant funding (a government grant, given to schools in challenging circumstances who are in danger of failing to reach examination floor targets, to facilitate supportive collaborative ventures to improve leadership) to participate in this section of the research study. Whilst all the headteachers were prepared to engage with the self-reflective opportunity provided by the instrument, an attempt to validate their personally reported views by anonymous triangulation from other school colleagues chosen by the respondent was less than universally successful. Although the 10 headteachers who agreed to participate were all personally known to the researcher and expressed full personal and professional confidence in his assurances of confidentiality and anonymity, it is significant that only 50% of the sample took up the opportunity of triangulation at all, and only 20% maximised their triangulation opportunities, a sign of anxieties about personal confidence, status and self-esteem that even anonymous and generally supportive feedback may create.

The School Mentor instrument was used to garner individual data, triangulated where possible, from the sample of 10 participating leaders of schools in challenging circumstances, drawn equally from the primary and secondary phases together with one special school, and equally balanced in terms of gender. Data may be analysed to produce graphical comparisons either as bar charts or radar diagrams, or as in this research, subjected to mathematical aggregation. Analysing such data, even from such a small and only partially triangulated sample, and calculating the average percentage score for each professional characteristic, aggregating these across each skills cluster, and comparing the cluster aggregate with the overall average for the sample of participants, allows conclusions to be drawn as to the dominant professional characteristics of these leaders to match against the views expressed by the wider interview sample. Such analysis reveals a clear skewing of professional characteristics towards the inter-personal skills domain for the sample of 10 participants, as shown in Table 5.3.

Cluster	Characteristic	1	2	3	4	5	6	7	8	9	10	avge
Extra-personal	Delivering results	96	77	75	96	85	94	90	57	70	94	83.4
	Flexible and adaptable	72	83	55	87	85	90	74	72	53	85	75.6
	Influencing skills	88	60	68	91	80	82	73	566	53	86	73.7
	Holding to account	87	58	86	93	92	98	86	60	41	95	79.6
	Developing others	93	59	73	86	98	97	54	62	50	86	75.8
Cluster average												*77.6*
Inter-personal	Communicating	85	70	75	96	92	90	62	70	61	98	79.9
	Teamwork	100	82	82	100	100	100	92	71	63	100	89.0
	Respect for others	92	83	88	100	96	100	98	75	70	100	90.2
	Building trust	83	72	59	90	96	94	96	79	59	100	82.8
	Empathy	98	72	64	100	98	79	72	68	44	96	79.1
Cluster average												*84.2*
Intellectual	Information search	75	70	31	81	79	98	68	64	50	79	69.5
	Analytical thinking	66	69	60	79	87	92	82	57	68	88	74.8
	Conceptual thinking	86	55	77	77	83	100	83	58	61	94	77.4
	Strategic thinking	83	79	66	96	91	96	79	74	65	87	81.6
	Decision making	79	61	57	73	76	90	61	63	38	84	68.2
Cluster average												*74.3*
Intra-personal	Self-management	86	72	50	91	86	97	44	72	63	88	74.9
	Self-confidence	87	77	75	100	87	98	75	66	35	94	79.4
	Initiative & innovation	93	75	91	95	88	100	55	75	57	82	81.1
	Passion and motivation	92	77	92	100	95	100	83	66	49	98	85.2
	Drive to improve	93	58	80	100	85	100	76	61	69	98	82.0
Cluster average												*80.5*
Total												*79.2*

Tab. 5-3. Analysis of professional characteristics

Analysis of Table 5.3 gives the following comparisons shown in Tables 5.4a-c:

Cluster	Cluster average	Comparison with overall sample average (79.2%)
Extra-personal skills	77.6	–1.6
Inter-personal skills	84.2	+5.0
Intellectual skills	74.3	–4.9
Intra-personal skills	80.5	+1.3

Tab. 5-4a. Skill set comparisons

This appears to confirm the hypothesis that there is a skew towards the people-oriented, inter-personal skills domain of the professional characteristics shown by such leaders of schools in challenging circumstances. If the data is disaggregated into gender-specific sets, Tables 5.4b (male) and 5.4c (female) result:

Cluster	Cluster average	Comparison with overall male average (72.5%)
Extra-personal skills	70.0	+2.5
Inter-personal skills	76.9	+4.4
Intellectual skills	71.2	–1.3
Intra-personal skills	72.0	–0.5

Tab. 5-4b. Gender comparisons: male

Cluster	Cluster average	Comparison with overall female average (85.8%)
Extra-personal skills	85.3	+0.5
Inter-personal skills	91.5	+6.2
Intellectual skills	77.4	−8.4
Intra-personal skills	89.0	+3.2

Tab. 5-4c. Gender comparisons: female

This shows a particularly marked skew towards the inter-personal domain amongst the five participant female school leaders. Whilst given the very small samples involved such results need to be treated with much caution, this suggests support for the Baron-Cohen (2003) hypothesis that 'empathising brains', on average but not exclusively found more amongst females, tend to be attracted to the more 'caring' professions such as teaching.

A more detailed analysis of the inter-personal skills cluster shows that respect for others and teamworking both feature towards the top of every respondent's analysis, with average scores of 90.2% and 89.0% respectively, and building trust (82.8%), empathy (79.1%) and communicating skills (79.9%) also feature strongly, confirming assertions made by the wider circle of interview respondents that high levels of emotional intelligence are felt necessary to lead such schools.

Within the intra-personal skills cluster, high levels of self-confidence (79.4%) are shown, together with passion and motivation for the role (85.2%), which again confirms the view that both personal self-confidence and self-belief, coupled with passionate motivation, are a *sine qua non* of such leadership. Initiative and innovation (81.1%), which might be considered as preparedness to engage in calculated risk taking, also confirms the previously described capacity to utilise self-confidence and amassed experience to seek out creative and innovative solutions to problems, whilst the low ranking for information search (69.5%) confirms the intuitive capacity displayed by many headteachers in their ability to respond instinctively to an emerging situation or operational necessity rather than through a more time-consuming logical and analytical approach.

Such intuitive inter-personal skills and self-knowledge are, however, tinged with operational hard-headedness, reflecting the presence of a utilitarian attitude deemed necessary to survive in an accountability culture, with a concern for strategic thinking (81.6%) in seeing the bigger picture, and a drive for continuous improvement (82.0%) to stay ahead of the game, thus delivering results (83.4%) and holding others accountable (79.6%) within that process. Interestingly, however, although teamworking (89.0%) was held to be a vital component of leadership, the importance of developing others cited in interviews featured less strongly in responses (75.8%). This may be a reflection of a short-term dominant need to make substantial progress in an early phase of development through a collective team effort, with individual development a more medium-term objective. The particularly low average score for decision making (68.2%) in the responses might appear to be peculiar unless it is recognised that this characteristic is construed as the taking of unilateral decisions unmediated by reflection and consultation with others, which would be at variance with the high levels of communicating and teamworking skills demonstrated. Equally, a relatively low score for the skill of adaptability and flexibility (75.6%) appears to be at variance with previous assertions in interview regarding "the excitement and unpredictability" of working in challenging circumstances "where no two days are ever the same", but may be explained by a dominant requirement to remain constant in the application of espoused core values irrespective of contextual circumstances.

To sum up, analysis of the aggregated average responses from this sample of leaders of schools in challenging circumstances indicates a skew in personal attributes towards the inter-personal skills end of the leadership spectrum, with a high focus on the promotion of teamworking, respect for others and building and maintaining trust through empathetic engagement with colleagues in effective and productive relationships. In demonstrating such social awareness, effective leaders confirm the view of Goleman et al (2003, 61), that leaders need to create a resonance with others through communicating their feelings with conviction and showing emotions which are clearly authentic through being rooted in deeply held values. In short, high levels of emotional intelligence appear to be required. These, however, need to be supplemented by high personal reserves of self-confidence, passion and motivation in the leadership role, and being prepared to take calculated risks in initiating innovative and creative solutions to ensure that continuous improvement and progress is maintained.

Given both the small size of this sample, the variability of access to triangulation and the occasional lack of consistency of reviewers, where actually used, in supporting the self-assessment of the headteacher, such results need to be treated with much caution. Nevertheless they do confirm the reported findings from interview and point up a potential area of future research using a wider sample base such as that available nationally through the LPSH programme across headteachers of a wider sample of schools in addition to simply those facing challenging circumstances. As Keys et al have cogently put it:

> Research into the leadership of schools in urban and challenging circumstances has produced a number of pointers concerning leadership style and effective strategies. What is less clear is the extent to which these are different from, or the same as, those adopted by successful leaders in other schools... There is a need for more research...[to] find out what is distinctive about leading a 'challenging' school...[and to] help to inform policy...as well as practice, to the benefit of schools, their pupils and communities. (Keys et al 2003, 20)

It is hoped that the present research study, by capturing through interviews the practitioner voice of headteachers serving in such 'challenging' schools, and providing a quantitative instrument to promote and analyse their self-reflection, may make some small contribution in this regard. It has been shown that such headteachers demonstrate the priority of a people-centred approach to school leadership; they establish a direction underpinned by a firm moral purpose; they engender motivation in themselves and their staff through a passion for progress; and they build capacity by promoting collaboration and teamworking. How these attributes differ from those of colleagues leading schools facing different circumstances must, however, be a matter for further ongoing consideration.

3. What sustains heads of schools in challenging circumstances

Having explored the specific professional characteristics and personal qualities displayed by leaders of schools in challenging circumstances in their work, interviews then focused on 'what' were the supporting and sustaining strategies used by such leaders to maintain their motivation and effectiveness. These may be considered in terms of informal personal and corporate sustaining strategies and more structured opportunities for reflective space provided by secondment and sabbatical participation.

3.1. Personal and corporate sustaining strategies

If headteachers of schools in challenging circumstances are motivated by their core values and the implementation of them in collaboration with colleagues, they are equally sustained in their task by the sharing of the fruits of success. *"Celebrating small victories"* can be an important sustaining factor across the school, demonstrating *"success against the odds"* (Maden and Hillman 1996) in *"making a difference"* in the face of challenging circumstances. It was felt that the capacity to make such a difference by *"having the chance to make rapid changes and see significant fast improvements"* allowed colleagues to sustain themselves in the task by being able to convert their motivational *"yearning to get things done"* into visible tangible progress as a result of *"quick fixes which gained us rapid recognition from the community"*. There was a universal and powerfully optimistic recognition that in such schools, for all their challenging circumstances, there remained a potential to succeed: *"you can feel it* here *[viscerally] that you can do it"*, and colleagues drew sustenance from what was termed *"the buzz...the adrenaline rush"* from realising that potential for success.

When asked to describe what was good about leading a school facing challenging circumstances, it was that *"capacity to have an immediate impact"* and the ability to gain rapid supportive feedback on success that sustained and reinforced motivation: *"You can see the changes; you can see your vision being realised as sustainable transformation"*. There was felt to be a favourable ratio of effort to progress: *"there is so far to go that it is easier to move it"* and a perceived collective acceptance of the need for change especially in a school facing negative Ofsted judgements creating what was termed *"a wide canvas of change potential"* within which *"you can have small tastes of success...and they taste good"*.

The *"excitement and unpredictability"* of working in such schools was also a sustaining factor. As one headteacher put it:

> *"Schools like this, facing challenging circumstances, are exciting places to be. We are the driving force [because] we have the power to make a difference...a difference to children's and the community's life chances...and to empower others to do the same... No two days are ever the same...it is never boring... Every day is potentially exciting as you can never guarantee what's going to happen...the adrenaline rush when crises develop is strangely alluring."*

That excitement, be it an adrenaline rush or a longer-term 'buzz', comes from the feeling of 'making a difference' reinforced by many cited examples of a wide range of successes often undetected by conventional success indicators, from the successful integration of behaviourally challenging pupils rejected by previous schools, to previously demoralised staff being given a new lease of professional life through seeing that they *can* make a difference: *"seeing the most difficult children achieve success...[and] receiving grateful affirmative feedback from a deprived community"*.

If the sharing of values provides collective motivation, and the experience of shared success provides sustenance, then headteachers also draw strength from the shared support that they receive from colleagues. "Teams not individuals change schools" (NCSL Leading Edge Workshop 2002), and this was a view echoed by the participants in the present study. Often such teams had been constructed on a deliberate basis to facilitate this. As two newly transferred headteachers candidly put it:

"I poached two key members of staff who I knew had the same values as me. They support and energise me."

"I brought some staff with me, my sort of people, motivated to do the job. After all, all's fair in love and war."

Support is similarly drawn from networks of headteacher colleagues with a similar mind-set and value system, either on an individual or collective basis: *"a supportive network of colleagues from schools in similar circumstances and facing similar issues, where you can have an open, honest relationship...more support than challenge"*. The capacity to grow one's own corporate networks of support, described by one head as *"an ad hoc networked learning community"*, was felt to be an essential skill. Externally imposed networks such as Leadership Incentive Grant groups or local authority clusters were felt not to work well unless there was a commonality of context and values, a porosity of geographical boundaries and above all a sympathy for bringing like-minded leaders together. (Indeed, two female headteachers spoke of the value of a self-generated informal network of specifically female heads, as *"a minority thing, where we can* really *be ourselves"*.) One such headteacher asserted: *"Our networks are strong because of the sort of people we are...our* chosen *networks we will* make *work"*, and others expressed the view that the informality of networks constituted their inherent strength: *"if you formalise it, you destroy it"*.

Such networks, as well as providing cathartic personal nurturing support, mutual reflection opportunities and information flow, also compensate for a perceived sense of isolation, especially in the aftermath of critical incidents, and permit valuable exchanges of knowledge and experience. *"I always know who will know. I don't have to know it all myself"* said one headteacher, and another particularly valued the exchange of experience through the retelling of leadership stories: *"Different ethnographies and stories let you get 'inside the soul' of schools and their leaders and help you identify the signposts of what is working"*. Indeed, sharing other leaders' stories of leadership in similar schools facing challenging circumstances is felt to be a powerful support mechanism (Gabriel 2000). As one headteacher asserted: *"Wrapping it up in a story makes it more powerful and memorable. It gives you self-confidence and an awareness that you are not alone"*.

Underpinning such professional networks, however, is the strongly expressed need to draw support from *"a life elsewhere"*. In common with other colleagues interviewed, there was *"a capacity to compartmentalise"*, *"to switch off into cut-off time, ruthlessly protected against time incursion and emotional leakage"* often in total immersion in something else quite different from professional life, be it church, sport, networks of friends or family life: *"as a dad not a head"*.

3.2. Secondment and sabbatical opportunities

In common with many of the 150 headteachers interviewed in total for this research, headteachers leading schools facing challenging circumstances particularly value the opportunity to step back on occasion from the day-to-day pressures of their role in order to find 'strategic sanctuary' (Lee 2005), *"space to be able to see the wood for the trees"*, as one headteacher put it, and to engage in reflection on and reinforcement of their strategic vision and the progress towards implementing it. Not only was the opportunity to engage with a personal reflective instrument such as School Mentor perceived to be of value in itself, headteachers also appreciated networking opportunities of peer support and reflection with like-minded colleagues who faced similar circumstances and who were 'on the same wavelength'. In addition, however, there was an appreciation of more structured opportunities to step back from the immediacy of ongoing day-to-day pressures and to engage with contexts beyond the immediate school situation. This could be achieved through access to a short-term secondment placement or sabbatical opportunity.

Perceptions of the value of such 'step-back' opportunities were gained from interviews with a further 10 headteachers who had participated in some way in them, together with a further 10 supporting educationists involved in enabling or evaluating this provision. All felt that, provided there was confidence in the remaining senior leadership capacity to ensure that the releasing school was not disadvantaged and that there was sensitivity to the potential problems of re-entry, such opportunities for the serving headteacher, especially when facing challenging circumstances, could have a significant impact on personal morale through giving space for reflection and renewal in a context 'at a distance' which allowed a reassessment, refocusing and reaffirmation of the substantive headship role.

Secondment opportunities

Secondment opportunities may take the form of support placements to assist the work of local authorities, the national education system or to wider contexts such as industry, commerce or international education. *Support placements* may last for between one day a week to short-term blocks of full-time commitment of up to a term or longer to provide practitioner expertise to specific projects such as Building Schools for the Future or succession planning, or system leadership roles as School Improvement Partners or National Leaders of Education. Those who have engaged with such opportunities report that impact on their professional and personal morale has been high through the motivating effect of new challenges, the cross-fertilisation of ideas and strategies between contexts, and an awareness of system issues which *"have helped to develop a sense of shared system leadership"*. That sense of shared leadership also extended back into the releasing school in the professional development of further leadership capacity in those senior staff 'acting up', albeit on a temporary basis, although seconded headteachers retaining a part-time commitment to the releasing school reported a significant pressure in maintaining dual roles, coupled with an element of personal destabilisation or frustration on return to full-time substantive service. As one head, who had been seconded two days a week for a year to the local authority to develop 'a new vision for learning' within a reorganisation context in a large rural county, described it:

> *"I relished the more creative opportunities to respond to wider system agendas and being in the forefront of change. However it's had a significant impact on my workload and work–life balance. You retain the full-time psychological commitment to both jobs... Overall, however, I have valued the excellent opportunities for reflection, analysis and critical thinking, and the experience has certainly retained me in headship but I have had to seek out ways of being able to continue the co-headship partnership with my deputy."*

However, the value of such secondments is to be seen not only for the individual concerned, but also to the releasing school. One headteacher interviewed has been seconded part-time for the last two years as co-director of schools in a Roman Catholic diocese, whilst retaining a substantive post as headteacher of a large urban secondary school. There he has developed a supporting leadership team of two associate headteachers that has allowed him to operate more in an executive role. Not only does he feel his secondment has allowed him *"to bring back into school examples of good practice from other schools"* but *"it allows investment in the development of other leaders and succession planning"*. He feels it ensures:

> *"my experience and knowledge is not lost to the system...but is offered as a way of motivating and developing less experienced leaders who just need a supportive nudge to prove that they* can *do it"*.

Opportunities in wider contexts such as *industry placements* are available through organisations such as Heads, Teachers and Industry (HTI), which offers interim management placements of between six weeks and 12 months to emergent as well as experienced school leaders. The programme aims to deliver not only the development of leadership skills in a different context, but also to provide an opportunity for renewal and reflection and a revitalisation of motivation. Evaluations (HTI 2004, 3) report that the majority of secondees have made changes to their leadership style as a result of the secondment experience. They report an increase in 'influencing power' and in personal authority and credibility. However, for longer-term placements, there is a reported paucity of applicants from leaders of schools facing challenging circumstances who tend to be mono-focused on the specific needs and demands of their immediate situation. For those leaders who do engage, however, the experience proves to be a valuable one, not only to themselves but also to the wider system. For example, a secondary headteacher of a school in challenging circumstances was seconded through HTI to Railtrack for 12 weeks as a project coordinator to work on anti-trespass and vandalism issues. Not only did she relish the socially responsible challenge and the education insights she was able to bring to bear, but her motivation and commitment were so enhanced that she felt subsequently able to accept being headhunted to an even more challenging school where her enhanced leadership skills have secured significant turn-around success in raising standards.

Short-term participation in *international placements* is also seen to bring extended benefits. International study visits such as those organised by the British Council in association with NCSL, and VSO opportunities developed in association with the National Association of Headteachers, allow *inter alia* the chance for reflection on self, skills and attitudes, and reappraisal of professional practice. Participants report *"a fresh appreciation of the job that has to be done"*, *"a life-changing experience"* creating *"an altered world-view and a sense of global fellowship amongst professionals"*. Such opportunities were felt to have had a positive impact in terms of regeneration in and commitment to the school leadership position, *"an oasis in the midst of hardship"*, providing a major stimulus to school leaders who might otherwise be getting stale and facing the 'plateau effect' or the temptations of early departure. As one participant revealed:

> *"It [a VSO placement in rural Africa] altered my approach to things when I returned. It made me appreciate more what we have here and often take for granted. It made me create more reflective space for myself...it will preserve me in education longer."*

Sabbatical opportunities

Sabbatical opportunities were also highly valued in 'recharging' school leaders, professionally, mentally and spiritually. As sabbaticals are not directly linked to a specific task, as is the case with secondments, they are seen to offer scope to pursue particular professional, research or personal interests, unfettered by specific outcome demands. Such opportunities are, however, considerably more rare in availability than secondments, particularly because of funding issues associated with them. Those that do exist may be codified as professional development sabbaticals, faith-based retreat sabbaticals and personal renewal sabbaticals (although the categorisations are clearly not mutually exclusive).

Professional development sabbaticals are where release is granted to pursue a specific programme of professional concerns. For example, a secondary school governing body, in discharge of its responsibility for the work–life balance of the headteacher, has granted a 'mini-sabbatical' of six weeks every three years to the headteacher to allow him to have 'headship time' to reflect on his own personal development as well as in particular to carry out self-initiated research relevant to the school development plan. The school is led in his absence by the deputy headteacher, with a concomitant concern for professional development and subsequent succession planning. Funding is provided by the governing body as a quid pro quo for the fact that any payments for consultancy work by staff are paid into the school budget. The scheme is seen both as a 'reward' and 'an incentive for retention' of a 'successful' headteacher. Its success has allowed its roll out to other members of the senior leadership team.

Faith-based retreat sabbaticals are available to those leading schools of a religious character. Examples are seen in both the Roman Catholic and Church of England sectors. The four Northern Roman Catholic dioceses have offered a three-week sabbatical programme annually for the last six years, which has been accessed by a total of 72 headteachers and 23 long-serving senior staff. The sabbatical programme is designed to offer 'spiritual and reflective opportunities to meet a need too often unmet during the day-to-day business of running a school'. Each of the three weeks has two days of planned group input plus a further three days of self-initiated content, providing *"time-out to reflect, to pray and just to be"*. This reflective space is seen to provide a valued opportunity for re-focusing, renewal and reinvigoration. Evaluation returns are enthusiastically positive; indeed some participants have indicated that were it not for the sabbatical experience, they would have resigned from headship or sought early retirement. One participant reported that after 14 years of headship in a primary school facing challenging circumstances, he felt he had reached a plateau and had lost some of his enthusiasm and sense of direction. The sabbatical *"has deeply affirmed me, refreshed and invigorated me and sent me back to my post with renewed optimism and hope"*. Its 'nourishment' had increased his morale and enthusiasm and had overcome any residual sense of disillusionment or burn out, and opened up wider horizons of possibility, so that he has recently transferred to a diocesan education post where he feels he can 'feed and support' other heads in a similar manner.

The Anglican Diocese of Bradford and Ripon and Leeds has run a small sabbatical programme for headteachers released from their normal duties for four weeks (including one week of half term) on the sole condition that they have no contact with their school, an obligation found very difficult to adhere to by committed and task-oriented leaders. There is an encouragement to participate through 'informal targeting' of leaders of schools facing challenging circumstances. Of particular interest has been the involvement of a spectrum of participants from differing faith perspectives and churchmanship, including one self-confessed 'non-practicing Christian'. A structured programme of optional activities involves 'quiet days' and the chance to talk to a confidential counsellor. The programme offers retreat spaces at a dissolved Cistercian Abbey and on the Holy Island of Lindisfarne. There is a focus on reflection on leadership story: *"on God the Father foundational to our story, God the Son active in the present reality of our story, and God the Holy Spirit at work in the rhythm of our life and journey"*. Participant evaluations are positive in terms of renewal of confidence, energy and vitality, providing *"space for me, away from the pressure of the next thing...and allowing me to learn that life goes on [at school] even if I am not there"*. One participant described it as:

> *"...a life-changing experience: you have made me question myself and reflect upon my role. I have realised that I must look after myself in order to run a [challenging] school and if I don't look after myself, how can I encourage others to do the same."*

Funding costs that need to be met by the school are seen as an obstacle, but governors are asked to consider them against the considerably greater cost of recruiting a new head. It is felt by the diocese that this scheme contributes significantly to a retention policy for heads by focusing attention on their pastoral as well as professional needs.

Personal renewal sabbaticals in the UK appear to be very rare and have to be personally funded. The wider community often view them with some suspicion. For example, one headteacher interviewed is a primary school headteacher of 14 years experience, now on his fourth headship. After six years of highly successful leadership of a school facing significant social deprivation, serving one of the most deprived wards of the inner city, he sought three months unpaid leave of absence to train abroad as a ski instructor. Although apparently far from his normal professional role, the experience of *"being a low status learner out of the comfort zone"* and the opportunity to transmit his skills to young French ski students in a teaching environment was a valuable professional one. Significant pre-planning and professional development with the deputy head ensured that the school was not disadvantaged by his absence. Although the subject of significant negative media publicity, he is adamant that the learning experience and the reflective space it provided gave a personal and professional refreshment opportunity that has re-energised and reinvigorated him. *"Without it I would have left headship within months"*, he avows.

What is of particular interest, however, is that although the school in question is not linked to a particular faith tradition, the headteacher is an active Christian and lay reader in the Church of England. Consequently he valued not only the space for reflection and reflective journaling, but also for meditation and prayer. He described his need for access to *"not doing but being"*, in order to engage in *"a spiritual health check...to ensure that everything had healed"* after a particularly difficult critical incident involving the sudden death of the baby son of a senior member of staff, and continuing day-to-day pressure over SATS outcome results and school failure to meet imposed targets. He was concerned to ensure that *"personal authenticity is still intact...that I am still happy with me...and that my motivational fire is still burning"*. In spite of being the victim of highly negative national press publicity, and suffering a sense of helplessness in not being able to rebut some of the ensuing ill-informed comments, he described the sabbatical experience as having:

> *"...refreshed my soul...reaching the parts that had not been reached. It allowed a 'retreat' experience in a particular sense: 'allowing God to re-treat [sic] me'. It provided an opportunity to slow down, to become more Mary than Martha (Luke 10, 38-42), and to ask God for the right speed in my life. I realised afresh that as a headteacher, preacher and worship leader, I am replaceable. But as a son and child of God, I am indispensable. I am in God's eyes irreplaceable."*

In spite of the media-distorted perceptions of the unpaid sabbatical being "the headteacher of a troubled school taking three months off to go skiing" (*Daily Mail* headline, cited in O'Connell 2008, 13) and giving the impression of a struggling school in difficulties with a headteacher who, rather than 'sorting it out', was disappearing into some kind of skiing holiday rather than the reality of a school with a recent Ofsted judgement of 'good with some outstanding features' in spite of its challenging circumstances, the headteacher has no regrets about engaging in the experience. He has successfully returned to school *"refreshed, reinvigorated, and retained"*, with the resilience to continue in headship and a clearer sense of future direction. *"It will motivate me for my fifth headship, but the next job will be four days with one day for voluntary and charity work, and above all, time to think"*. He urges other school leaders of schools facing challenging circumstances of whatever kind to contemplate engaging in similar experiences, not necessarily as a leadership entitlement simply to be taken for granted but as a proactive *"working out your own salvation"*.

Conclusion

This chapter has explored the professional characteristics and personal qualities revealed by a sample of leaders of schools facing challenging circumstances, defining such schools not simply in terms of levels of academic attainment or measures of social deprivation, but by the range of contextual difficulties, both within the school and beyond, that they are called on to face. Through the use of semi-structured interview, it has sought to capture the views of such leaders and to demonstrate that they are primarily concerned more with guidance than control, and with spiritual and moral leadership (defined in a secular sense) than with simply operational management issues. It has shown that they are motivated in their leadership by a people-centred set of values which display a strong sense of 'inclusive individualism' which respects the worth of every individual and seeks to maximise their potential for development by 'making a difference' to individual lives and community circumstances. This strong moral purpose is supported through the sharing of this vision with colleagues and the promotion of collaboration and teamworking in achieving it. Such leaders of schools in challenging circumstances feel they are supported by informal networks of professional colleagues both within and beyond the school, who face similar circumstances and who are 'on the same wavelength'. Nevertheless, many would value the occasional opportunity to 'step back' from the pressures of leadership in challenging circumstances to have more structured and extensive reflective space through the provision of sabbatical and secondment opportunities, provided that funding and temporary replacement issues do not compromise the onward progress of their schools.

Interview data shows that such leaders are characterised by their capacity to sustain a strong vision in the face of challenging circumstances, in developing others to work with them, and in showing empathy to support the building of appropriate relationships. They have the capacity to maintain a rectitude of moral purpose in spite of the pressures of external events, are capable of maintaining effective relationships at both an individual and team level, and are prepared to engage in calculated risk taking in order to move the school forward. These personal characteristics have been substantially confirmed through the application of a self-reflective analytical instrument to a small sub-set of headteachers. This confirms the views expressed in interview of the dominant importance of high levels of emotional intelligence and inter-personal skills, supported by personal attributes such as self-confidence, passion and motivation, and a willingness to engage in innovation to maintain continuous improvement.

In common with their counterparts operating in the secular sphere or within a faith-based milieu, leaders of schools facing challenging circumstances are motivated by a vision of hope in the prospect of a better future and a passion to make a difference to the communities in their care. They are imbued with a strong moral compass that is predicated on respect, redemption and renewal, the pursuit of excellence and the courage to take risks to ensure success against the odds. They apply high levels of emotional intelligence to develop and maintain effective inter-personal engagement in strong relationships founded on trust, in seeking to deliver with colleagues that vision of hope, no matter what the external pressures and circumstances. They are prepared to empty themselves in the service of this ideal, and have developed robust sustainability strategies to ensure that their personal reservoir of hope is replenished and sustained. Chief amongst these sustainability strategies is the maintenance of structured space for reflection, and access to wide networks of sustaining relationships, together with a capacity to compartmentalise professional problems so that they do not impinge on other areas of personal life. The essential difference, however, between the 150 school leaders interviewed is not in 'what' they do to sustain themselves, nor indeed 'how' they exercise their spiritual and moral leadership role, but rather in 'why' they feel called to service in the particular context in which their leadership is set.

Irrespective of their context, above all, such emotionally intelligent leaders feel called on to maintain hope in the capacity of the institution wherever it is set to bring about redemptive renewal, where all can seek to maximise their potential and move forward, in spite of the challenging circumstances being faced. This is summed up well by Boyatzis and McKee as they postulate a resonant form of leadership in which leaders renew themselves and connect with others "through mindfulness, hope and compassion":

> In addition to knowing and managing themselves, emotionally intelligent leaders manage others' emotions and build strong, trusting relationships... They inspire through demonstrating passion, commitment, and deep concern for people and the organisational vision. They give us courage and hope, and help us to become the best that we can be. (Boyatzis and McKee 2005, 4-5)

The next chapter moves on to offer a theological reflection on hope as it is revealed in the spiritual and moral leadership of headteachers. It applies a lens of practical theology and engages the concepts of kerygma, kenosis and koinonia to argue that a message of hope is the essential motivation for spiritual and moral leadership, providing the source reservoir which sustains the leader as he or she is prepared to empty himself or herself in the service of others: a reservoir of hope which is replenished and renewed by networks of supportive relationships of fellowship and community.

CHAPTER SIX

HOPE SPRINGS ETERNAL

This chapter offers a theological reflection on hope as it is revealed in the spiritual and moral leadership of headteachers, in order not only to locate the data from the preceding three chapters within a theological framework, but also to provide a connecting bridge between educational leadership and theological perspectives. This will be done first through the lens of *practical theology*, exploring how the various facets of practical theology may be applied to spiritual and moral leadership—as theology in context, as 'ordinary theology' and as narrative theology that is informed by reflection on practice, and which in aggregate results in an operating theology that preserves and promotes personal authenticity. It will be shown that the emergent 'theology of hope' looks not just to future things but also needs to focus on and inform leadership actions in the present.

Second, the theological concepts of *kerygma*, *kenosis* and *koinonia* will be applied to the central metaphor 'reservoirs of hope', arguing that they provide integrative themes running through the spiritual and moral leadership of headteachers. These three concepts have been selected because they may be used to describe what can be considered to be the essentials of the spiritual and moral leadership of headteachers, namely, the importance of having a coherent vision or core message (kerygma) which underpins leadership actions; a way of working which is prepared to adopt a self-emptying servant leadership role in subjugating the needs of self to the needs of others (kenosis); and a source of support which draws on networks of sustaining relationships with professional colleagues and faith communities (koinonia). Thus it is suggested that the belief systems of headteachers can be seen as the essential kerygmatic message of their leadership, acting as the source reservoir of their principled leadership actions. When confronted by critical incidents and unrelenting systemic pressures, the headteacher is prepared to drain that reservoir in a spirit of kenotic self-emptying in the service of others. One replenishment strategy valued by headteachers to refill their personal reservoirs of hope is the fellowship gained from networks of relationships, a koinonia or 'communion in community' of like-minded individuals.

Finally, the chapter explores three enduring concepts which form threads throughout this examination of spiritual and moral leadership: namely, a capacity for bilingualism in expressing the universal *Golden Rule* of 'love your neighbour as yourself' which underpins leadership actions, a faith in the possibility of *redemption* which motivates them and the power of *covenantal relationships* within a framework of grace which supports them, to show how 'hope springs eternal' within the challenges and pressures of school leadership.

The aim in this chapter therefore is to use these theological concepts to shed further light on the 'why', 'how' and 'what' of spiritual and moral leadership, by considering the theological framework which underpins it, the self-emptying leadership actions which result from it and the replenishing strategies which sustain it.

1. Spiritual and moral leadership as practical theology

Practical theology straddles a perceived fault line between theory and practice in theology, what Veling (2005, 5) identifies as the longstanding division of theology into 'systematic theology' with its concern for theoretical discussions of systematics, church history and scriptural studies, and 'pastoral theology', the translation of this theory into practice through the application of pastoral skills, and the presumption that theory informs practice and not vice versa. Practical theology, however, seeks to bridge this fault line by integrating theory and practice through the engagement of theological reflection with pastoral experience. It has been termed 'theology in context', a 'conversation' between experience and tradition that sees "ordinary life itself" and the stories that emerge from it as "the primary locus of our spiritual health" (Astley 2002, 49). Practical theology therefore requires us not only to address the question 'what do I believe?' but also 'what should I do?'; to be concerned not only with theories of personal belief but the stories of their practical outworking in action. It therefore offers a theology for the 'real world' context of the hard-pressed school leader as well as the theologian: it is a concern not simply for 'philosophical purity' but also for 'practical realism', a concern, as one science educator (Smithells 1921, 25) writing in a different milieu put it, of both "professors and practical men".

Headteachers are required to be such 'practical men' [sic], but their practice is infused with values and belief. They recognise, when critical incidents and day-to-day pressures hit the school community, the necessity of maintaining the balance between acting as the practical external 'reservoir of hope' for their school in their leadership actions and of simultaneously sustaining their own personal internal reservoir with replenishment from the wellsprings of their own individual belief systems. All the headteachers interviewed for this research were able to articulate without hesitation a belief system on which they stand. They could all see their lives and the space in which they live those lives as having a moral and spiritual shape. Although their belief systems were drawn from a multifarious set of sources, some tethered to a specific religious tradition, others less so and some determinedly secular, all were able to describe the hopes, beliefs and ideals which gave purpose to their personal and professional lives and in particular underpin and inform their leadership actions. This underpinning spirituality has been termed the 'fifth dimension' (Hick 1999), a universal spirituality that underlies, interpenetrates and gives meaning to the four spatial and temporal dimensions of the physical world. It can be seen as analogous to Senge's (1990) 'fifth discipline' of systems thinking which provides a conceptual cornerstone that integrates the theory and practice of leadership and manages and resolves the tension between personal vision and the actions required by current reality.

Headteacher success in maintaining this balance between personal belief and leadership action is shown in behaviours exhibited under the pressure of critical incidents, where faith from whatever source is tested in the fire of practice. Belief in such circumstances becomes not just a set of values subscribed to but what Taylor (2007, 8) has called "a lived condition", which resonates with the definition of secular spirituality as 'a lived faith in action' being used throughout this study, so that how espoused belief plays out in practice becomes a test of the personal authenticity of the leader. If then, as for Astley (2002, 143), "spirituality is the engine that drives not only religion and morality, but all fulfilled living", then critical reflection on the beliefs underpinning that spirituality and the behaviours emanating from it may be described as the 'engine oil' which maintains and reveals personal authenticity. Astley (2002, 103) therefore argues the need to study theology in its 'ordinary' context by capturing through empirical research the descriptive stories of leadership subjected to constructive conceptual reflection, and revealing through it the personal authenticity of leaders. The present research study follows that approach.

Practical theology is thus 'ordinary theology' in Astley's (2002) seminal term: "the content, pattern and processes of ordinary people's articulation of their religious understanding...the theology of the non-theological adult" (Astley 2002, 56). Such 'ordinary theology' is learned from experience, is tentative in its expression and is significant and meaningful for everyday life, in that it takes the ordinary everyday experiences of the workplace world and promotes theological reflection on them. Fundamental to this process is the capturing of stories of everyday practice. Astley (2002, 132) therefore argues that "a person's ordinary theology is often expressed in autobiographical mode", what might be termed 'life-story theology', a form of "theology as biography" (after McClendon 1974, 37) in which "stories as well as images and metaphors...illuminate and express the learner's experience so as to capture the heart of the matter" and "entering the space of the image" or "exploring the world of the metaphor" can enable the correlation between personal life experience and the theological tradition (Astley 2002, 132). Participation in such a reflective process generates a greater awareness of what Fowler (1981, 277) has termed our "master stories", the stories by which we live our lives. Within the present research study, the opportunity for such critical reflection on leadership story and underpinning belief structures through guided interview, the value of the metaphor 'reservoirs of hope' in promoting such reflection and the appreciation of the ensuing analysis by fellow practitioners in informing their own leadership reflection on practice has demonstrated the power of 'story-telling' as a vehicle for both individual and collective personal and professional development, supporting Astley's view (2002, 133) that "stories invite participation and evoke response. They take us up into ourselves".

Practical theology is therefore also 'narrative theology' or, as it has been called, "the theology of story" (Fuller and Vaughan 1986, 1), a theology which uses the narration of events and the telling of stories as the fundamental data of a theology rooted in the basic structure of daily human experience and as such corresponds with the oral tradition underlying many of the earliest expressions of faith. "Stories create order and meaning out of the scattered fragments of human existence. They provide spaces in which to remember our past and rehearse our future" (Lynch and Willows 2000, 181) and as such are 'agents of transformation' in that not only through them can "we locate ourselves in the world, know who we are, where we have been, and where we are going, in and through the stories that we tell about ourselves and through the meta-narratives by which we choose to live" (Willows and Swinton 2000, 15), but we can also, in the experience of engaging with the stories of others, transform our own future actions. Narrative theology has both subjective and objective components: it "speaks to both head and heart" (Fuller and Vaughan 1986, 6) in that the stories told may not only create empathy between the sensitivities and feelings of participants and hearers, but must also be amenable to intellectual scrutiny and be capable of having a rational impact on future leadership practice.

The practice of narrative theology without the safeguard of such intellectual scrutiny can degenerate into a mere cathartic off-loading of problems and concerns, even if such relief is collaterally drawn from unlikely sources of succour as research interviews in what one headteacher described as an 'Elijah moment', recalling the Old Testament description of the prophet being fed by ravens whilst in the wilderness (I Kings 17, 1-6). In circumstances of professional crisis, immediate or remembered, what colleagues need most of all is to recall and reflect on their story. This can be through an 'Elijah's cave' revelation (I Kings 19, 9-13a) where overwhelmed by the pressures of critical incident survival and uncertainty of purpose and response, what is required is not to be found in the clamour of "earthquake, wind and fire" in recalling what has been experienced, but a use of the silence of "the still small voice of calm" to promote self-reflection on its purpose and meaning. Equally, however, the presence of a 'friendly outsider' beyond the immediate professional circle can provide a non-threatening opportunity to engage in a 'Road to Emmaus' experience in which a story of a critical incident can be retold, reviewed, reassessed and reflected back (Moody 1992, 93) so as to reveal influences at work which had been hidden or obscured from view at the time of the incident itself.. The role of the interviewer in the Emmaus process becomes one of listening to the retold story of the experience with all its disappointments and pressures, drawing it out further in dialogue, analysing its content and meaning, reframing it and re-envisioning it for the teller, and then 'breaking bread' together (often literally as well as metaphorically) in a new covenantal relationship of 'shared praxis' (Groome 1999).

The hallmarks of the Emmaus experience point up the essentials of the reflective interview process: a focus on guided reflection, a vision of growth emerging from the darkness of the immediate critical moment, a self-emptying of ego by both the teller of the story (resisting the temptation to present flawed leadership actions in the best possible light) and also the listener to the story (resisting the temptation to trump with a better story from one's own experience) and a cathartic fellowship in communion between colleagues. But the danger is of collusive selectivity in the way in which the narrative material is selected, processed, reflected on and interpreted (Carr 1997, 95). The role of the 'friendly outsider' in the interview situation is, both through the common bond of shared experience and hierarchical equality, to elicit the detail of the story—the 'what' of leadership actions—but also to be concerned with the 'how', creating empathy and facilitating catharsis through 'listening' so that "listening becomes a mark of respect...a deeply affirming act that tells people that they and their stories matter" (Astley 2002, 147). The over-riding aim is nevertheless to maintain a degree of professional distance which will enable the essential detail of the story to be teased out, the critical questions to be asked and effective reflection which can impact on future practice to ensue.

Practical theology is therefore 'reflective theology' in that it encourages such reflection on practice in order to illuminate belief and to promote a gain in what Astley (2002, 140), following Farley (1998, 90), has termed "reflective wisdom". For Willows and Swinton (2000, 14), "practical theology is a praxis-based discipline", drawing the distinction between practice as the non-reflective performance of a task in a value-free manner and praxis which is "value directed, value-laden and profoundly saturated with meaning". For Browning (2000, 9) "critical reflection on praxis lies at the heart of the practical theological task" and such reflection is concerned not only with the means by which particular ends are achieved, but with the validity of those ends and means in the light of the underlying value system. Praxis "is not just reflective action, but reflective action which is laden with belief" (Swinton 2000, 11).

Engagement with such praxis results in the development of phronesis, an Aristotelian cardinal virtue of moral thought, often translated as 'practical wisdom' concerned with how to act in situations previously unseen. Practical wisdom (phronesis) therefore informs practice as distinct from wisdom (sophia) being sought for its own sake. Practical wisdom accumulates through experience and reflection on it. For Walker (2005, 23-4), it is "grounded in everyday life", is "researchable through narrative and biographical methodologies" and is "related to continuity" in that it is formed and developed as the result of one's inner systems and resources being tested by critical incidents, by the experience of managing change or by embarking on 'a second journey' (after O'Collins 1995). It is "related to quality of life" being linked to notions of wholeness and balance, and can be seen as "the outcome of the spiritual quest, containing the answers to meaning and purpose in human life and affecting our most basic assumptions and outlook" Walker (2005, 23-4). Practical wisdom as the capacity to act wisely in uncharted territory is a function of experience and maturity. Indeed Casey (1990, 146) has called this capacity "moral imagination": the ability to see "what is at stake where the application of rules may not be at all obvious, and to know how to respond". Such practical wisdom then underpins the instinctive 'risk taking' which experienced, confident and self-aware headteachers are prepared to engage in: *"the courage to take risks which are true to your values,* knowing *what*

is right", as one headteacher put it, yet with the realism to recognise that
"it is not over until the fat lady sings".

Effective spiritual and moral leadership in such circumstances is
prepared to work with the ambiguity and uncertainty of not having total
awareness or control of all the factors involved. It accepts, exposes and
shares the vulnerability implicit in the knowledge that the decision taken
may be flawed and that things may go 'wrong', yet strives to apply
contextual intelligence to the prevailing circumstances to generate what is
judged to be the 'best' decision at the time. For the inexperienced
headteacher, however, such decision making may be uninformed, full of
'unknown unknowns' which allows calculated risk taking to shade into
foolhardiness. A growth in practical wisdom as a capacity 'to think and act
outside the box' arises from the growth in confidence and self-awareness
that professional experience and maturity brings, the change from 'doing
headship' to 'being the head', and the courage, as one experienced
headteacher put it, *"to be prepared to take risks to break the rules if it is
for a higher purpose"*, and can be seen in what has been termed
"breakthrough leadership" (Hay Group/HTI 2002) which is prepared to
cross boundaries, challenge the status quo and take calculated risks in
pursuit of improvement which remains true to personal values.

Practical theology is also therefore a 'theology of personal
authenticity', for the journey of development into practical wisdom can be
linked to identified stages of the development of emergent personal
authenticity described by West-Burnham (2002, 5). He posits a pivotal
movement from external authenticity derived from the trappings and
symbols of leadership power to internal authenticity through "the capacity
to reflect on self, to move towards an authentic awareness and
understanding...[so that] understanding of self allows the possibility of a
life driven by a clear ethical purpose...and the pursuit of the ethical
becomes the dominant purpose". Putting this principle into practice
"allows...the development of [practical] wisdom: intuitive understanding
that informs every aspect of life. Such wholeness and authenticity
approaches transcendence: the fully authentic self".

For Macquarrie (1977, 74), an authentic self is one which is able to
hold in balance and bring to fulfilment "the polarities of existence",
including the tensions of community and individuality, for authentic
selfhood can never be developed solely in a solitary individualistic way
but is only fully possible in a "community of selves". In asserting that an
individual is only a person in so far as he or she stands in relation to other
individuals, he is echoing the concept of 'ubuntu', that "a person is a
person through other people", existing in what Tutu has memorably called

"a delicate network of interdependence" (Tutu 1999, 196). Tutu draws a thought-provoking distinction between the Western view of personhood centred on the value of the product one produces, and the African view of a person's meaning and identity being drawn from the human community in which the individual is set (Tutu 1991, 20, cited in Battle 1997, 36). It is a distinction that can be nicely illustrated by the difference between the questions '*what* do you *do*?' (which tends to be the default introductory position in Western conversation), that is, 'what gives you *value*?', and the African concern for '*who are* you?', that is, 'what gives you *values*?'. For Macquarrie (1998, 94), the conditions for attaining authentic selfhood are acceptance and commitment: acceptance of the present context in which we find ourselves, and commitment not only to a belief system which gives meaning to that context but also to the potentiality of its development to create a better future. Thus formal beliefs and contextual circumstances combine to produce operational actions.

In their responses to a wide range of critical incident situations as they lead that 'community of selves' which is their school, headteachers reveal their personal authenticity at the point where their formal theology of belief, the source of their values, is mediated through the pressures and constraints of context to generate an operating theology which emanates in praxis: practical leadership action in response to the situation which is informed by reflection, tested by context, yet has to remain consonant with the underlying belief system if the integrity of personal authenticity is to be maintained both for self and in the eyes of others. This interrelationship can be seen in Figure 6.1.

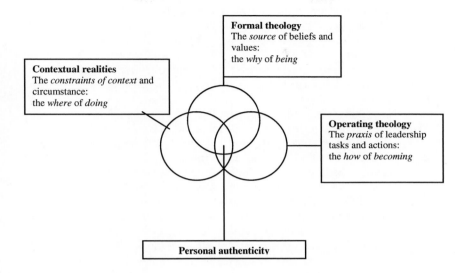

Fig. 6-1. Personal authenticity as source, context, praxis

'Formal theology' is the belief system which individual leaders espouse, rooted and formed in their previous upbringing or present spiritual practice, and which provides 'the *why* of their *being*'. It may be metaphorically termed the 'biology of belief': the values which are hard-wired into the cellular structure of being to provide the bedrock of enduring conviction which determines why they take a specific course of leadership action described in the biography of their leadership story. It is the source or sources of their personal reservoir of belief and meaning, sustained by the tradition or traditions, the resources and the stories that they appeal to as authoritative for them, that they draw sustenance and support from and that influence their ways of thinking and behaving. It is fed by the influence of a number of 'significant others' who have acted and continue to act as role models—for many this may be a parent; for Christians this will be above all Christ. But 'formal theology' is mediated through the culture and context of the workplace, the commitment to work within the often conflicting and contradictory pressures from parents, pupils, government and other stakeholders, within which leaders are required to operate and which requires the translation and accommodation of these multiple and complex contextual realities and expectations into an acceptance of 'the *where* of *doing*': the leadership arena in which one is required to operate.

'Operating theology is the '*how* of *becoming*': the way in which leadership behaviour is worked out in practice within its specific context to ensure that developments are secured, improvements made and the vision progressed through leadership actions which remain consonant with personal and collective values. Such leadership behaviour might be termed (after Nye 2008) 'contextual intelligence', as it draws on the leader's stock of knowledge, experience and fundamental values (formal theology) to make what is *felt*, both cognitively and viscerally, to be the best decision according to the context prevailing at the time.

'Operating theology' is therefore synonymous with practical theology in that it straddles the potential fault line between the 'theory' of formal theology and the 'practical' demands of the operating context. It engages in a continuing reflective dialogue to synthesise theory and practice: a "critical conversation between context and tradition, leading to revised theological understandings and ways of being in the world" (Willows and Swinton 2000, 14). It does not separate but rather strives to mediate between the two, so that understanding continually informs practice and practice impacts on understanding in a symbiotic loop of onward spiritual development. For example, the headteacher faced with a staffing disciplinary issue or a demand for pupil exclusion is required to balance his or her awareness of the personal factors involved, often not in the public domain, and his or her belief in a redemptive, forgiving 'gospel of the second chance' for the individual concerned, with the pressures of both public expectation and the greater good of the wider community. The resultant balance, often a messy compromise, then has to be justified to oneself within the wider parameters of one's structure of belief: why one has privileged one value at the expense of subordinating another. Yet out of the seed bed of such reflection comes personal spiritual growth that can inform future leadership actions.

An individual operating theology may be directly consonant with the practices of a formal embedded institutionally-resourced theology arising out of a specific faith community, informed by its coherent world-view and expressed in the language of faith, as is the case with headteachers who are self-confessed 'cradle Catholics' who have remained active within their faith community. Alternatively it may have developed away from that faith community whilst still being reliant on the 'cradle capital' laid down in a faith-based upbringing, for example the atheist headteacher who recognises that he still espouses the values of his erstwhile religious upbringing, and even continues to express them in the language of faith, whilst rejecting any concept of a Higher Being or worship practices associated with it. Or whilst being based firmly in a religious tradition, it may be couched in the secular language of the profession, yet retain a bilingual capacity to be translated into the language of faith and vice versa as circumstance and context dictate. This concept of bilingualism is returned to later in this chapter.

Where there is congruence between the formal theology, however derived, expressed and presently exercised, and the operating theology either in its day-to-day context or when tested by the pressures of a critical incident, what is done, how it is done and particularly why it is done reveals the personal authenticity of the leader, both in his or her own eyes and in the perception of others. Where congruence between publicly espoused values and leadership practice is clearly visible, personal authenticity is preserved and reinforced and "belief becomes a lived condition", in Taylor's phrase (2007, 8), not just a set of beliefs nominally espoused. As one headteacher put it: *"Every decision has to stand the test of comparison against your publicly avowed principles"*, whilst recognising the complexity, ambiguity and clash of values that are inherent in many leadership situations.

Where there is dissonance between those principles and actual practice, personal authenticity is weakened or destroyed. For example, the story was recounted by one headteacher of the behaviour of a stridently evangelical Christian teacher found abusing the school postal system for the despatch of inappropriate literature which destroyed any credibility he, and more importantly the message of his belief system had built up over the years. The expressed response to his behaviour from staff was couched not in the specifics of the offence, nor as a concern for the detail of his actions, but more as a judgement on his personal authenticity: "But he calls himself a Christian?". In such circumstances there is a necessity for there to be a match between the meaning of the 'message' as expressed through the espoused value system, the character of the communicator, that is, his perceived trustworthiness in being true to his value system when it is seen played out in both verbal and non-verbal actions, and the concomitant judgement his audience brings to bear as a result of witnessing those actions. If this match breaks down, due to human fallibility and shortcomings, as in this example, then the personal authenticity of the 'messenger' is destroyed or undermined, the promulgated meaning is compromised and the audience loses any receptiveness for the 'message' both in the present and often in the future. The person of faith operating in the real world must therefore accept the high risk strategy of preserving the balance so that word and deed do not conflict, values are seen played out in action and personal authenticity is maintained. Nowhere must this be more evident than in the spiritual and moral leadership role of the headteacher. A mismatch between promulgated values and leadership actions damages not only personal effectiveness but also personal authenticity, both in the eyes of self and the estimation of others.

As they operate as spiritual and moral leaders in confronting the day-to-day pressures and critical incidents of school leadership, headteachers may be said to be engaged in practical theology (although some would resist any notion that they are engaged in theology of any kind!)—a theology responsive to context; a theology concerned with the ordinary as well as the extraordinary; a theology of reflection on practice through the narration of leadership story to inform, enhance and enable further professional and spiritual development; and an operating theology which holds in synergy both fundamental beliefs and contextual pressures so as to maintain both personal authenticity in the present and a vision of hope for the future.

Yet in exercising spiritual and moral leadership, the operating theology of the headteacher can be viewed as not only practical theology but also as 'liberation theology'. It has been suggested (Gorringe 2000, 134) that liberation theology is a synonym for contextual theology, due to its methodological rooting in and growth out of experience. It is a narrative theology rooted in the storytelling of that experience. It is therefore more an inductive theology than a deductive one (with interesting parallels to the working of the scientific method). But for headteachers, it is an operating theology formed by the mediation of context through the lens of belief. It is a theology of praxis, of commitment and action springing from reflection on a personal value system and faith perspective but tailored to context—'what can be made to work in this place' as opposed to a 'one size fits all' model. It is also a liberation theology with a concern for the needs of the poor and the oppressed and so is a theology seen particularly at work in those who lead schools facing challenging circumstances as a result of the socio-economic environment in which they are set. It is not just pastoral care in such circumstances, but pastoral care with a moral imperative, concerned not only with the compassionate support of people in need but with their transformation to more wholesome ways of living (Goodliff 1998, 91). As a theology of context, having been described as "theology from below" (Bosch 1991, 439) rather than imposed from above, it is a theology which is 'issue-based', starting its reflection from the realities of human life by analysing the socio-economic situation in order to produce new modes of social transformation (Althaus-Reid 2000, 388). It is a countercultural model of contextual theology (Bevans 2002): a theology of 'revolution' rather than conformity, being prepared to challenge or subvert the existing social order in order to fulfil the hope of a better future. Experienced headteachers consequently speak of being prepared 'to subvert the system' in order to improve the life chances of the students in their care.

For Moltmann, however (1972, 56), writing from a Christian faith perspective, "liberation theology…is a theology which radically focuses on Christian hope". This is more than a belief that there is a meaning to existence and a final fulfilment awaiting us, what Polkinghorne (1994, 66) has called "the intuition of hope". It is a belief that recognises that Christ's Cross and Resurrection are the beginning and promise of that which is to come, and generates a yearning to look forward, confident in the memory of what God has already achieved in Jesus Christ, to the fulfilment of God's creation. Christians therefore look back to the Cross and forward to the Eschaton. With Parker (2002, 3), they recognise that "how we work depends on who we are, which in turn is a product of what we have been", but with Pannenberg (1968, 169) they accept that "what things are is decided by what they will become". Christians operate, however, in the present world, within which eschatology cannot be seen as 'the last chapter' but as the perspective from which all else is to be understood and given its proper meaning. For Christians, with Moltmann, Christian eschatology does not mean "the future as such"; it sets out from "a reality in history" and announces "the future of that reality in its future possibilities and its power over the future" as an active doctrine of hope: "From first to last and not merely in the epilogue, Christianity is eschatology, is hope" (Moltmann 1967, 16-17).

Therefore this 'formal theology' cannot restrict itself simply to an eschatological hope for the last things at the end of time but must also be based in the context of the present circumstance. It is not only a visionary hope in an eternal future when all will be revealed and made new, but also a practical hope for a more immediate future and the possibility of transforming it through present action. It is theology predicated on faith, hope and love. In the words of Pope Benedict (2007):

> Redemption is offered to us in the sense that we have been given hope…by virtue of which we can face our present. The present can be lived and accepted if it heads towards a goal…if we can be sure of this goal [faith]…and if this goal [love] is great enough to justify the effort of the journey.

Thus formal theology and present circumstance must interact in an operating theology of both naming the present context (Tracy 1995) and transforming the immediate future, for "the future is not a matter of some far-off divine event. The future is the reality that encounters us as we put our hope and anticipation to the test" (Taylor, no date 132, cited in Polkinghorne 1994, 66).

For the headteacher operating within a secular milieu, the techniques of Appreciative Inquiry offer a similar perspective, albeit couched in the language of transformational change and organisational development. Appreciative Inquiry (Cooperrider and Srivastva 1999) is based on a paradigm of social constructivism that treats organisations as a set of interlocking organic relationships that contain within themselves pockets of excellence that provide 'seeds of hope' for the future. Such organisations should seek out and nurture, from examples and stories of present good practice, such 'seeds of hope' in order to create images of future excellence. Thus Appreciative Inquiry is rooted in the key concepts of valuing what is ('appreciative') and explorative seeking out of new potentialities ('inquiry'). It is based on a four-stage process of Discovery, Dream, Design and Destiny. Discovery involves gathering stories of best practice in order to appreciate the best of what is, of immersing oneself in the stories and practices of the 'tradition' in whatever belief system it is found; Dream involves envisioning an image of an ideal future, envisioning what might be; Design is the conversion of the dream into reality, grown from the seedbed of existing practice in a mutual co-constructing of a way forward and establishing how it can be; Destiny is the reiterative, regenerative process which delivers and sustains the final vision of what will be. Luckcock (2007) has linked these four stages with the theological virtues of Faith, Hope and Love. He argues that the Discovery stage is linked with Love: the loving of what is, regardless of imperfections and resisting the cynicism and fatalism that Halpin (2003, 18-21) has identified as amongst the enemies of hope. The Dream stage of Appreciative Inquiry can be linked with Hope: our hope in the prospect of a better future and our vision of what it might be like. Design, however, involves Faith: what we really believe we are capable of growing from the seeds of hope, and our individual and collective self-belief in our capacity so to do. To this analysis, however, must be added Destiny: for Christians the delivery of a hope not only worked out in the present but ultimately fulfilled in a Christ who promises to transform individual lives and to make all things new.

A theology of hope speaks of hope as 'performative' and not just 'informative' (Pope Benedict 2007). It is based on a gospel that does not just 'make things known' but 'makes things happen'. It is inclusive as well as individualistic, concerned with 'we' as well as 'me'. It is realistic as regards the present as well as idealistic for the future. It takes sufferings and setbacks and uses them to transform social structures. It is this belief in the transformational power of hope which makes it an important underpinning philosophical theme for Christians and non-Christians alike, providing a unifying 'theology of hope' for hard-pressed headteachers of whatever faith perspective as they face the task of transforming the exigencies of their present situations. We have seen that the Christian view of hope, as expressed by the so-called 'theologians of hope' Moltmann and Pannenberg, conceives of both 'future hope' in the 'last things', or as Halpin (2003, 16, following Godfrey 1987) terms it 'ultimate hope', but also 'present hope' or, as Halpin (again following Godfrey) terms it, 'absolute hope': "a positive orientation to the world…that enables an openness or readiness of spirit towards the future" (Halpin 2003, 16). But this positive orientation is not a naive or simple hope; rather it is what Grace has called a 'complex hope': "an optimism of the will that recognises the historical and structural difficulties which need to be overcome" (Grace 1994, 59) and as such "draws into the equation the importance of grounding one's aspirations for the future in a comprehensive analysis of those factors which structurally inhibit reform…in an intelligent as opposed to evangelistic engagement with the possibilities of change" (Halpin 2003, 20).

Such an orientation offers Christians the opportunity to participate in the creative, transforming activity of a God with the capacity 'to make all things new' not simply in the future but in the present moment. For Jews, the future hope for the coming of the Messiah is complemented by a recognition that "hope is best understood as a vital part of living to the full in the present—a form of *realised* eschatology without which it is not possible to engage either meaningfully or *authentically* with one's immediate life or the contemporary world" (Halpin 2003, 18, citing Benjamin 1997 who writes from a personal commitment to Judaism; emphasis added). For Muslims, belief in resurrection and judgement carries with it a concomitant obligation not to withdraw from the world but, as one of the five pillars of Islam, to actively participate in improving the lot of the less fortunate within it, against which one will be judged. For humanists also, with a belief that morality is a natural product of our social instincts and not divinely inspired, hope should be for the improvement of human welfare and fulfilment (Copson 2008). So the concept of hope within a vision of a better future to be worked for now in the present is a unifying theme across all the faith perspectives espoused by the headteachers in this study. Indeed Bloch (1985), arguing from a Marxist perspective, avers that hope is a *universal* characteristic of human existence, an important driver of our present actions, and as a consequence, Fergusson asserts "human existence *in the present* assumes a definite importance in the light of an expected future...a time in which present imperfections and injustices can be overcome" (Fergusson 1997, 233; emphasis added).

To sum up, it has been argued that in their spiritual and moral leadership, headteachers may be said to be exercising a practical 'theology of hope' which filters their formal theology of belief through the contextual realities of circumstance to ensure a maintenance of the vision of hope in the prospect of a better future and the transforming power of present action in bringing it about. But how is this universal theme of hope seen to be worked out within the day-to-day pressures of school leadership as headteachers act as the 'reservoirs of hope' for their schools? The integrative concepts of kerygma, kenosis and koinonia can provide a template that can be applied to such spiritual and moral leadership based on hope. This will now be explored.

2. Kerygma, kenosis and koinonia

The theological concepts of kerygma, kenosis and koinonia may usefully be applied to the metaphor 'reservoirs of hope' to link it both with metanoia and kairos.

Kerygma

When exercising spiritual and moral leadership as they act as 'reservoirs of hope' in leading their schools, headteachers are required constantly to convey a consistent and coherent message of hope, a message based on their core values which are preserved in spite of the pressures of context and circumstance. This constant message of hope may be conceived of as a *kerygma*, to use the term applied to the essential gospel message preached in the New Testament. Bultmann (1975) argued the necessity of 'recovering' this kerygma from the historical and linguistic contextual trappings of the particular New Testament world-view, in order to 'demytholologise' it and make the message meaningful, significant and accessible to a contemporary audience. In this, he strove to be a 'bridge builder', attempting to span differing faith perspectives and world-views. Hence the kerygma is not to be defined just in terms of specific content but more in terms of its effect in bringing about a transformation in the hearer, or, as Bultmann would express it, 'the experience of redemption'. Similarly, headteachers exercising spiritual and moral leadership act as 'apologists' for their core value system, translating it in accordance with the needs of the specific context and interpreting it to be meaningful for the audience of the school community, yet defending it against assaults from others with differing perspectives and views. Through the constant application of the essential message of their value system, they seek the redemptive 'turning around' and 'moving forward' of both that school community and the individuals within it towards their embedded vision of a better future.

Nowhere is this seen more strongly than in response to incidents which could lead to potential pupil exclusion, where headteachers strive to maintain their core values of inclusion and individual worth, to maintain the vision of a redemptive 'gospel of the infinite second chance' against insistent pressures from staff and parents often seeking instant retribution. Heads have to interpret and balance the needs of the individual against the needs of the wider community, to reconcile however imperfectly, leadership actions with a vision of a better future for all. They have to justify those actions both privately and publicly in language that is accessible to their hearers. They have to defend those actions against both private and public challenge, and maintain their individual sense of self-belief and self-worth against pressures to convince them that 'they have got it wrong'.

Kenosis

Such pressures are of themselves draining, but headteachers in exercising such spiritual and moral leadership are prepared willingly to empty themselves in the defence of and service to others, a form of *kenosis*, defined as "a letting go or emptying of our self-possession" (Veling 2005, 36) in a demonstration of servant leadership. For Christians inspired by the example of the self-emptying servant leadership of Jesus Christ, the call is to abandon the privilege of rank and status and to be prepared to reveal a capacity for pain and suffering—as one headteacher put it *"to be prepared to let my humanity show"*, whilst remaining true to one's fundamental values. This may be seen in some small way as analogous to the Christian view that in Christ, God "set aside (or became emptied of) the divine *metaphysical* attributes (such as omnipotence, omniscience and omnipresence) in Christ, whilst retaining the *moral* attributes (such as the divine love, righteousness and holiness)" (McGrath 1997, 260; emphasis added).

The metaphor of the 'reservoir of hope', with its opportunity for visualisation of self-emptying, provides a conceptualisation of the kenotic process for Christians and non-Christians alike. The renunciation of the external trappings of headteacher authority and power, whilst retaining the essential core values and moral attributes, displays personal authenticity as a human being as well as a leader. However, this process can lead to a position of vulnerability. The inexperienced headteacher is often tempted to take refuge behind the bulwark of 'authority' and feels that to admit weakness and seek support is a sign of leadership failure. The experienced headteacher, however, is prepared to admit vulnerability, to take risks with self-image and to seek out support without shame. This is encapsulated in the contrast between the new headteacher who confidently stated *"the head has to remain upbeat in his public face day after day...otherwise it soon gets round"*, compared to the more experienced colleague who testified that *"my staff say we draw strength from you because you are ready to admit your own weaknesses. By showing your human frailty, you give us the courage to reveal our own"*.

Koinonia

Self-giving in the service of others thereby impacts not only on self but also on the relationships in the community in which that self is set. For Macquarrie (1977, 336) "the very notion of a self-giving implies going out from the individual existence". Writing of salvation, in the sense of 'making whole', he argues that the polarities of the individual and the community have to be brought into balance: "there can be no genuine salvation (making whole) for an individual apart from the community of faith...a community of the Spirit which becomes the agency by which the Spirit works in the world and by which it continues the work of reconciliation begun by Christ" (Macquarrie 1977, 336). This 'fellowship of the spirit' or *koinonia*, can be described in secular terms as 'a community of shared values', united in a common purpose in working towards an agreed vision of 'making things whole'. The term 'koinonia', derived from the Greek word for 'common', implies not only that sharing of values but an acceptance of a share in working towards the outcome of the joint enterprise to deliver them. It is thus a relational 'partnership in common', an alignment of relationships in the service of a higher purpose or mission, a 'fellowship' not of hierarchical command but of distributed leadership which focuses energies and aligns actions within a covenant of shared values. If, then, the building of this covenantal community is based on mutual subscription to these shared values, then "spiritual and moral leaders must be consummate relationship builders with diverse people and groups, especially with people different than themselves" (Fullan 2001, 5). This must be more than relationship building, but rather 'fellowship building', a moral activity in which the leader enters into what has been termed a "covenantal relationship" (Sergiovanni 1992, 102, developing de Pree 1989), by establishing, renewing and reasserting a collective understanding of its central meaning, purpose and values.

Metanoia

If unchallenged by the impact of critical incidents or systemic pressures, values may, however, become ossified and potentially irrelevant; attitudes and relationships may become cosy, comfortable and exclusive; self-emptying actions may become seen as facile, fruitless and ineffective: not so much 'the way we do things around here' as 'the way we have always done things'. But under the pressure of events, the unpredictable and uncertain conditions of critical incidents may force paradigm shifts which stretch personal boundaries beyond their comfort zone and lead to reassessment, radical revision, renewal and redemption, the possibility of restoration and reintegration into the full life of the community through a demonstration of 'the gospel of the chance to change' in action. The term 'metanoia', or 'conversion' in the sense of change of heart, change of attitude and change of behaviour, may be used to describe this. It is more than a breakdown of prior understanding; it is a breakthrough into new understanding, a process of release from past positions and conceptual frameworks into new vistas of insight and recognition. It is more than simply a change of mind; it is a change of heart, a 'turning around' or 'repentance' so that new ways of thinking and acting can emerge.

The term 'metanoia' has not only faith but also secular connotations; it was used by Deming, the business economist, to describe the need for a cultural change in organisations, a reorientation or transformation of outlook from mutually destructive competition (which he termed win-lose) to the win-win situation of mutually interdependent cooperative support (Deming 1993). A similar cultural change has to be engendered by spiritual and moral leaders of schools if they are to move from being isolated outposts of competition to integrated communities of love. For Veling (2005, 189) the concepts of mercy and metanoia are intimately linked. For, as we ourselves recognise our own inadequacies yet feel the merciful generosity of God's forgiveness, so "the metanoia demanded by the kingdom takes concrete form in empathy with and dedicated commitment to one's fellow human beings" (Schillebeeckx 1979, 165). Veling also cites Chappell (2001, 6):

> ...mercy requires something of us: that we relent, that we change our mind and heart, that we give up a previous understanding of another, that we

release them from the bondage of our preconception, and finally that we stoop down and bear with them in their suffering.

This may be seen as an encapsulation of the essential values-driven message of the spiritual and moral leader (kerygma), their modus operandi in empathetic relationships (koinonia) and their capacity for self-emptying (kenosis) to stand in solidarity with others in their suffering.

Stamp and Todd (1996, 42) consider this from a managerial perspective and link it to the ministerial role. They conceptualise the operation of organisations as being based primarily on 'people in working relationships' and have synthesised a 'tripod of work' based on 'tasking', 'trusting' and 'tending' to describe those relationships:

> In the Tripod, people task and are tasked, share intention, limits and resources; trust and are trusted with the purpose ('vision') of the organisation and to use their best judgement in serving it; tend and are tended provide and use the space, the information, the waiting upon (ministering), the watching over (episcope) that keep the enterprise on course.

Using these insights, it is possible to identify 'tasking'—the maintenance of a coherence of direction, energy and understanding—with the sharing of the vision expressed as its kerygma; to link 'trusting' as the empowerment of colleagues through distributed leadership in discerning the best course of action to deliver the vision in specific circumstances, with koinonia; and to link 'tending' as symbiotic self-emptying in the mutual support and care of others, with the concept of kenosis. Metanoia, then, is seen in the reviewing of the vision through an inbuilt capacity to pause, reflect, forgive and learn, leading to ongoing transformation. Figure 6.2 shows the interaction of these concepts.

Stamp and Todd (1996, 53) draw attention to the fundamental stability of the tripod arrangement, where even if the three 'legs' of tasking, trusting and tending are not equally fully developed, balance may still be maintained, even when the equilibrium of the system is disturbed by the unpredictable uncertain conditions of critical incidents. Whilst they point to the essential role of the leader in 'waiting on' or 'ministering' to colleagues in such situations, and 'watching over them' (episcope) in order to keep the collective enterprise on course, they do not address the support needs of the leaders themselves. There is a need to consider who ministers to the leader and who has 'episcopal' oversight of their needs, to answer the question 'who cares for the carers?' and to devise strategies to respond positively and proactively to it, not simply during and in the aftermath of critical incidents, but in the day-to-day pressures of the leadership situation, when self-emptying kenosis can threaten to drain the reservoir of hope.

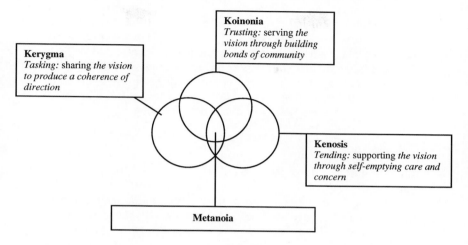

Fig. 6-2. Metanoia as kerygma, kenosis, koinonia

Such caring demands a corporate culture of collaboration, a koinonia of common mutually supportive relationships to combat feelings of personal isolation and to replace collective competition with collaboration. School leaders draw the support they need from informal self-generated and home-grown networks of colleagues with common interests and mind-sets. They draw strength from individual peer support structures and appreciate the listening ear of a non-judgemental critical friend. They value access to communities of support far beyond the remit of the professional role, be they networks of engagement within a particular faith tradition, voluntary interest groups or charitable work. All contribute through such networks of relationships to refilling and sustaining the personal reservoir of hope (Flintham 2008a, 26-7).

In summary, kerygma is the essential message of belief: the source on which the school leader draws as the reservoir of core values and the vision of a desired future on which leadership actions are based and by which he or she is tasked and tasks others. It is the source of the call or sense of vocation to the leadership role in the first place, be it within a school of a particular faith tradition or one facing particular challenging circumstances. It underpins the imperative to serve in such communities and to act as the reservoir of hope for them. Kenosis is the self-emptying role of spiritual and moral leadership which ministers to and supports others, tending them and caring for them in their difficulties and needs and acting as the reservoir of hope when critical incidents impinge, preserving the vision and maintaining the hope, both individually and collectively. Koinonia is the mutual solidarity of interdependent trusting relationships, providing networks of mutual support and resulting in a collective approach to thinking, behaving and belonging which refills the reservoir of hope of school leaders when it is in danger of running dry.

Kairos

But overlaid on this is the concept of *kairos*, the 'right' or opportune moment, the 'special time' for action. For Tillich (1957, 173), "Ethics in a changing world must be understood as the ethics of the *kairos,* of the God-given moment". Successful headteachers not only have a capacity to identify 'why' and 'what' needs to be done and 'how' to do it effectively, but also an intuitive sense of '*when*' the moment is right to engage with a window of opportunity to advance the vision, or when it is better simply to pause and take stock, to react or to reflect. Kairos, that sense of when is the appropriate 'right' time, is then combined with ethos, the purpose, vision and community which creates the contextual atmosphere for appropriate engagement in 'why' and 'with whom' to act, and logos, the articulation of 'what' are then the appropriate ethical actions in the circumstances and 'how' they should be undertaken to ensure engagement with and movement towards the collective vision. Successful leadership is therefore displayed at the confluence of logos, ethos and kairos, as shown in Figure 6.3.

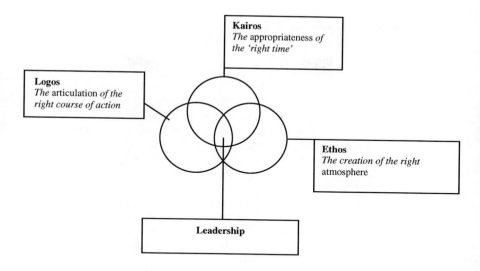

Fig. 6-3. Leadership as logos, ethos, kairos

Leadership is then the summation of kairos, ethos and logos so that the whole becomes greater than the sum of its parts.

3. The Golden Rule, redemption and covenant

In addition to the integrative themes of kerygma, kenosis and koinonia which have been explored above, it is also possible to discern a further three enduring concepts which have emerged as continuing threads within discussions of spiritual and moral leadership with headteachers; namely, the prevalence of the *Golden Rule* in guiding leadership actions, a belief in the importance of the possibility of *redemption* and renewal as a motivating factor, and the value of *covenantal relationships* in supporting community values and aspirations. These, although underpinned by a universal belief in fairness, justice and equality of opportunity, may be expressed in a variety of forms, depending on the faith perspective from which they emerge. It is possible, however, to be able to translate between secular or professional expressions of this philosophy and their counterparts in the language of faith. A capacity for bilingual fluency in this regard has proved invaluable in conducting interviews for this research study. It has permitted the emergence and non-threatening exploration of themes such as redemption and covenant in dialogue with a range of headteachers from a variety of faith and secular perspectives.

Within the 'mixed economy' of education, with schools of a faith-based character co-existing with those standing on a more secular foundation, there is a paucity of shared language to enable effective communication. Across all the school contexts of those headteachers interviewed it was accepted that, as one headteacher put it: *"there is a collective need for a shared and consistent language across how we deal with a series of practical incidents and learning experiences, even if we do not yet have a fully shared vocabulary of the language of learning"*, a shared vocabulary which is capable not only of expressing present experience but of shaping future experience. For Pinker (2007), our propensity for metaphor in enabling us to grasp complex and abstract concepts through simpler analogies, and the combinatorial power of language allowing an infinite variety of formulations, permits such communication by providing the tools we need to think outside the boxes of our differing positions. The metaphor of 'reservoirs of hope' and the capacity for bilingualism in applying and interpreting it in differing contexts provide some readily available tools to enable such communication.

The commonality of values demonstrated across the faith spectrum by those interviewed, even if motivated by different belief systems and articulated in different language and vocabulary, is evidence in support of the contention that in the same way as with our capacity for spoken language, where the details vary from culture to culture yet the underlying deep structure of grammar is universal, so also there is a 'universal moral grammar' (Hauser 2007) which drives our moral judgements, a set of fundamental principles out of which can be built a range of possible moral value systems and which form a set of deep moral 'intuitions' which underlie cultural and religious variations in social norms of behaviour.

This 'universal moral grammar' can then be seen to emanate in those 'universal verities' described by several of those interviewed for this present study, demonstrating what Dawkins (2006, 263) has termed "the broad liberal consensus of ethical principles" centring round the philosophy of 'do not do unto others what you would not want them to do to you'. This is a modern-day humanist restatement of the so-called 'Golden Rule' of 'do as you would be done by' which underpins almost all belief systems. Although the accounts given of the universe, of human nature, of the goals of life and of the ways that lead to salvation or enlightenment are fundamentally and often irreconcilably different, the adherents of these belief systems all strive to live out their faith in adherence to the Golden Rule variously expressed in the Hindu

Mahabharata as 'do nothing to others which if done to you could cause you pain', in the sayings of the Buddha as 'do not hurt others with that which hurts yourself' or of the Prophet Mohammed as 'none of you truly believes until he wishes for his brothers what he wishes for himself', or by Jesus of Nazareth, quoting the Jewish Torah, as the commandment to 'love your neighbour as yourself'.

The all-pervasiveness of the Golden Rule across so many responses of headteachers interviewed, be it expressed in its Christian formulation of 'love your neighbour as yourself' or the more neutral secular rendering of 'do as you would be done by', shows its universal appeal as a dominant thread within the broad liberal consensus of educational values, irrespective of the faith perspective being held or the language in which it is described. Sullivan (2008a) has used the Hegelian term 'sublation' to describe ways in which one concept may not only stand alone, but may be integrated within a different concept to serve not only its own purpose but also a higher unity. Headteachers with a personal faith perspective who operate within a school of similar faith tradition are able openly and overtly to express themselves and their values in the language of faith amongst those who are comfortable with its articulation in such terms, being able to sublate professional language within the language of faith. For other leaders, operating in more secular environments, there is a necessity to practice 'bilingualism', to retain so-called 'religious language' for the private domain and to use conventional secular language 'in the public square' of professional life (Sullivan 2010). Indeed, for headteachers fluent in the languages of both domains, there is often a need to practice what could, after Darwin, be termed linguistic 'cryptic colouration', to moderate language and vocabulary to fit the expectations and mind-set of the listener.

For example, one secular headteacher interviewed about his spiritual and moral leadership was relieved by the all-encompassing definition of 'secular spirituality' being applied, for otherwise he indicated that if it had been about religion, it would have been the shortest interview on record! To have revealed the status of the interviewer as an Anglican priest would have further exacerbated the situation. Equally, a secular head of a school facing challenging circumstances, whose office wall displayed a Bob Marley poster for the 'Redemption Song' adjacent to a poster of a skydiver casting himself into the void in a 'parachutist's faith', may have been repelled by a theological discussion of redemption or of the value of trust, in the context of a redemptive faith, in 'the eternal everlasting arms', but was happy to accept the validity of articulating his belief in the essential redeemability of his pupils if given confidence in their ability to succeed, through the words of the poem by Guillaume Apollinaire, which was the caption to the poster:

> "Come to the edge", he said.
> They said: "We are afraid".
> "Come to the edge", he said.
> They came. He pushed them.
> And they flew.

In capturing, analysing and promulgating the leadership experiences of those who had faced critical testing times when they had had to 'come to the edge' in defence of their values, the capacity for such 'bilingualism', the ability to mediate a discourse between those who use 'insider' religious language (for example, terms such as 'gospel values' and 'what would Jesus do?') in addressing their professional role, and those who use secular language (for example, terms such as 'inclusion' and 'equality of opportunity') becomes crucial. This may be illustrated by the example of two headteachers interviewed who had faced a similar critical incident of sudden and violent pupil death and had led their school communities through its trauma. One, standing on a foundation of a formal 'secular' theology, described the aftermath as 'sharing our humanity'; the other from a formal faith perspective spoke of 'evangelisation by witness' in describing his role. Both felt encouraged by the 'bilingual' capacity of the interviewer to be capable of operating effectively within either of these linguistic codes, to be able to share similar deep personal feelings of loss, vulnerability and hope in a language of expression and response that was comfortable to each. This ability to 'translate' faith through sensitivity to the local context, thereby mediating between faith and culture through the use of appropriate language, can be seen as a form of 'inculturation'. It requires, adapting a telling terminology of Bosch (1991, 453), the capacity of the 'padre' and of 'compadre'.

Underpinning this common collective endeavour is the concept of a covenant of mutually shared values in which "the covenant partners are bound together not by a set of legal requirements but by the relational nexus of gracious initiative followed by thankful response" (Bridger 2003, 16). Such a covenantal relationship goes further than the carefully defined obligations of the contract to a commitment to actions underpinned by agape: love which is freely offered as a gift, not contractually prescribed; relationships which are based on faithfulness and constancy; vision which is open to the possibilities of continual growth. Spiritual and moral leadership in such circumstances is thus not simply a matter of adherence to contractual rules; it is an ethical orientation that gives moral direction to leadership actions, especially when they are tested by challenging circumstances. "The character of the professional is as important as the code to which he or she adheres. The ethics of conduct must be shaped by the ethics of character and the ethics of integrity" (Bridger 2003, 19). In other words, what we do is governed by who we are: the beliefs we hold and the 'habits of the heart' that instinctively inform our actions.

For de Pree (1989, 12, cited in Sergiovanni 1992, 73), "a covenantal relationship rests on a shared commitment to ideas, to values, to goals…covenantal relationships reflect unity, grace and poise". The covenantal relationship between the headteacher and the community he or she leads is based on matter and spirit, head and heart, doing and being. It can be conceived of as both 'a covenant of works', the actions the community takes or upholds in the light of those shared values in 'the way we *do* things round here', but also 'a covenant of grace' in which the possibility of forgiveness, renewal and transformation is paramount in 'the way we *are* towards people round here'. This synthesis of 'doing' and 'being' thus "changes the root metaphor for schools from organisation to community" (Sergiovanni 1997, 238) and the role of those who lead them from efficient management functionaries into spiritual and moral leaders. For Christians, this ethical framework is constructed on a foundation of grace. As in the biblical model of covenant, where the covenantal relationship between God and His people is founded on grace, the free self-giving of God in Christ and the active presence of God suffusing the whole of creation and transforming human lives, so the school leader is called, challenged and empowered to be a vehicle of grace in giving himself or herself in love and service to those entrusted to his or her care. And when faith in that calling is tested through critical incidents and challenging circumstances, when leadership is painful and personally draining, leaders may draw strength from the belief poetically expressed by Hicks (2008), that:

> It may well be that from this time of hurt,
> You will be led in ways you would not choose,
> So grace may seed its hope within life's dirt…

Conclusion

This chapter has sought to apply concepts of practical theology to the spiritual and moral leadership of headteachers. This has generated a chapter that is in a somewhat different key and language to the previous data chapters on 'reservoirs of hope', 'foundations of faith' and 'labours of love'. Nevertheless, in continuing to surface some of the voices of headteachers as they exercise their leadership role especially when faced with critical situations, it has particularly sought to provide a bridge between educational expressions of that leadership role and theological perspectives on it. It has shown the value of structured and guided reflection opportunities in articulating the 'ordinary theology' of narratives of leadership story, providing supportive 'Road to Emmaus' learning experiences that can impact on future praxis, and generate a growth in practical wisdom and personal authenticity. It has recognised the necessity for that personal authenticity, and the underpinning formal theology that may underpin it, to be consistent in the face of critical contextual realities.

By applying a lens of practical theology to such circumstances, it has been possible to outline a 'theology of hope'. In order to make this applicable and relevant to as wide a range of faith perspectives as possible, the concern has been less with hope in the 'last things' of an eschatological future, and more with the hope of leaders for their present situations. However, it is accepted that for many, the relevance of hope in the present is linked to a view of an eternal hope, in that "without a genuinely future consummation of God's purpose for the world and for individuals, his purpose in the present becomes pointless" (Travis 1980, 137). However, whilst concentrating on hope within present contextual realities, this does not obviate a concern for future potentialities, for a theology of hope and its outliers in liberation theology and political theology can encapsulate both a hope for the present and a hope which springs eternal, so that hope in the anticipation of a better future is linked to investment in the present situation.

The theological concepts of kerygma, kenosis and koinonia have been applied to the spiritual and moral leadership of headteachers. It has been argued that their core vision of the prospect of a better future may be described as a kerygma that informs and imbues their leadership, providing the reason 'why' a particular course of action is favoured in the cockpit of swirling contextual realities. The chapter has explored 'how' such leadership is applied in the face of critical incidents and external pressures, suggesting that as the headteacher is prepared to drain the personal reservoir of hope to maintain an external reservoir of hope for the school, he or she is engaged in a form of kenotic self-emptying in the service of others. It has been suggested that from the descriptions of 'what' sustaining strategies are used by headteachers to replenish their personal reservoirs of hope, that paramount are opportunities for reflection and support from within a koinonia or 'fellowship in communion' of networks of mutually supportive relationships.

Finally, it has been possible to discern three further enduring concepts that have suffused discussions on spiritual and moral leadership with headteachers from a range of faith perspectives. The universal applicability of the Golden Rule of 'love your neighbour as yourself' in guiding leadership actions gives support to the view that there is a 'universal moral grammar' which underpins them. In seeking to explore this across a variety of faith perspectives, a capacity for 'bilingualism' in translating enduring concepts such as redemption from a faith-based perspective to a secular context and vice versa requires interviewers to be "bilingualists who are fluent in the metaphors of management but can readily switch into alternative discourse according to context" (Hoyle and Wallace 2007, 437). Above all, underpinning the common collective endeavour of effective school leadership is a covenantal relationship between headteachers and those they lead, a synthesis based in grace, of head and heart, doing and being, faith and works, which together ensures that (after Sergiovanni 192, 108): "the heart of the school as a moral community is its covenant of shared values".

A concluding chapter now endeavours to sum up the findings in order thence to identify the key messages for practitioners and policy makers that have emerged.

CHAPTER SEVEN

LAST THINGS

We saw in the previous chapter that a theology of hope is a theology of the present and what it can be made to become, not merely an eschatological hope for the 'last things' at the end of time. It is therefore not simply a visionary hope in the prospect of a distant future when all will be revealed and made new, but rather a practical hope for a more immediate future and the practicalities of transforming it through present action. It is not only a future to be prayed for, and a future to be hoped for, but also a future that has to be worked for.

In that context, it is hoped that the findings of this research study will provide a contribution to that work. This concluding chapter therefore provides an overview of the book as a whole, in particular by summarising the findings from its three main data chapters on 'reservoirs of hope', 'foundations of faith' and 'labours of love', relating these to the four original research questions and offering a theological perspective on them. It identifies the emergence of three common themes: the importance of *vision*, the value of *reflection*, and the necessity for *renewal*, and the importance of their contribution to the support, sustaining and effective functioning of school leaders. It indicates how these three themes provide essential key messages from practitioners to those who are charged with policy making and professional development in this area. It concludes by arguing that as we confront the imminent 'demographic time bomb' of headteacher recruitment and retention within the education system in England, these findings are timely in focusing on the importance of spiritual and moral leadership, driven by hope, underpinned by faith and fuelled by networks of relationships, as an essential attribute for the school leaders of the future.

1. Overview of findings

This book has explored the spiritual and moral leadership of headteachers across a range of school leaders, from those still serving as headteachers to those who left their headship post early. It has engaged with those who run their 'secular' schools from a particular personal faith perspective and those charged with the leadership of schools of a specific religious character, as well as those leading schools facing particularly challenging circumstances due to their social context.

In addressing the first of the research questions, namely, 'what are the spiritual and moral bases on which headteachers stand, from whence are they derived and how do they impact on leadership?', it has been argued that spiritual and moral leadership is not simply a preserve of those active in the religious domain, nor still less linked solely to schools within a particular faith tradition. All the 150 headteachers who were interviewed, irrespective of their personal faith perspective, were able to articulate without hesitation a personal value system on which they based their leadership actions, whether explicitly or implicitly. This value system may be generationally-based, faith-based or based on the egalitarian Golden Rule of 'love your neighbour as yourself', or a combination of these, which results in leadership actions based on the premise of respect for all, a concern for inclusion and social justice, and renewal and development through constant opportunities for forgiveness and the prospect of a fresh start. The coherence of vision and integrity of values that this ethical base provides thereby equips all headteachers with a cohesive underpinning foundation for their leadership actions. This has been termed a 'secular spirituality' that allows them to hold true to those values as 'a lived faith in action' (the definition of spirituality being used throughout this study) as they act as spiritual and moral leaders of their schools when faced with both critical incidents and day-to-day systemic pressures. In such circumstances, professional colleagues and the wider community within and beyond the school look to the headteacher to maintain the personal and collective vision, to facilitate effective inter-personal engagement in the common task and to sustain institutional self-belief in the face of such external pressures.

In response to the second research question as to the perceived value of reflection, headteachers interviewed relished the opportunity to reflect on critical incidents in their leadership story and to be able to consider how their value system of fundamental belief had withstood the pressures of events and had been revealed in their leadership actions in response to them. Use of the metaphor 'reservoirs of hope', which identifies the headteacher as not only the external reservoir of hope for the school in maintaining its collective vision, morale and direction, but also suggests the necessity for the retention and replenishment of a personal internal reservoir of hope, was felt to provide a ready visualisation and valuable structure to aid such reflection.

In considering the third research question as to the sustainability strategies and support structures which are deployed and valued by headteachers, all headteachers interviewed were able to articulate a range of sustainability strategies which they used to maintain and replenish their internal reservoirs. Such strategies have been codified as participation in belief networks of like-minded colleagues, support networks of families, friends and peers and involvement in external networks beyond the world of education. Such networks provided opportunities for reflective space and professional renewal, as well as personal refreshment. In response to the fourth research question, it can therefore be argued that the perceived need for such opportunities provides key messages regarding the value of reflection, the importance of networking and the primacy of relationships, within a shared vision of the hope of a better future, to inform future generations of headteachers and those charged with their identification, formation, development and support.

The opportunity for practitioner reflection and the subsequent analysis of interviews with a range of headteachers of varying experience across a variety of school circumstances and contexts has provided an extensive empirical database of practitioner voice on which to draw. From it, the following detailed conclusions may be summarised. It is possible first to tabulate the findings from the 'reservoirs of hope' data set of headteachers leading predominantly secular schools and those who had left their headship early, second to move on to those leading schools from the 'foundations of faith' of a specific faith perspective, and then third to consider those who lead schools facing particularly challenging circumstances as 'labours of love'. In each case, the findings detailed in Chapters Four to Six are summarised, and linked respectively to three facets of hope: a sustaining hope, a believing hope and a covenantal hope.

1.1. Summary of 'reservoirs of hope' findings from interviews with headteachers leading predominantly 'secular' schools

Utilising a total of 50 interviews with representative samples of 25 serving headteachers and 15 headteachers who left headship early in advance of the normal retirement age in England, together with a further 10 Australian school principals, the following conclusions have been drawn:

- All heads interviewed could articulate an individual personal value system that underpinned their approach to spiritual and moral leadership. This could be categorised as either generational, faith-based and/or egalitarian-based.

- All found the 'reservoirs of hope' metaphor useful in considering their role and promoting reflection on it.
- All could describe a range of sustainability strategies without which their effective functioning would have been impaired. These relied on belief networks, support networks and external networks of engagement beyond the school.
- All were able to offer micro-narratives of critical incidents in which their sustainability strategies had been tested and valued the opportunity for guided reflection on what had sustained them through these.
- All identified a development of capacity to act in a spiritual and moral leadership role as headship progressed, and many identified with a transition from 'doing headship' to 'being the head' around the four to five year mark and the possible emergence of a plateau effect after 7-10 years.
- Heads leaving headship early could be seen as 'striding', 'strolling' or 'stumbling' from headship:
  —'strider' heads had a proactive exit strategy and moved on after successful experience;
  —'stroller' heads walked away from headship with concerns over work–life balance or pressures;
  —'stumbler' heads suffered burn out through failure of their sustainability strategies to cope.
- Such heads had similar value systems to their serving colleagues and had faced similar issues. They showed a difference in the adequacy of sustainability strategies in coping with critical incidents and the day-to-day pressures of headship:
  —'strider' heads had robust replenishment mechanisms and were able to compartmentalise their responses so that their sustaining reservoirs did not fail;
  —'stroller' heads recognised the continual draining of their emotional reservoir and its potential for eventual failure and left headship before this could occur;
  —'stumbler' heads had non-existent or inadequate sustainability strategies to replenish their reservoir, and suffered emotional or physical collapse 'when the reservoir of hope ran dry';
  —'sprinter' heads adopt a time-limited post-modernist portfolio approach to headship, matching their perceived skill set to the short-term needs of the school, and then moving on elsewhere, not necessarily within headship.

- All heads had key messages regarding the value of professional development when reinforced by strategic reflection opportunities and an infrastructure of peer support in sustaining both themselves and future generations of headteachers.

Although expressed in professional secular language rather than the language of faith, these headteachers articulate what might be termed *"a sustaining hope"*: the consistent message of hope in the possibility of a better future for the community in their charge, a kerygma which they were able to maintain even in the face of critical incidents which threatened to destroy that hope. When faced with such pressures, they were prepared to empty themselves in an act of kenosis, to drain temporarily their own personal reservoirs in the service of others. However, they felt able to refill those reservoirs from networks of peers, colleagues and families, a koinonia of mutual solidarity, support and growth. Only when such replenishment strategies were insufficiently robust did the personal reservoir of hope threaten to run dry.

1.2. Summary of 'foundations of faith' findings from interviews with headteachers leading schools from a personal faith perspective

Findings may be grouped in terms of the career development paths of a further 60 headteachers interviewed in England and Australasia who were leading schools from an individual faith perspective, the foundations of spiritual belief on which their school leadership stands and the attributes which they feel called on to display in exercising it, and how those attributes withstand the test of critical incident situations where rhetoric is required to become reality and leadership skill is pushed to the edge. Views were sought as to what sustainability strategies were effective both in crisis mode and in the face of day-to-day pressures, and what corporate support mechanisms should be available and how these might be modified and improved to meet the recruitment and development needs of potential school leaders.

Headteachers operating from a personal faith perspective identify bases of belief which are couched in a specific language of faith yet show a commonality of fundamental adherence to the Golden Rule of 'love your neighbour as yourself', encompassed within gospel imperatives of inclusion and justice. Leaders of schools of a specifically religious character display similar professional attributes to their secular colleagues and find them tested by facing a similar range of critical incidents. The essential difference is in the capacity to articulate, fluently and without embarrassment, such deeply personal attributes and values in the language of faith, and to seek out and draw succour from sustaining refreshment opportunities from the faith community where such language is a natural part of the *zeitgeist*.

Specific findings that emerged from the study may be summarised as follows:

- Career courses of headteachers interviewed were characterised by a strong sense of call to a particular type of school, be it secular or of a specific religious character, to a particular area, or to communities facing challenging circumstances. Headteachers were motivated by a passion 'to make a difference', having the power 'to make it happen' and having the capacity to deliver progress in the face of challenging circumstances and entrenched attitudes.

- Bases of belief were predicated on gospel imperatives of inclusion, invitation and social justice. These were seen to be worked out particularly when facing pupil exclusion or admission pressures.

- Foundations of faith, irrespective of espoused faith perspective, focused around the themes of respect for all, through the application of a unifying philosophy of inclusion, redemption seen through the belief that all deserve forgiveness in some form, and renewal seen in the need to offer a fresh start from mistakes and new opportunities to move forward.

- Attributes needed by headteachers of faith were felt to revolve around courage, vision and capacity, supplemented by reserves of resilience required when facing parish pressures and moral tensions, and the perceived requirement to be 'a moral icon' in the community. It was accepted that these were not specific to leaders of schools of a religious character; however, what was unique was the underpinning framework of faith and its expression in the language of faith.

- The implication of these beliefs and attributes in practice, the 'rhetoric into reality', was seen in terms of preferred leadership style, approaches to assessment, admissions and exclusions, and in the application of a 'universal moral grammar' underpinning leadership actions: the so-called Golden Rule of 'do as you would be done by', which, although expressed in different language, pervaded all the faith perspectives represented.

- Testing times in the form of severe critical incidents were experienced by these headteachers as by many others. The pressures of critical incidents that pushed leaders 'to the edge' tested their faith in terms of the retention of these core beliefs of respect, redemption and renewal, but led to eventual reconciliation. Such pressures were withstood by a majoring on relationships and a falling back onto personal foundations of faith.

- Sustaining strategies included reinforcement from peer networks and the support of the parish; renewal through sabbatical and retreat opportunities; refreshment through the creation of reflective space; and the ability to switch off from problems through compartmentalisation.

- Of support structures provided corporately, the most valued were spiritual development opportunities. It was felt necessary to be individually proactive in seeking out and accessing these. There was some suggestion (although not universally supported) that this should be addressed through making such activities mandatory or setting targets for participation.

- The essential difference between colleagues holding different faith perspectives was seen not in the 'what' of their leadership, nor in 'how' it is exercised, but in the 'why': the underpinning belief structure that governed their actions and the language and vocabulary in which this is expressed.

- All the headteachers interviewed, however, recognised that the passion and power of their spiritual and moral leadership and its underpinning foundational values of respect, redemption and renewal, leading to reconciliation, needed to be imbued with what was seen as an essential ingredient of leadership: 'a sense of hope' in the possibility of a better future for the individuals and communities entrusted to their care.

Headteachers leading their schools from a personal faith perspective see hope as "the inseparable companion of faith" (Moltmann 2002, 5), what might therefore be termed *"a believing hope"* to parallel and support the "sustaining hope" articulated by the successful leaders of secular schools. Although the belief system from which that hope is drawn varies from individual to individual, with in some cases an explicit linkage to a particular faith tradition and in other cases untethered from it, there is universal acceptance of the commandment to apply the Golden Rule of 'love your neighbour as yourself', or, as one headteacher cogently put it: *"If I would not wish this done to my own children, why am I doing it to someone else's?"*.

Equally, whilst not expressed in theological language, there is an all-pervasive belief in the possibility of redemption. This may be viewed in the New Testament sense of 'buying back', a sense which draws on the two Old Testament concepts of "freeing by payment" and "fulfilling a promise" (O'Collins 2000, 598). For the hard-pressed school leader, especially when faced with pressures for pupil exclusion, the fulfilled 'promise' is one of equality, inclusion and the possibility of infinite forgiveness to enable restoration into the life of the community, as the demonstration of 'the gospel of the second chance' in action. The 'payment', however, may have a cost in staff disaffection, community morale and leadership loneliness when faced with the righteous anger of those who ask: 'how many "last chances" should there be?', to which the scripturally-based implicit response must be "seventy times seven" (Matthew 18, 22), that is, with no reckonable limit to forgiveness.

O'Collins (1983, 160), in commenting on how the three classical models of redemption, namely liberation, expiation and transforming love, complement each other, admits the priority of the third model: for love opens up for others the freedom to live, love cleanses and purifies, and love transforms selfish hearts in metanoia to bring about a new unity. Nowhere can this be seen more clearly than in the work of those leading schools in challenging circumstances as 'labours of love', a summary of which follows.

1.3. Summary of 'labours of love' findings from interviews with headteachers leading schools facing challenging circumstances

Schools facing challenging circumstances may face a range of contextual difficulties but are conventionally identified as those failing to meet government 'floor targets' for academic attainment, or serving communities with high levels of social and economic deprivation, as indicated by the proxy free school meal entitlement indicator. In addition to 10 headteachers and 10 supporting educationists involved in participating in, enabling or evaluating secondment or sabbatical activities, a further 30 headteachers of schools facing challenging circumstances in the UK were interviewed for this part of the study, making a total sample of 40 headteachers. They demonstrated the following characteristics over and above the generality of their colleagues:

- Headteachers interviewed describe themselves as people-centred, recognising the individual worth of each member of the community and being prepared to place human needs above organisational needs and outcome measures. They operate a philosophy of 'inclusive individualism' coupled with a concern for the availability of personalised learning and developmental opportunities.

- They combine moral purpose and a passion 'to make a difference' with a willingness to collaborate and promote collaboration with colleagues to achieve that end. They place a high value on the pursuit of excellence no matter what the countervailing circumstances.

- They display a high degree of confidence in standing by their values in the face of external pressures and seek to engender a unity of collective purpose, strengthened by mutual subscription, solidarity and support.

- They are sustained by a sense of 'success against the odds', being motivated by small incremental steps of improvement and by affirmative feedback on progress, however slight.

- They are motivated by a strong belief system and a vision of a better future, high levels of self-confidence, a passion to see progress, a tenacity to pursue it and a willingness to take calculated risks to bring it about.

- Quantitative analysis, using a commercially available online instrument, of the professional characteristics of a sub-set of 10 of these school leaders, substantially drawn from one local authority area, shows that they are characterised by high levels of inter-personal skill, majoring on the primacy of respect for others, teamworking and building trust through empathetic engagement to develop effective and productive working relationships. These findings are validated by qualitative interviews with the remainder of the sample of leaders of schools facing challenging circumstances.

- Such leaders draw personal sustenance from opportunities for reflection (corroborated by interviews with a sample of a further 10 headteachers who had also experienced sabbatical or secondment opportunities and 10 supporting educationists involved in enabling or evaluating them), the ability to compartmentalise and switch off from immediate problems and the availability of non-judgemental networks of support from colleagues facing similar circumstances who are felt to be 'on the same wavelength'.

Leaders of schools facing challenging circumstances display what might be termed a *"covenantal hope"*. As with their colleagues in other schools supported by sustaining hope and believing hope, they connect faith and works by standing with their staff within a framework not only of shared values, a 'covenant of works' which inspires and informs collective actions, but also in a 'covenant of grace', founded on a nexus of faithful and trusting relationships and inspired by a vision which is open to the possibility of redemptive growth. That covenantal relationship, supported by high levels of inter-personal leadership skill and emotional intelligence, not only sustains the leader in the task of renewal and validates what is done in furtherance of it, but also allows a remaining true to a personal value system and a capacity to take calculated risks in the maintenance of it, by giving what might be termed (after Tillich 1952) 'the courage to be' as well as to do.

1.4. Emergent common themes that provide messages for policy makers and those charged with the professional development of headteachers

Although varying in degree and perspective, there are emergent common themes arising from the data summarised above which provide key messages from practitioners to policy makers, namely, the importance of *vision*, the value of *reflection* and the necessity for *renewal*. These themes will now be considered in turn and linked to the concepts of kerygma, kenosis and koinonia outlined in the theological reflection of Chapter Six.

The importance of vision

Headteachers recognise the importance of having a clear vision and sense of direction for their work, which stands on a firm and clearly articulated ethical and moral base to provide the philosophical rationale for their often instinctive responses to external pressures. That ethical and moral base may for some be linked directly to a particular religious tradition, whereas for others it may sit more loosely or be completely disconnected. However, across all headteachers interviewed, there is a unifying raison d'être of 'being here to make a difference' which maintains their clarity of vision and purpose against the buffeting of external events and establishes and underpins the promulgation of 'a sense of hope' in a better future to be collectively worked for. This belief in the capacity to make a difference and the vision of a preferred future that it predicates provides the reservoir of hope on which headteachers draw to sustain their own self-belief and from which they energise, empower and enable others. As Duignan (2006, 21) has put it:

One of the distinguishing characteristics of successful educational leaders is their capacity to provide a vision for the future and inspire hope in those with whom they work. They also lift the spirits of their people and help them translate the vision into the daily practices of their work. In this way they help to inject meaning into the daily grind of getting the work done, thereby providing a sense of purpose and direction.

The core kerygma message of hope provides that necessary sense of purpose and direction, the enabling and sustaining power for action. It is underpinned by a motivation not only to strive for the best that can be realised in the present, but by a transforming hope of a better life in the future and the possibility of creating it.

Moltmann (1967, 19) points up the transformational nature of such hope:

> Hope cannot cling rigidly to the past and the given and ally itself with the utopia of the status quo. Rather, it is itself summoned and empowered to creative transformation of reality... It constantly provokes and produces thinking of an anticipatory kind...in order to give shape to the newly dawning possibilities in the light of the promised future.

The value of reflection

That hope in the prospect of a better future is, however, filtered through the rocks of contextual reality, be they the pressures of challenging circumstances or the specific expectations of the distinctive milieu of the faith school, so that leadership action becomes a practical theology of 'the art of the possible', whilst remaining consonant with personal and collective values. Such mediation of leadership values against contextual circumstance is facilitated by the opportunity for reflection, either before or after events, individually or collectively with like-minded colleagues. Headteachers value such opportunities to be 'far from the madding crowd', be it in periods of snatched withdrawal from the immediate pressures of the working day or through more structured long-term engagement in mentoring and coaching (either as donor or recipient), non-judgemental peer support, secondment or sabbatical retreat, so that the troubled surface of the reservoir might be stilled and personal equilibrium restored. They would echo the words of Pope Benedict XVI (2006):

> We have to guard ourselves against the dangers of excessive activity, regardless of the office one holds, because too many concerns can often lead to hardness of heart and suffering of the spirit. Instead we should put aside time for prayer and contemplation.

Spiritual and moral leadership demands not only a kenotic self-emptying of the personal reservoir in the service of others, but also the opportunity to refill it through reflection opportunities which can give space to shape our deepest desires, aspirations and concerns. Storr (1988), writing from a psychologist's perspective, has argued that valuable though inter-personal relationships may be in sustaining individual wellbeing, the 'solitude' and opportunity for reflection and 'self-realisation' that it brings is equally fundamental to development. The capacity to seek out and profit from such reflection opportunities is as much a mark of maturity as the ability to sustain productive relationships with others. For the theist, in such reflection "we confront our inner emptiness in the hope of kenosis: that is offering our emptiness to God to receive God's fullness" (Alford and Naughton 2001, 224). It is significant, however, that such self-emptying opportunities for reflection and meditation are valued not only by those with a religious faith perspective, for, as Goleman et al (2003, 50) assert:

> Many outstanding leaders, in fact, bring to their work life the thoughtful mode of self-reflection they cultivate in their spiritual lives. For some this means prayer or meditation; for others it is a more philosophical quest for self-understanding...to enable them to act with conviction and authenticity.

Such reflection must not be used simply to retreat from the world, but rather to sustain continued engagement with it. For spirituality is more than simply the possession of a static set of ethical and moral values; it is a commitment to their dynamic application, and an acceptance that they will be tested, moulded and tempered in the fires of the harsh realities of leadership. Hope in a better future requires not only anticipation of that future but investment in it in the present: "Kingdom participation as well as Kingdom expectation" (Volf 1991, 100). Thus:

> Spirituality is not a retreat or escape into an inner world, for spirit is precisely the capacity to go out, and the truly spiritual person is the one who is able to go out or to *exist* in the full dynamic sense. (Macquarrie 1977, 498)

The necessity for renewal

The praxis of spiritual and moral leadership demands the leader being prepared to exercise a self-emptying role which ministers to and serves others and which is prepared temporarily to see the draining of the personal reservoir when critical incidents strike. However, if leadership burn out or drop out is to be avoided, that personal reservoir must be replenished and renewed. Whilst a variety of sustainability strategies are cited by headteachers, dominant amongst them is the value of self-generated networks of support—the opportunity to draw on the mutual solidarity of interdependent trusting relationships in networks of collegial and extra-curricular engagement within a covenant of shared values. The image of the 'stand-alone' individualistic headteacher, aloof from the impact of external events and systemic pressures, is a dated one; indeed a parallel may be drawn with the changing circumstances of the computing world (Carr 2008, 12):

> Over the last 10 years the nature of computing has changed... Instead of relying on software installed on our hard-drives, we increasingly tap into software that streams through the internet... Our PCs are no longer self-contained devices. They are terminals that draw most of their usefulness not from what's inside them *but from the networks they are hooked up to.* (emphasis added)

Such networking should be seen in the context of what Putnam (2000; Putnam et al 2003) has seminally termed 'social capital': the nexus of relationships that bond and link individuals and build communities. Field (2003, 1) sums the concept up:

> The theory of social capital is, at heart, most straightforward. Its central thesis can be summed up in two words: *relationships matter.* By making connections with one another, and keeping them going over time, people are able to work together to achieve things that they either could not achieve by themselves, or could only achieve with great difficulty. People connect through a series of networks and they tend to share common values with other members of these networks...

Networks provide a koinonia or 'communion in community' to support and sustain the individual leader. Such networks may be simply informal and transient, formed by *"jockeying for position for who you sit next to at conferences and meetings, because you know they will be on the same wavelength"*, as one headteacher put it; they may be structured networks of peer support; or they may be provided by relationships drawn from formal membership of communities beyond the world of education, such as the church. All contribute, however, to the replenishment and sustaining of the individual reservoir of hope.

Archbishop Rowan Williams (2008) usefully provides a link with personal authenticity by drawing the distinction between an individual and a person:

An individual is someone who occupies space. To be a person is to be
someone who hears and answers, to be someone who doesn't occupy a
territory but more a place in a network... The human enterprise is about
those exchanges and relations whereby we build each other up, we take
responsibility for each other's flourishing.

This collective engagement and responsibility surely provides a welcome
corrective to a view of education that too often has focused on competition
rather than collaboration, entrepreneurship rather than empathy,
management of initiatives rather than leadership of communities.

Key messages for policy makers

These three themes of the importance of vision, the value of reflection and
the necessity for renewal provide key messages from practitioners to those
charged with their ongoing professional development and those responsible
for the preparation and induction of the school leaders of the future.
Although headteachers interviewed clearly valued networking and
reflection opportunities as vehicles for renewing and restoring their faith in
their vision and their sense of hope in developmental progress towards it,
there was still seen to be a necessity of individual proactivity in seeking
out and accessing such activities. Doing so often engendered a sense of
guilt in headteachers, even when participation in the reflection opportunity
came with the blessing of those such as governing bodies to whom they
were accountable. This guilt was persistent due to the pressing concerns of
the immediate school situation they had left behind, what one head
memorably termed *"the pull-back to the now"*. For example, participants
in a sabbatical retreat experience for church school heads reported their
sense of guilt at having a 'free' day unencumbered by immediate school
responsibilities; as one put it: *"I had a wonderful day walking alone, but
guilt almost had me ringing school in the middle of it"*. Nevertheless at the
end of the experience, participants were able to report *"a return to school
with renewed energy, enthusiasm, resilience and more importantly a far
deeper spirituality"*.

Another headteacher of considerable experience participated in regular
networking opportunities with long-standing colleagues who he had first
met at his headteacher residential induction many years before.
Networking occurred at a termly extended lunch in a pub remote from the
school and its pressures. In spite of valuing enormously this networking
opportunity for its informal interchange of leadership ideas, problems and
solutions, he nevertheless lacked the confidence to 'confess' to his
colleagues back at school his need for participation, and in particular the

venue in which it occurred, preferring to take refuge in the obfuscatory description of a 'headteachers' meeting' at one of the constituent schools. Yet such lunchtime information exchange, support and bonding opportunities would not be seen as abnormal within a business environment.

Headteachers therefore reaffirmed the view that it should not be necessary for them to have to be proactive in seeking out such reflection and networking opportunities, nor for them to feel guilty or stigmatised by accessing them, but rather that they should be legitimised as a normal part of the leadership entitlement package and funding provided directly to facilitate them. This could be achieved in two ways: both within existing structures and through a development of them. Existing short-term professional development provision for headteachers should be remodelled to move beyond simply the transmission of information and discussion around it, to incorporate formal opportunities for 'time-out' reflective space, time for 'being' as well as 'doing'. Equally, networking opportunities, which presently take place in the refreshment interstices of conferences, should be formalised, extended and legitimised. From one headteacher came the call for *"more events with a spiritual heart"*, and if the definition of spiritual as a secular construct being used throughout this study were applied, this would command support from many headteachers interviewed. And for those who do not yet recognise their need for such reflection and networking opportunities, such events would provide them through what has been memorably termed 'the pill in the jam'.

Equally, headteachers interviewed supported the extension of existing local schemes of peer support to all headteachers irrespective of length of experience, as a way of not only encouraging collaborative linkages and networking, but of stimulating self-reflection and mutual support in a non-judgemental and hence non-threatening forum. The proposed piloting of a national version of the Nottinghamshire 'Heads Count' scheme (evaluated for Nottinghamshire Local Authority by Flintham 2005) under the auspices of the National College in partnership with the National Association of Headteachers, is therefore to be applauded.

On a longer time scale, the opportunity for the 'release into retreat' that a short-term secondment or sabbatical opportunity can provide should be extended. There are presently some innovative in-house solutions being applied to this: for example the headteacher of a large secondary school being granted by his governing body in their statutory concern for his work–life balance the entitlement to 'headship release time' for a mini-sabbatical of six weeks every three years, funding for which comes from revenue earned through consultancy work in the intervening period. Whilst recognising the benefits of this pioneering approach to the wellbeing of the headteacher and the professional development of the deputy head acting up in his absence, it is sad that the motivation for this initiative arose out of the sudden death in post of the previous headteacher.

It would therefore be far better to provide on a national basis an amount of ring-fenced funding for ongoing headteacher wellbeing purposes. This might be memorably termed 'Tail Lamp' funding for experienced headteachers to rival the former 'Head Lamp' funding for newly appointed heads (now less evocatively termed Early Headship Provision Funding). One more cynical experienced headteacher has suggested the alternative term 'Fog Lamp' funding! Irrespective of nomenclature, the financial costs involved would be relatively insignificant compared to the human and financial costs of headteacher burn out, drop out and replacement. For example, to offer a six-week sabbatical to every headteacher once in a 10-year headship career in order to obviate the well-documented 'plateau effect' occurring around that time would require around £5,000 in individual supply cover costs. This equates to less than 1% of the headteacher salary costs over that period and is on a par with the overall cost of advertising, interviewing and selecting a replacement.

Making such opportunities nationally available would bring the education system in England into line with Australia, where there is an entitlement to study leave accruing at one month for every five years of service. Such opportunities are highly valued by Australian school leaders, permitting, as one put it, *"the resurrection of the phoenix from the fiery flames of principalship"*. It is recognised, however, that such provision for headteachers would bring with it concomitant pressure for similar provision for all staff. Those with long memories will recall such a recommendation for a one-term sabbatical for all teachers every seven years of service being made in the James Report of 1972, and it being rejected on the grounds of cost. It is interesting, however, to observe the resurgence of the idea in some present-day academies, facilitated by their so-called 'uplift' funding.

The key messages from practitioners to those charged with the professional development of existing headteachers and the preparation and induction of future generations of school leaders thus focus on the importance of maintaining a vision of hope and sense of purpose, the value of structured reflection opportunities in facilitating this, and the necessity to provide renewal opportunities through engagement with networks of peer support, both formal and informal. It is argued that the legitimisation and funding of such reflection and renewal opportunities as part of a leadership entitlement package (such as that proposed by Pass 2009 on an individual headteacher basis or as described by Newman and Koerner

2010 for a whole-school professional learning community) would be highly cost-effective in both recruitment and retention terms.

Conclusion

Growing tomorrow's leaders of schools has become a significant national imperative, given the contextual reality of potential school leadership shortage—a 'demographic time bomb' predicted to peak between 2009-11, and fuelled by the fact that over 25% of serving headteachers in England are presently above the age of 55, that many existing deputy headteachers evince no desire to seek promotion to headship and there is a decline in the number of serving teachers in their late thirties and early forties (the peak years for leadership development to deputy headship and potentially beyond), and that an increasing number of existing headteachers are seeking early retirement (NCSL 2008, 28). The literature consistently reveals that the factors which drive headteachers to leave headship and limit recruitment to it focus on a perceived lack of support, excessive workload, personal stress and a lack of recognition. Conversely, retention and recruitment are stimulated by a sense of achievement in a capacity 'to make a difference', a reservoir of commitment springing from a firm base of core values and beliefs, a sustenance from a clear vision of a better future together with recognition and praise for often small incremental 'steps of success' towards it, and an awareness of the sustaining power of strong networks of supportive relationships and mutual reflection opportunities.

These positive factors are clearly related to the themes that have been articulated throughout this book. The imperative therefore is not only to recruit to headship but to sustain and support headteachers in it; not only to engage with management competencies but to equip with leadership capabilities (Duignan 2006, 120); not only to focus on operational and accountability pressures but also on spiritual and moral leadership issues. The requirement is to inculcate in our school leaders, both present and future:

- a *hope* in the dream of a better future, a clarity of vision in describing it, and a capacity to make a difference as the sustaining reservoir of hope in the journey towards it;
- a *faith* in an underpinning moral purpose which provides the foundations of the reservoir of hope, and maintains individual and collective self-belief that the dream is achievable;

- a *love* which majors on networks of caring relationships to replenish the reservoir of hope in difficult circumstances, and sustains and supports self and others in the task to turn the dream into reality.

Faced with the contextual realities of economic crisis, recruitment difficulties, critical incidents and systemic pressures, and a collective sense of apparent 'hopelessness' in the face of them, those called to be the spiritual and moral leaders of our schools may maintain their hope and preserve their faith in their capacity to make a difference. In the words of Martin Luther King (1963):

> I have a dream... This is our hope. This is the faith... With this faith we will be able to hew out of the mountain of despair, a stone of hope.

This book has endeavoured to contribute to the hewing of that stone from the leadership stories of 150 serving headteachers, so that out of it may be built the reservoirs of hope without which successful headship cannot be sustained. The final words of Mo Mowlam's autobiography *Momentum* (2002, 320) may be as appropriate for school leaders as for politicians to sum it all up:

> Although life does contain many difficulties and there is not always a 'happy ending', I hope that the story I have told shows more hope than despair—shows that people working together can overcome many obstacles, often within themselves, and by so doing can make the world a better place.

APPENDIX

The data for the chapters 'Reservoirs of hope', 'Foundations of faith' and 'Labours of love' are based on seven separate research samples as follows:

1. Reservoirs of hope
2. When reservoirs run dry
3. Retaining the reservoirs of hope
4. Foundations of faith
5. Grounded in faith
6. Leading schools in challenging circumstances
7. Sabbatical and secondment experiences

Chapter Three: Reservoirs of hope draws on research samples 1, 2 and part of 3 (secular school principals).

Chapter Four: Foundations of faith draws on research samples 4, 5 and part of 3 (faith school principals).

Chapter Five: Labours of love draws on research samples 6 and 7.

Details of composition and acknowledgement of participation are given below.

1. Reservoirs of hope

The research sample

A cross-sectional sample of 25 serving headteachers was constructed, drawn from all phases of compulsory-age education from infant school to independent school, from a variety of contexts from inner-city deprivation (free school meal indicator 45%) to suburban social advantage (free school meals 2%) and a range of school sizes ranging from 60 to 1,600 pupils on roll, and from a wide geographical area from Devon to Durham, Lancashire to London.

The initial sample base was drawn from participants in an NCSL Leading Edge Seminar on Leadership and Spirituality held in July 2002. This opportunity sample of 14 headteachers, including three from church schools, was then supplemented from other networks using recommendations from diocesan directors of education, local education authority advisers and personal knowledge to produce a more representative sample. The headteachers interviewed during Autumn 2002 ranged in experience of headship from one year in post to 20 years, with an age range from mid thirties to late fifties. A number of colleagues were in their second headship, with two into their third headship. Three colleagues had previously been deputy head in the same school as their eventual headship, including one who had also held a middle management post, a length of service to the same school thus totalling almost 28 years.

The detailed composition of the sample of 25 heads was as follows:

School type		School area		School headteacher	
Primary		Inner city	10	Female	11
Infants	2	Suburban	9	Male	14
First school	1	Rural	6		
Junior	1				
All-through	7	**Free school meal indicator**		**Length of headship**	
Total	**11**	0-9%	7	1-4 years	5
		10-19%	9	5-8 years	8
Secondary		20-29%	2	9-12 years	4
11-16	3	30-39%	3	13-16 years	3
11-18	8	40-49%	4	17-20 years	5
CTC	1				
EBD	1	**School faith perspective**		**Previous experience**	
Independent	1	Church	8	2nd headship	5
Total	**14**	Secular	13	3rd headship	2
Sample total	**25**	High ethnic	4	Same school	3

The interview schedule

Colleagues were asked to respond to the areas of questioning indicated below, which had been sent to them in advance. Interviews were conducted over a four-week period and as interviewing progressed supplementary questioning regarding the emerging themes took place. The main areas of focus were as follows, as specified on the provided interview schedule:

- Please give some background about yourself: length of headship, type and character of school, faith perspective if any (remembering that the definition of spiritual leadership being used does not have exclusively religious connotations but seeks to embrace a broader concept of secular spirituality). Where would you say you derive your own spiritual/moral base from?

- Do you find of value the concepts of an internal 'personal reservoir of hope' (the calm centre at the heart of the individual leader from which their values and vision flow and which enables effective inter-personal engagement no matter what the external pressures) and the external 'reservoir of hope' for the institution (where the head acts as the wellspring of self-belief and directional focus for the school) in thinking about your role in spiritual and moral leadership, or are there alternative metaphors that would better describe your own approach to spiritual and moral leadership?

- Could you give examples of sustainability strategies you use to preserve and replenish your personal reservoir of hope in the face of external pressures? How does the success of these strategies manifest itself internally for you personally/externally for the school?

- Could you give examples of critical incidents in your 'leadership story' of how you have acted as the reservoir of hope for the institution yet preserved your own internal reservoir of hope?

- Has there been a development of your capacity to do this as your headship has gone on, and if so, to what do you attribute this? Does this link to any perceived stages of headteacher development?

- What mechanisms do you think are possible for the transference of your spiritual and moral leadership qualities to other members of your leadership team, and to aspirant and newly appointed headteachers?

Acknowledgements

Thanks are due to the National College under the auspices of whose research associate scheme this research was conducted. Especial thanks to the following headteachers who participated in this study and through their co-operation and openness have made possible this rendering of practitioner voice and have validated its outcomes.

Headteacher	School at time of interview
Ann Anderson	Hatfield Manor CE Junior School, Doncaster
David Atton	The Park Community School, Barnstaple
June Austin	Manor Lees Infants School, Lincoln
Dianne Barker	Violet Lane Infants School, Burton-on-Trent
David Bowes	Tapton School, Sheffield
Tom Clark	George Spencer Technology School, Nottingham
Harry Goddard	Derby High School for Girls, Littleover, Derby
John Grove	Belleville Primary School, London SW11
Carole Gumbley	Shenley Court Specialist Arts College, Birmingham
David Hall	Aughton Town Green Primary School, Lancashire
Vanessa Huws Jones	Easingwold Primary School, Easingwold, North Yorkshire
Max Kay	The Nottingham Bluecoat CE School, Nottingham
Janet Lewis	Sandringham School, St. Albans
Jackie Mills	Netherthong Junior and Infants School, Holmfirth
Gerard Moran	St. John's RC Comprehensive School, Bishop Auckland
Richard Parker	Lodge Park Technology College, Corby
Maria Parr	Newbold CE Primary School, Chesterfield
Rosemary Potter	Djanogly City Technology College, Nottingham
Christopher Reynolds	St. Benedict Catholic School, Derby
Steve Robinson	Chaucer School, Sheffield
Linda Rockey	St. John's CE Primary School, Sparkhill, Birmingham
Martin Sutton	Beech Hill Special School, Mansfield
David Taylor	Tysoe CE Primary School, Warwickshire
Lindsey Weimers	Windmill First School, Headington, Oxford
Neil Whitehead	Canon Williamson CE High School, Eccles

2. When reservoirs run dry

The research sample

A cross-sectional sample of 15 headteachers who had left their headship in advance of the normal retirement age, or were committed to do so, was constructed, drawn from all phases of compulsory-age education, from infant school to large secondary school, with numbers of pupils on roll ranging from 60 to 2,000, and from a variety of social contexts from inner-city deprivation to suburban social advantage within the East Midlands.

The detailed composition of the sample of 15 heads was as follows:

School type		School area		School headteacher		Age on leaving	
Primary		Inner city	8	Female	6	45-49	3
Infants	1	Suburban	6	Male	9	50-55	10
Junior	1	Rural	1			56-59	2
All-through	5					Mean	52
Total	7	Free school meals		Length of headship			
		0-9%	2	1-4 years	3	Reasons for leaving	
Secondary		10-19%	5	5-8 years	1	Career plan	5
9-13	1	20-29%	4	9-12 years	7	Disengagement	5
11-16	2	30-39%	2	13-16 years	2	Health/stress	4
11-18	4	40-49%	1	17-20 years	2	School closure 1	
Total	7	50-60%	1	Mean	10		
						Destinations	
Special		School faith		Experience		Consultancy	5
All-age EBD	1	Church	2	2nd headship	5	Inspection etc	5
		Secular	12	3rd headship	2	LEA (part-time)	3
Sample total	15	High ethnic	1	Same school	3	Unemployment	2

The interview schedule

Colleagues were asked to respond to the areas of questioning indicated below, which had been sent to them in advance. Interviews were conducted over a four-month period during Spring 2003 and as interviewing progressed supplementary questioning regarding the emerging themes took place. The main areas of focus were as follows, as specified on the provided interview schedule:

- Please give some background about yourself: length of headship, type and character of school, reasons for leaving headship, what you have done since or intend to do.
- Where would you say you derive your own spiritual/moral base from? (remembering that the definition of spiritual leadership being used does not have exclusively religious connotations but seeks to embrace a broader concept of secular spirituality)
- Do you find of value the concepts of an internal 'personal reservoir of hope' (the calm centre at the heart of the individual leader from which their values and vision flows and which enables effective inter-personal engagement no matter what the external pressures)

and the external 'reservoir of hope' for the institution (where the head acts as the wellspring of self-belief and directional focus for the school) in thinking about your role in spiritual and moral leadership, or are there alternative metaphors that would have better described your own approach to spiritual and moral leadership?

- Could you give examples of sustainability strategies you used to preserve and replenish your personal reservoir of hope in the face of external pressures?
- What difficulties may arise should these sustaining mechanisms fail? Could you give examples of critical incidents in your 'leadership story' that would illustrate this?
- Was there a development of your capacity for spiritual and moral leadership as your headship went on, and if so, to what do you attribute this? Does this link to any perceived stages of headteacher development?
- From your experience, what messages would you want to transfer about spiritual and moral leadership to aspirant and newly appointed headteachers?

Acknowledgements

Thanks are due to the National College under the auspices of whose research associate scheme this research was conducted. Especial thanks are given to the following individuals who participated in this study for their co-operation and openness in discussing their reasons for leaving headship:

Participant	Former school
Greg Abbott	Annesley Primary School, Nottinghamshire
Mike Armstrong	Wilford Meadows Comprehensive School, Nottingham
Penny Bassey	St. Andrew's Primary School, Skegby, Nottinghamshire
Gerry Blinston	Sneinton Primary School, Nottingham
Gill Empson	High Oakham Middle School, Mansfield, Nottinghamshire
Kath Hatfield	Lake View Primary School, Rainworth, Nottinghamshire
Andrew Kawalek	Bracken Hill School, Kirkby-in-Ashfield, Nottinghamshire
Graham Miller	Dalestorth Primary School, Sutton-in-Ashfield, Nottinghamshire
Andy Mortimer	Sutton Centre Community College, Sutton-in-Ashfield
Keith Poyser	Hartland Comprehensive School, Worksop, Nottinghamshire
Sheila Roser	South Wolds Community School, Keyworth, Nottingham
John Round	The Holgate Comprehensive School, Hucknall, Nottinghamshire
Peter Scott	Prospect Hills Junior School, Worksop, Nottinghamshire
Michael Shaw	Merrill Community College, Derby
Linda Trapnell	Alderman Pounder Infants School, Nottingham

3. Retaining the reservoirs of hope

The research sample

A sample of 20 Australasian school principals and a further 20 Australian educationists were interviewed as part of a Churchill Travelling Fellowship to Australia carried out in October-November 2005. The principals interviewed had an average age of 54 and a range of total headship experience of between three and 32 years (mean 12), with a range of 1-21 years (mean 7) years spent as principal of their present school. Fifty per cent of the sample was on their second or multiple experience of headship. There was consequently a considerable depth of school leadership experience on which to draw.

School phase	School faith perspective	Educationists
Primary 7	Anglican 2	Male 11
Secondary 8	Catholic 2	Female 7
All age 5	Charismatic Christian 1	
	Christian Scientist 1	**Type of organisation**
School type	Jewish 1	Government 4
Government 12	Methodist 1	Faith sector 6
Catholic 2		Professional associations 6
Private 6	**School principal**	Universities 3
	Female 8	Other 1
School location	Male 12	
Australia 18		
New Zealand 2	**Total principals** 20	**Total educationists 20**

The interview schedules

Interviews were conducted using a semi-structured interview schedule as reproduced below, which had been sent to participants in advance. Educationists received a truncated version of the schedule as shown. As the interviewing sequence progressed, supplementary questioning regarding the emerging themes was inserted into the interview process. In the case of the principals interviewed, interviews were tape recorded to supplement the contemporaneous notes taken and, following respondent validation, to provide the source of the direct quotations cited, and to provide an authentic rendering of principal practitioner voice.

Principals' interview schedule

- Please give some *background* about yourself: length of principalship, type/character of school, faith perspective if any (remembering that the definition of spiritual leadership being used does not have exclusively religious connotations but seeks to embrace a broader concept of secular spirituality).
- Where would you say you derive your own spiritual/moral base from?
- Do you find of value the *concepts* of an internal 'personal reservoir of hope' (the calm centre at the heart of the individual leader from which their values and vision flows and which enables effective inter-personal engagement no matter what the external pressures) and the external 'reservoir of hope' for the institution (where the leader acts as the wellspring of self-belief and directional focus for

the school) in thinking about your role in spiritual and moral leadership, or are there alternative metaphors that would better describe your own approach to spiritual and moral leadership?

- Could you give examples of *sustainability strategies* you use to preserve and replenish your personal reservoir of hope in the face of external pressures? How does the success of these strategies manifest itself internally for you personally/externally for the school?

- Could you give examples of *critical incidents* in your 'leadership story' of how you have acted as the reservoir of hope for the institution yet preserved your own internal reservoir of hope?

- Has there been a *development* of your capacity to do this as your school leadership has gone on, and if so, to what do you attribute this? Does this link to any perceived stages of leadership development?

- What mechanisms are in place in your area for the *collective support* of school leaders? How effective do you think they are? How might they be enhanced?

- What mechanisms do you think are possible for the *transference* of your spiritual and moral leadership qualities to other members of your leadership team, and to aspirant and newly appointed school principals?

- Are there any *other points* you wish to record?

Educationists' interview schedule

- Please give some *background* about yourself and your organisation.

- Do you find of value the *concepts* of an internal 'personal reservoir of hope' (the calm centre at the heart of the individual leader from which their values and vision flows and which enables effective inter-personal engagement no matter what the external pressures) and the external 'reservoir of hope' for the school (where the leader acts as the wellspring of self-belief and directional focus for the school) in thinking about the spiritual and moral leadership role of school principals and their support needs?

- What mechanisms do you provide in your area for the *collective support* of school principals in maintaining their 'internal reservoirs of hope'? How effective are they? How might they be enhanced?

- What mechanisms do you think are possible for the *transference* of spiritual and moral leadership qualities to aspirant and newly appointed school principals?

- Are there any *other points* you wish to record?

Acknowledgements

Especial thanks are due to the Winston Churchill Memorial Trust for the grant of Churchill Travelling Fellowship funding which permitted this study to take place and to all those colleagues identified below who so generously gave of their time and hospitality to be interviewed as part of this research.

Australasian principals

Headteacher	School	Area
Sholto Bowen	Huntingtower School, Mount Waverley	Melbourne
David Loader	formerly Wesley College, Melbourne	Melbourne
Kevin Mackay	Dandenong North Primary School, Dandenong	Melbourne
Meenah Marchbank	Cambridge Primary School, Hoppers Crossing	Melbourne
Ken Thompson	Gladstone Park Secondary College, Gladstone Park	Melbourne
Harvey Wood	Fairhills High School, Knoxfield	Melbourne
Jim Davies	Australian Science and Mathematics School, Flinders University	Adelaide
Kaye Johnson	Woodville Primary School	Adelaide
Helen Seretis	Lockleys North Primary School	Adelaide
Deb Graham	Hallett Cove R-12 School, Hallett Cove	Adelaide
Kim Hebenstreit	Thebarton Senior College, Torrensville	Adelaide
Jenny Sommer	Wirreanda High School, Morphett Vale	Adelaide
Dennis Flannery	Belconnen High School, Hawker	Canberra
Moira Najdecki	Mackillop Catholic College, Tuggeranong	Canberra
Andrew Newman	Tuggerah Lakes Secondary College, Wylong	New South Wales
Sharon Parkes	Warners Bay High School, Newcastle	New South Wales
Phil Roberts	Mount Sinai College, Manoubra	Sydney
Lynne Stone	St Catherine's School, Waverley	Sydney
Graham Preston*	Bethlehem College, Tauranga	New Zealand
Tali Temese*	Porirua Primary School, Wellington	New Zealand

Note: * Interview conducted by email.

Australian educationists

Educationist	Position	Area
Debra Brydon	iNet and cybertext Online Conference Manager	Melbourne
Brian Caldwell	Director, Educational Transformations, formerly University of Melbourne	Melbourne
Joe Fleming	Visiting Scholar Cambridge University, formerly Archdiocese of Melbourne	Melbourne
Neil Wright	Project Co-ordinator, Principals First, Council for Christian Education in Schools	Melbourne
Anne Barkaway	Education Social Worker, Dept Education and Training Southern Sea and Vines District	Adelaide
Christine Budd	Inclusion Well-Being Co-ordinator, District Team, Southern Sea and Vines District	Adelaide
Wendy House	Leadership Consultant, South Australian Centre for Leaders in Education	Adelaide
Jeremy Hurley	Profess. Officer, Australian Principals Associations Professional Development Council	Adelaide
Nancy Schupelius	Principal, South Australian Centre for Leaders in Education, Department of Education and Children's Services	Adelaide
Wendy Teasdale-Smith	Vice-President Australian Secondary Principals Association and Principal Aberfoyle Park School	Adelaide
Allan Shaw	Chief Executive, Association of Heads of Independent Schools of Australia, formerly Foundation Principal, Peter Moyes Anglican Community School, Perth	Canberra
Dennis Sleigh	Principal Human Resources Officer, Catholic Education Office Archdiocese of Canberra formerly Principal, Saints Peter and Paul RC Primary School, Garran	Canberra
Chris Bonnor	President, New South Wales Secondary Principals' Council, formerly Principal Davidson High School	Sydney
Tony Bracken	Head of Professional Development, Catholic Education Office, Parramatta	Sydney
Tony D'Arbon	Deputy Director, Flagship for Creative and Authentic Leadership, Australian Catholic University	Sydney
Patrick Duignan	Director, Flagship for Creative and Authentic Leadership, Australian Catholic University	Sydney
Tracey Hayne	Principal Liaison Officer, Office of Schools, NSW Department of Education and Training	Sydney
Kerryanne Knox	Principal Liaison Officer, Office of Schools, NSW Department of Education and Training	Sydney

Anthony Steel	Leader, Spirituality Team, Catholic Education Office, Archdiocese of Sydney	Sydney
Robert Tobias	Member, Spirituality Team, Catholic Education Office, Archdiocese of Sydney	Sydney

4. Foundations of faith

The research sample

A sample of 27 headteachers representing a range of personal faith perspectives was interviewed as detailed below. Their interviews were supplemented with data from some 10 Australian faith school principals (Anglican 3, Roman Catholic 3, Christian Scientist 1, Methodist 1, Evangelical Christian 1, Jewish 1) drawn from the 'Retaining the reservoirs of hope' sample. The headteachers were aged between 40 and 60 (mean age 52). The total length of experience as a headteacher ranged from 1-27 years (mean 10 years). Length of headship in the present school also ranged from 1-27 years (mean 6 years). Some nine headteachers had experience as head of more than one school, with five 'serial offenders' now being in their third headship. Most heads interviewed had followed a 'conventional' career route to headship through deputy headship, although some also had cross-phase and advisory work experience. One colleague had been promoted to headship from deputy headship in the same school.

School phase		School context		Headteacher faith	
Primary	13	Rural	3	Anglican	7
Secondary	12	'Affluent' suburban	8	Roman Catholic	7
All age	1	'Deprived' suburban	5	Charismatic	2
Home school	1	Urban	5	Jewish	3
		Inner city	6	Muslim	2
School size				Methodist	1
Primary 76-500 (mean 264)		**Headteacher gender**		Hindu	1
Secondary 190-2,000 (mean 800)		Female	12	Sikh	1
All age 470		Male	15	Buddhist	1
Home school 3				Humanist	1
		Headteacher location		Atheist	1
		School of same faith	15		
		School of different faith	5		
Total headteachers 27		Secular school	7		

The interview schedule

Interviews were conducted on a face-to-face basis and each lasted for approximately one hour. A semi-structured interview schedule, sent to participants in advance, was used as reproduced below. Interviews were conducted between October 2004 and June 2010. As the interviewing sequence progressed, supplementary questioning regarding the emerging themes was inserted into the interview process. Interviews were tape recorded to supplement the contemporaneous notes taken, and following the opportunity for respondent validation, were used to provide the source of the anonymised direct quotations cited, and thus hopefully to offer an authentic rendering of practitioner voice.

- Please give some *background* about your professional self: length of headship, type and character of school, outline of career development to this point etc.
- What are your *foundations* of faith: the spiritual, ethical and moral bases on which you stand?
- How did the *development* of these foundations come about? How were the foundations laid down? Who or what were the formative influences? What were the epiphanies or turning points? Are there examples of specific incidents, life-changing events or developing philosophies that illustrate this?
- What brought you to this *present* place? Why this school at this particular time? What decisions led to your arrival here? What sustains you that it was the 'right' decision?
- How are your spiritual and moral bases of faith *evidenced* in: your leadership style in this school; your approaches to learning; the nurturing of staff and pupils; the sharing of your vision and values with colleagues and the community, that are different from that found in the commonality of schools?
- Can you give an example of a critical incident in your leadership story that *tested* your foundations of faith? What sustained and supported you through it? What did you learn from the experience?
- How could that learning be transmitted to other leaders?
- Where do you see yourself going to next in the *future*, professionally and personally?

Acknowledgements

Sincere thanks are due to those colleagues listed below who gave so generously of their time and insights to be interviewed as part of this research.

Headteacher	School at time of interview	Location
Peter Barton	Peckham Park Primary School, Peckham	London
Nigel Bishop	Keelby Primary School, Keelby	Grimsby
Hasan Chawdhry	Edinburgh Primary School, Walthamstow	London
Elisabeth Gilpin	St. Augustine Joint CE/RC Upper School	Oxford
Rosalind Goulden	Kerem School, Hampstead	London
Karol Grabowski	St. Michael's Catholic and CE High School	Barnsley
Bernie Groves	Big Wood School	Nottingham
John Honey	St. George's Catholic Primary School	Littleover, Derby
Anne Hudson	Burtonwood Community Primary School	Warrington
John Illingworth	Bentinck Primary School	Nottingham
Kate & Mark Illsley	Home school	Ashby de la Zouch
Daniel Kerbel	Broughton Cassel Fox Primary School	Salford
Tim Luckcock	St. Paul's CE Primary School	Salford
Peter Murdock	The Dharma School	Brighton
Wendy Parmley	Archbishop Michael Ramsey Technology College	London
Firdos Qazi	Gatton Primary School, Upper Tooting	London
Helen Robson	Christ The King School, Arnold	Nottingham
Rajinder Sandhu	The Guru Nanak Sikh Secondary School	Hayes
Mahendra Savjani	The Swaminaryan School, Neasden	London
David Shannon	The National CE Technology College	Hucknall
Alan Shaw	The Moriah Jewish Day School	Pinner
Gillian Simm	Rosehill Methodist Community School	Ashton under Lyne
Brigid Smith	King David High School	Liverpool
Sue Sowden	St. Mary's School	Wantage
Michael Thompson	St. Ambrose College	Hale Barns
Jane Tiller	Feversham College	Bradford
Chris Williams	King Edward VII School	Melton Mowbray

5. Grounded in faith

The research sample

Some 23 headteachers leading Roman Catholic schools drawn from 12 Roman Catholic dioceses in England and Australia were interviewed, together with a further 10 supporting local, diocesan and national educationists as detailed below.

School phase	School context	Educationists
Primary 12	Rural 4	Male 5
Secondary 11 (4 single sex)	'Affluent' suburban 6	Female 5
	'Deprived' suburban 6	
	Urban 2	**System represented**
	Inner city 7	Australian dioceses 1
School size		English dioceses 4
Primary 220-835 (mean 390)	**Headteacher gender**	English national 2
Secondary 800-1,200 (mean 1012)	Male 11	
	Female 12	**Total educationists 10**
HT diocesan representation		
English RC dioceses 9	**Headteacher location**	**Diocesan represented**
Australian dioceses 2	English principals 15	English dioceses 9
	Australian principals 8	Australian dioceses 3
Total headteachers 23		**Total dioceses 12**

The principals had an age range of between 41 to the 'staggering' (at least to UK eyes) 71 of an Australian colleague (mean age 55.0). The total length of experience as a principal ranged from 1-35 years (mean 13 years). Length of principalship in the present school ranged from 1-20 years (mean 9 years). Some 10 principals had experience as principal in more than one school, with one 'serial offender' now being in his fifth principalship. Most principals interviewed had followed a 'conventional' career route to principalship through deputy principalship, although some also had cross-phase and advisory work experience. Two colleagues had been promoted to principalship from deputy principalship in the same school.

The interview schedules

Interviews were conducted in the vast majority of cases on a face-to-face basis (with the exception of two interviews which for reasons of timing or geographical constraints were conducted by telephone) and each lasted for approximately one hour. Semi-structured interview schedules, sent to participants in advance, were used as reproduced below. Interviews were conducted between June 2006 and April 2007. As the interviewing sequence progressed supplementary questioning regarding the emerging themes was inserted into the interview process. Interviews were tape recorded to supplement the contemporaneous notes taken, and following the opportunity for respondent validation, were used to provide the source of the direct quotations cited, and thus hopefully to offer an authentic rendering of practitioner and educationist voice.

Principals' interview schedule

- Please give some *background* about your professional self: length of headship, type and context of school, career development to date, why you chose to be a Catholic school head.
- What would you say are the *foundations* of your faith: the spiritual bases on which you stand?
- What values and attributes does a Catholic school leader specifically need to possess?
- How did the *development* of these foundations come about: how were they laid down, who or what were the formative influences, what were the epiphanies or turning points?
- What areas of your *own spiritual formation* and development have assisted in your role as spiritual leader of a Catholic school community? Which areas could be further developed?
- How are your spiritual bases of faith *evidenced* in your leadership style, your approaches to learning, the nurturing of staff and pupils, the sharing of your vision and values with colleagues?
- Can you give an example of a critical incident in your leadership story that *tested* your spiritual leadership? What supported and sustained you through it? What did you learn?
- What *mechanisms* are provided *for supporting and sustaining* you as a Catholic school principal in your spiritual leadership? How effective are they? How might they be developed?

- What *main messages* would you wish to give from your experience to the dioceses about the preparation and spiritual formation of *aspirant* and newly appointed Catholic principals?

Educationists' interview schedule

- Please give some *background* about yourself and your role in forming, supporting and sustaining Catholic school principals in their spiritual leadership of their schools.
- What *values and attributes* in the spiritual leadership of a school do you feel a Catholic school leader needs to possess over and above the generality of school principals?
- What *mechanisms* are provided *for supporting and sustaining* Catholic school principals in their spiritual leadership? How effective are they? How might they be further developed?
- What *mechanisms* are provided *for spiritual formation* of aspirant and newly appointed Catholic school principals? How effective are they? How might they be further developed?
- Are there any *other points* you would wish to record?

Acknowledgements

Thanks are due to the East Midlands Leadership Centre (EMLC), Liverpool Hope University, the Diocese of Parramatta and ACU National, the Australian Catholic University, for the grants of research funding, and provision of accommodation and travel expenses, which allowed this section of the study to occur. The efforts of Dr. Tony Bracken, Head of Professional Development, Catholic Education Office, Diocese of Parramatta, and Professor Patrick Duignan and Mr. Soma Nagappan of the Flagship for Creative and Authentic Leadership, ACU National, the Australian Catholic University, in making the logistical arrangements for the Australian leg of the research were most warmly appreciated. Above all, most sincere thanks are due to all those colleagues listed below who gave so generously of their time, hospitality and insights to be interviewed as part of this research. Without them, it would not have been possible.

UK school principals

Headteacher	School	Diocese
Stella Adcock	St. Dominic's Primary, Stone	Birmingham
John Cape	Holy Family Primary, Worksop	Hallam
Jim Conway	Notre Dame High School, Sheffield	Hallam
Catherine Fields	English Martyrs Secondary, Leicester	Nottingham
John Flower	St. Paul's Catholic College, Burgess Hill	Arundel and Brighton
Michael Gallagher	St. Cuthbert's Primary, Sunderland	Hexham and Newcastle
Patricia Mason	St. Thomas More Primary, Leicester	Nottingham
Christine McCann	Notre Dame Catholic College, Everton	Liverpool
Pat McDermott	St. Joseph's College, Bradford	Leeds
Rosie McGlynn	St. Joseph's Junior, Leyton, London	Brentwood
Mike McKeever	Trinity School, Nottingham	Nottingham
Philomena Mullins	St. Francis of Assisi College, Aldridge	Birmingham
Eileen Rogan	St. Gregory's Primary, Longton, Stoke	Birmingham
Pauline Sammon	St. James' Primary, Orpington	Southwark
Ken Smithson	St. Gregory's Primary, South Shields	Hexham and Newcastle

Australian school principals

Principal	School	Diocese
Lynn Bard	Marian Catholic College, Kenthurst	Parramatta
Chris Dutfield	St. Paul's Catholic College, Greystanes	Parramatta
Jennifer Fraser	St. Michael's Primary, Baulkham Hills	Parramatta
Bernadette Florence	St. Monica's Primary, Wodonga, Victoria	Sandhurst
Kevin Holohan	McCarthy Catholic College, Emu Plains	Parramatta
Christine Howe	Caroline Chisholm College, Glenmore Park	Parramatta
Richard McGuiness	St. Andrew's Primary, Marayong	Parramatta
John Spadbrow	St. Matthew's Primary, Windsor	Parramatta

UK educationists

Interviewee	Role	Organisation
Sue Benson	Leadership Consultant	National College
Margaret Buck	Diocesan Deputy Director of Education	Birmingham
Edward Hayes	Diocesan Director of Education	Nottingham
Frank McDermott	Diocesan Director of Schools	Hallam
Jenny Pate	Diocesan Deputy Director of Education	Hexham and Newcastle
Oona Stannard	Chief Executive	Catholic Education Service, England

Australian educationists

Interviewee	Role	Organisation
John DeCourcy	Head of Strategic Accountabilities, Catholic Education Office, formerly Principal of St. Andrew's College, Marayong	Diocese of Parramatta
Stephen Marchant	Head of Staff Services, Catholic Education Office	Diocese of Parramatta
Leonne Pallisier	Education Officer, Professional Learning	Diocese of Parramatta
Greg Whitby	Executive Director of Schools	Diocese of Parramatta

6. Leading schools facing challenging circumstances

The research sample

A sample of 30 headteachers leading schools facing challenging circumstances were interviewed. Some 8 of these formed part of National College research into 'What's good about leading schools in challenging circumstances' and were supplemented by a further 12 researcher-generated interviews. A further 10 headteachers engaged with the School Mentor online self-reflective instrument and participated in follow-up interviews. The headteachers in the overall sample had lengths of total headship experience ranging from 2-22 years (mean 8 years). Length of service in the present school in challenging circumstances ranged from 1-15 years (mean 5.5 years). In addition, four colleagues had also previously been deputy head in the school in which they were now headteacher. Fifty per cent of the sample was on their second or multiple headship, with one self-confessed 'serial offender' having served as headteacher in five schools in challenging circumstances and who was shortly to move on to a sixth. This constitutes a significant experience base of such schools to draw on.

School phase		School context	
Primary	14	Rural	5
Secondary	14	'Deprived' suburban	9
Special	1	'Deprived' urban	8
Middle	1	Inner city	8
School size		**Deprivation index (free school meals)**	
Primary/Special 16-540	(mean 284)	Primary/Special 6-54% (mean 34%)	
Secondary/Middle 400-2,450	(mean 920)	Secondary/Middle 11-45% (mean 26%)	
Headteacher participation		**Headteacher gender**	
Schools in challenging circumstances interviews	12	Female 14	
What's good about leading schools in challenging circumstances	8	Male 16	
School Mentor reflective instrument and interview follow-up	10		
		Total sample of headteachers 30	

The interview schedule

The following generic semi-structured interview schedule was used:

- Please give some *background* about yourself: length of headship, type/character of school, faith perspective if any (remembering that the definition of spiritual leadership being used does not have exclusively religious connotations but seeks to embrace a broader concept of secular spirituality).
- Where would you say you derive your own spiritual/moral base from?
- Do you find of value the *concepts* of an internal 'personal reservoir of hope' (the calm centre at the heart of the individual leader from which their values and vision flows and which enables effective inter-personal engagement no matter what the external pressures) and the external 'reservoir of hope' for the institution (where the leader acts as the wellspring of self-belief and directional focus for the school) in thinking about your role in spiritual and moral leadership, or are there alternative metaphors that would better describe your own approach to spiritual and moral leadership?
- Could you give examples of *personal sustainability strategies* you use to preserve and replenish your personal reservoir of hope in the face of external pressures?
- Are there *corporate support strategies* that have assisted in maintaining your personal reservoir of hope? How effective do you think they are? How might they be enhanced?
- Could you give examples of *critical incidents* in your 'leadership story' of how you have acted as the reservoir of hope for the institution yet preserved your own internal reservoir of hope?
- Are there any *specific professional characteristics* you would feel are desirable if not essential in an approach to spiritual and moral leadership specifically in a school in challenging circumstances?
- Has there been a *development* of your capacity as your school leadership has gone on, and if so, to what do you attribute this? Does this link to any perceived stages of leadership development?
- What mechanisms do you think are possible for the *transference* of your spiritual and moral leadership qualities to other members of your leadership team, and to aspirant and newly appointed headteachers working in schools in challenging circumstances?

In addition to asking whether there were any *other points* they would wish to have recorded, those interviewed for the 'what's good about leading schools in challenging circumstances' research were additionally asked:

- What's good about leading a school facing challenging circumstances?
- What would you say is particularly good about leading *this* school?
- Could you give examples of incidents or events that made you feel particularly good?

Those involved with Leadership Incentive Grant groups (who also engaged with School Mentor analysis of professional characteristics) were also asked:

- Has corporate membership of a Leadership Incentive Grant group been of value compared to individual reflection opportunities provided by LPSH?

Interviews were conducted on a 1:1 face-to-face basis (with the exception for logistical reasons of those with colleagues in Shetland and Wales which were conducted by email). 'What's good about leading schools in challenging circumstances' interviews were carried out in January 2006. Interviews and School Mentor participation with the sub-sets of those leading schools in challenging circumstances were substantially held between April and June 2005.

Acknowledgements

Grateful thanks are due to Katie Verity of Mentus for permission to use the School Mentor instrument, and to her, together with Sue Craggs, Derek Blackman and Chris Housden of the Nottinghamshire Local Authority Continuing Professional Development Team, for assistance with its administration with some 10 headteachers in the total sample. Above all, particular thanks are due to all the 30 headteachers who participated in some way in the various sections of this research as follows.

Schools in challenging circumstances

Headteacher	School at time of interview	Location
Phil Austin	Eastwood Primary School, Eastwood	Nottinghamshire
Kate Coutts	Uyeasound Primary School, Unst	Shetland
Ian Fraser	Ashfield School, Kirkby in Ashfield	Nottinghamshire
Rob Kenney	The Holgate School, Hucknall	Nottinghamshire
Bill Morris	Fullhurst Secondary School	Leicester
Callum Orr	The Wheldon Secondary School	Nottingham
Val Penny-Stewart	Elliot Durham Secondary School	Nottingham
Jean Pope	Rhws Primary School	Glamorgan
Hazel Pulley	Caldecote Primary School	Leicester
Keith Sudbury	The Newark High School, Newark	Nottinghamshire
Lewis Walker	Dukeries Community College, Ollerton	Nottinghamshire
Craig Weaver	Brierton Secondary School	Hartlepool

'What's good about leading schools in challenging circumstances?'

Headteacher	School at time of interview	Location
Irene Baldry	Portsdown Primary School, Cosham	Portsmouth
Jan Fleming	Somers Park Primary School, Southsea	Portsmouth
Jenny Francis	Collenswood Secondary School	Stevenage
Mandie Haywood	Langley St. Leonard's Primary, Dawley	Telford
Polly Honeychurch	Cottage Grove Primary School, Southsea	Portsmouth
Gerry Hudson	Bentley Drive JMI School	Walsall
Eric Jackson	Queen Elizabeth Secondary, Middleton	Manchester
Paul Rushforth	Minehead Middle School	Minehead

School Mentor participants

Headteacher	School at time of interview	Location
Rob Bailey	Quarrydale School, Sutton-in-Ashfield	Nottinghamshire
Colin Bowpitt	Uplands Junior School	Leicester
Martin Cray	Bagthorpe Primary School, Selston	Nottinghamshire
Sharon Jefferies	Orchard Special School, Newark	Nottinghamshire
Sue Osborn	Ollerton Junior School, Ollerton	Nottinghamshire
Jenni Page	Lafford High School, Billingshay	Lincolnshire
Lynn Parkes	Kirkby College, Kirkby-in-Ashfield	Nottinghamshire
Clive Richardson	Bishop Alexander Primary School, Newark	Nottinghamshire
Di Stendall	Matthew Holland School, Selston	Nottinghamshire
Andrew Swirles	Robert Jones Junior School, Blidworth	Nottinghamshire

7. Leaders who had engaged in or supported a sabbatical or secondment experience

The research sample

Some 10 headteachers who had recently participated in secondment or sabbatical opportunities were interviewed or provided written case study materials (as asterisked). A further 10 educationists with responsibility for or an interest in the provision of secondment or sabbatical opportunities were also interviewed.

School phase		School context		Educationists	
Infant	1	Rural	2	Female	4
Primary	4	Suburban	4	Male	6
Middle	1	Urban	2		
Secondary	4	Inner city	2		
School size		**Secondment location**		**System represented**	
Infant/Primary 45-480 (mean 340)		Local authority	1	Faith sector	3
Secondary/Middle 615-1,080 (mean 880)		VSO	2	Professional associations	3
		Research	2	Local authorities	1
Headteacher gender		Professional association	1	Leadership centres	2
Male	3	Study visit	2	Academies	1
Female	7	Industry	1		
		Self-generated	1		
Total sample of headteachers 10				**Total educationists 10**	

The focus of interview with these participants was specifically on the value of sabbatical or secondment opportunities as a personal sustainability strategy. Interviews regarding sabbaticals and secondments were largely conducted by telephone between April and July 2008 or in the cases asterisked were generated primarily from provided written case study materials.

Acknowledgements

Particular thanks are due to the 10 headteachers and 10 educationists who participated in some way in this section of the research as follows.

Sabbatical/secondment participants

Headteacher	School at time of interview	Location
Wendy Garrard	St. Mary's Primary School, Mildenhall	Suffolk
Ken Gill	Macarthur Girls High School, Parramatta	Sydney, Australia
Jill Hudson*	Pegasus Primary School	Oxford
Chris Hummerstone*	The Arnewood School	Hampshire
Linda Latchford*	Newton Solney CE Aided Infant School	Derbyshire
Jane Lees	Hindley High School	Wigan
Pauline Munro	Roundhills High School, Thurmaston	Leicestershire
Julia Shepard*	Beechwood School	Slough
Andrew Warren	Mill Hill Primary School, Tunstall	Stoke on Trent
Liz Youngman	Hucknall National Primary School	Nottinghamshire

Sabbatical/secondment supporting educationists

Name	Position	Organisation
Fiona Beevers	Schools Adviser	Bradford CE Diocese
John Cape	Co-director of Schools	Hallam RC Diocese
Bob Carstairs	Assistant General Secretary	ASCL
Jim Conway	Co-director of Schools	Hallam RC Diocese
Anne Evans	Chief Executive	HTI
Julia Hurlbut	HT Wellbeing Support Officer	Norfolk Local Authority
Mike Parkhouse	Senior Assistant Secretary	NAHT
Karen Robinson	Principal Officer-Primary	NUT
Peter Smith	Head of Research and Innovation	East Midlands Leadership Centre
David Triggs	Principal and CEO	Academies Enterprise Trust

Overall therefore, the totality of the research stands on the foundation of interviews with 150 school leaders and a further 40 supporting educationists. Sincere thanks are due to all these colleagues, for without their ready willingness to participate, generosity of time, and openness of response, the writing of this book would not have been possible.

BIBLIOGRAPHY

Aburdene, P. 2005. *Megatrends 2010: The Rise of Conscious Capitalism.* Charlottesville VA: Hampton Road

Ackerman, R. and P. Maslin-Ostrowski. 2002. *The Wounded Leader: How Real Leadership Emerges in Times of Crisis,* San Francisco, CA: Jossey-Bass

Adey, K. 2007. Unpublished lecture to The Friends of Melbourne Parish Church, Melbourne, Derbyshire, 8 September

Alford, H.J. and M.J. Naughton. 2001. *Managing As If Faith Mattered: Christian Social Principles in the Modern Organisation.* Notre Dame, IN: University of Notre Dame Press

Allix, N.M. 2000 Transformational leadership: democratic or despotic? *Education Management and Administration* 28 (1): 7-20

Althaus-Reid, M. 2000. Liberation theology. In *Oxford Companion to Christian Thought,* eds A. Hastings, M. Mason and P. Pyper, 386-90. Oxford: Oxford University Press

Aquinas, Thomas. 1997. Summa Theologica. In *Basic Writings of St. Thomas Aquinas* volume 2, ed. A.C. Pegis. Indianapolis, IN: Hackett Publishing

Aristotle. 2004. *The Nicomanchean Ethics,* trans. J.A.K. Thomson. London: Penguin Classics

Armstrong, K. 2006. *The Guardian* 26 August

Arnold, R. 2005. *Empathic Intelligence: Teaching, Learning, Relating.* Sydney: University of New South Wales Press

Astley, J. 2002. *Ordinary Theology: Looking, Listening and Learning in Theology.* Aldershot: Ashgate

Averill, J.R., G. Catlin and K.K. Chon. 1990. *Rules of Hope.* New York: Springer-Verlag

Bakewell, J. 2005. *Beliefs.* London: Duckworth

Baron-Cohen, S. 2003. *The Essential Difference.* London: Penguin Books

Bass, B. and P. Steidlmeier. 1999. Ethics, character and authentic transformational leadership. *Leadership Quarterly* 10 (2): 181-217

Battle, M. 1997. *Reconciliation: The Ubuntu Theology of Desmond Tutu.* Cleveland, OH: Pilgrim Press

Beare, H. 2004. The management metaphors leaders use. Paper presented to i-net conference on educational leadership, 6-12 December

Beatty, R. 2000. The emotions of educational leadership: breaking the silence. *International Journal of Leadership in Education* 3 (4): 331-57

Beck, L.G. and J. Murphy. 1993. *Understanding the Principalship: Metaphorical Themes 1920's-1990's.* New York: Teachers College Press

Begley, P.T. 2001. In pursuit of authentic school leadership practices. *International Journal of Leadership in Education* 4 (4): 353-65

Bell, J. 2002. *Church Times* 30 August

Benjamin, A. 1997. *Present Hope: Philosophy, Architecture, Judaism.* London: Routledge

Bevans, S.B. 2002. *Models of Contextual Theology* 2nd edn. Maryknoll, NY: Orbis

Bloch, E. 1985. *The Principle of Hope*, trans. N. Plaice et al. Oxford: Blackwell

Block, P. 1993. *Stewardship: Choosing Service over Self-Interest.* San Francisco, CA: Berrett-Keohler

Bolton, G. 2000. *Reflexive Practice: Writing and Professional Development.* London: Paul Chapman Publishing

Bosch, D.J. 1991. *Transforming Mission: Paradigm Shifts in the Theology of Mission.* Maryknoll, NY: Orbis

Bourdieu, P. 1977. *Outline of a Theory of Practice*, trans. R. Nice. Cambridge: Cambridge University Press

Boyatzis, R. and A. McKee. 2005. *Resonant Leadership: Renewing Yourself and Connecting with Others Through Mindfulness, Hope and Compassion.* Boston, MA: Harvard University Press

Boyatzis, R., D. Goleman and K. Rhee. 2000. Clustering competence in emotional intelligence: insights from the emotional competence inventory. In *Handbook of Emotional Intelligence: Theory, Development, Assessment and Application at Home, School and in the Workplace*, eds R. Bar-On and J.D.A. Parker, 343-62. San Francisco, CA: Jossey-Bass

Bracken, A.J. 2004. The principal's leadership role in the spiritual formation of teachers in Catholic schools: a case study in one educational system. Unpublished PhD thesis, Australian Catholic University

—. 2006. Personal correspondence 18 April

Breton, D. and C. Largent. 1996. *The Paradigm Conspiracy: Why Our Social Systems Violate Human Potential – And How We Can Change Them.* Minnesota: Center City, Hazelden

Bridger, F. 2003. A theological reflection. In *Guidelines for the Professional Conduct of Clergy*, 13-22. London: Church House Publishing

Briggs-Myers, I. 1993. *Introduction to Type: A Guide to Understanding Your Results on the Myers-Briggs Type Indicator*, 5th edn. Oxford: Oxford Psychologists Press

Brookes, M. 2008. General Secretary's speech to Annual Conference of National Association of Headteachers. *Leadership Focus* 32, July: 9

Browning, D. 2000. Foreword. In *Spiritual Dimensions of Pastoral Care: Practical Theology in a Multidisciplinary Context*, eds D. Willows and J. Swinton, 9. London: Jessica Kingsley Publishers

Bultmann, R. 1975. *Jesus and the Word*. London: Macmillan

Bush, T. and D. Glover. 2003. *School Leadership: Concepts and Evidence*. Nottingham: National College for School Leadership

Byers, P. 1992. The spiritual in the classroom. *Holistic Education Review* 5 (1): 6-10

Canavan, Brother Kelvin. 2006. Leaders for the future: an innovative program for teachers under 30. *Perspectives on Educational Leadership* 6. Sydney: Australian Council for Educational Leaders, 27 October

Caperon, J. 2007a. *The Spiritual Dimension of School Leadership*. Project Paper 38. Oxford: Bloxham Project

—. 2007b. *The Bloxham Project Director's Newsletter* April

Carr, D. and J. Haldane, eds. 2003. *Spirituality, Philosophy and Education*. London: Routledge

Carr, N. 2008. *The Guardian* 3 January, summarising *The Big Switch: Rewiring the World, From Edison to Google*. N. Carr. 2008, 12-14. London: Norton

Carr, W. 1997. *Handbook of Pastoral Studies*. London: SPCK

Casey, J. 1990. *Pagan Virtue: An Essay in Ethics*. Oxford: Oxford University Press

Chappell, H. 2001. Conversion *by* mercy and *for* a praxis of mercy. Paper presented at the Catholic Theological Society of America, 8 June

Chodorow, N. 1978. *The Reproduction of Mothering*. Berkeley, CA: University of California Press

Claxton, G. 2005. *The Wayward Mind: An Intimate History of the Unconscious*. London: Little Brown

Coleman, A. 2008. Senior Research Officer, National College for School Leadership, Nottingham, personal communication, 7 October

Coleman, M. 1996. Management style of female headteachers. *Education Management and Administration* 24 (2): 163-74

—. 2002. *Women as Headteachers: Striking the Balance*. Stoke: Trentham Books

Conger, J.A. and R.N. Kanungo. 1998. *Charismatic Leadership in Organizations*. Thousand Oaks, CA: Sage Publications

Cooperrider, D.L. and S. Srivastva. 1999. *Appreciative Management and Leadership: The Power of Positive Thought and Action in Organisations*. Euclid, OH: Williams Custom Publishing

Copson, A. 2008. Face to faith. *The Guardian* 17 May

Cottingham, J. 2005. *The Spiritual Dimension: Religion, Philosophy and Human Values*. Cambridge: Cambridge University Press

Craig, C.L., B. Duncan and L.J. Francis. 2006. Psychological type preferences of Roman Catholic priests in the United Kingdom. *Journal of Beliefs and Values* 27: 157-64

Crosby, J.F. 1966. *The Selfhood of the Human Person*. Washington: Catholic University of America Press

Crossman, J. 2003 Secular Spiritual development in education from international and global perspectives. *Oxford Review of Education* 29 (4): 503-20

Crouch, D. 2005. Sacred spaces in everyday life. Unpublished lecture, University of Derby, 13 October

Cuban, L. 1988. *The Managerial Imperative and the Practice of Leadership in Schools*. Albany, NY: State University of New York Press

Danzig, A. 1999. How might leadership be taught? The use of story and narrative to teach leadership. *International Journal of Leadership in Education* 2 (2): 117-31

Davie, G. 1994. *Religion in Britain Since 1945: Believing without Belonging*. Oxford: Blackwell

Dawkins, R. 2006. *The God Delusion*. London: Bantam

Day, C. and M. Schmidt. 2007. Sustaining resilience. In *Developing Sustainable Leadership*, ed. B. Davies, 65-86. London: PCP/Sage Publications

Day, C., A. Harris, M. Hatfield, H. Tolley and J. Beresford. 2000. *Leading Schools in Times of Change*. Maidenhead: Open University Press

de Pree, M. 1989. *Leadership is an Art*. New York: Doubleday

Deming, W.E. 1993. *The New Economics for Industry, Government and Education*. Cambridge, MA: Massachusetts Institute of Technology

Dennett, D. 1988. Conditions of personhood. In *What is a Person*, M.F. Goodman, 145-67. Totowa, NJ: Humana Press

DfES (Department for Education and Skills). 2004. *National Standards for Headteachers*. London: DfES

Ditch, H. 2006. Relishing the tough times. *LDR Magazine* 23 (September): 26-9. Nottingham: National College for School Leadership

Duignan, P.A. (2003) Authenticity in Leadership: Encouraging the Heart, Celebrating the Spirit, paper presented to the Lutheran Principals National Conference, Canberra Australia, 27-29 August

—. 2006. *Educational Leadership: Key Challenges and Ethical Tensions.* Cambridge: Cambridge University Press

Duignan, P.A. and N. Bhindi. 1997. Authenticity in leadership: an emerging perspective. *Journal of Educational Administration* 35 (3): 195-209

Duignan, P.A., J. Butcher, B. Spies-Butcher and J.F. Collins. 2005. *Socially Responsible Indicators for Policy, Practice and Benchmarking in Service Organisations.* Sydney: ACU National

Earley, P. 2006. Headship and beyond: the motivation and development of school leaders. Professorial Lecture delivered at the Institute of Education, University of London, 21 June

Eliot, T.S. 1936. *Four Quartets* (1959 paperback edition). London: Faber

EMLC (East Midlands Leadership Centre). 2006. Established Leaders Programme for senior staff in Catholic schools. Northampton: EMLC

Evans, D. 1993. *Spirituality and Human Nature.* New York: State University of New York Press

Farley, E. 1998. *The Fragility of Knowledge: The Fragmentation and Unity of Theological Education.* Philadelphia: Fortress Press

Faulks, S. 2006. *Human Traces.* London: Vintage

Fergusson, D. 1997. Eschatology. In *The Cambridge Companion to Christian Doctrine*, ed. C.E. Gunton, 226-44. Cambridge: Cambridge University Press

Field, J. 2003. *Social Capital.* London: Routledge

Flanagan, J.C. 1954. The critical incident technique. *Psychological Bulletin* 51: 327-58

Fletcher, J. 1979. *Humanhood: Essays in Biomedical Ethics.* Buffalo, NY: Prometheus

Flintham, A.J. 2003a. *Reservoirs of Hope: Spiritual and Moral Leadership in Headteachers.* NCSL Practitioner Enquiry Report. Nottingham: National College for School Leadership

—. 2003b. *When Reservoirs Run Dry: Why Some Headteachers Leave Headship Early.* NCSL Practitioner Enquiry Report. Nottingham: National College for School Leadership

—. 2004. Post-modernist portfolio people: sustainability and succession in school leadership. *Management in Education* 18 (3): 16-19

—. 2005. Heads Count: an evaluation of a Nottinghamshire model for headteacher sustainability, support and development through peer support. Unpublished evaluation report. Nottinghamshire Local Authority

—. 2006a. *Retaining the Reservoirs of Hope: Supporting School Principals in Australia in Spiritual and Moral Leadership*. Winston Churchill Travelling Fellowship Report. London: Winston Churchill Memorial Trust

—. 2006b. *What's Good about Leading Schools in Challenging Circumstances*. Nottingham: National College for School Leadership

—. 2007a. *Grounded in Faith: the spiritual formation, development and sustainability of Catholic school principals across 12 dioceses in England and Australia*. Northampton: East Midlands Leadership Centre

—. 2007b. Nottinghamshire head teacher peer support: a model for headteacher collaboration, sustainability, and development. *Head Teachers of the Future*, 46-8. Bagshot: Westminster Education Forum

—. 2008a. Who cares for the carers? *School Leadership* 23: 26-7

—. 2008b. Reservoirs of hope: sustaining passion in leadership. In *Passionate Leadership in Education*, ed. B. Davies and T. Brighouse, 57-72. London: Sage Publications

—. 2009. Faith, hope and spirituality in school leadership. Unpublished PhD thesis, University of Liverpool

Fowler, J.W. 1981. *Stages of Faith: The Psychology of Human Development and the Quest for Meaning*. San Francisco, CA: Harper Collins

Francis, L.J., C.L. Craig, M. Whinney, D. Tilley and S. Slater. 2007. Psychological typology of Anglican clergy in England: diversity, strengths and weaknesses in ministry. *International Journal of Practical Theology* 11: 226-84

Frankel, V.E. 1959 (reprinted 2004). *Man's Search for Meaning*. London: Rider

Fullan, M. 1993. Why teachers must become agents of change. *Educational Leadership* 50 (6): 12-17

—. 2001. *Leading in a Culture of Change*. San Francisco, CA: Jossey-Bass

—. 2005. *Leadership and Sustainability: System Thinkers in Action*. Thousand Oaks, CA: Corwin Press

Fuller, J. and P. Vaughan. 1986. *Working for the Kingdom: The Story of Ministers in Secular Employment*. London: SPCK

Gabriel, Y. 2000. *Storytelling in Organisations: Facts, Fictions, Fantasies*. Oxford: Oxford University Press

Gardner, H. 1983. *Frames of Mind*. London: Heinemann

—. 1995. *Leading Minds: An Anatomy of Leadership*. New York: Basic Books

Geltner, B. and M. Shelton. 1991. Expanded notions of strategic instructional leadership. *Journal of School Leadership* 1: 338-50

Glaser, B. and A. Strauss. 1967. *The Discovery of Grounded Theory*. Chicago, IL: Aldine

Godfrey, J.J. 1987. *A Philosophy of Human Hope*. Dordrecht, The Netherlands: Martinus Nijhoff

Goldsmith, M. 1994. *Knowing Me: Knowing God: Exploring Your Spirituality with Myers-Briggs*. London: Triangle

Goldsmith, M. and M. Wharton. 1993. *Knowing Me: Knowing You: Exploring Personality Type and Temperament*. London: SPCK

Goldsmith, O. 1770. *The Deserted Village*: London: W. Griffin

Goleman, D. 1996. *Emotional Intelligence*. London: Bloomsbury

Goleman, D., R. Boyatzis and A. McKee. 2003. *The New Leaders: Transforming the Art of Leadership into the Science of Results*. London: Time Warner Paperbacks

Goodliff, P. 1998. *Care in a Confused Climate: Pastoral Care and Postmodern Culture*. London: Darton Longman & Todd

Gore, J. 2007. Quality teaching. Paper delivered at an in-service event for schools, Westfield, Diocese of Parramatta, Australia, 23 March

Gorringe, T.J. 2000. Contextual theology. In *Oxford Companion to Christian Thought*, eds A. Hastings, M. Mason and P. Pyper, 133. Oxford: Oxford University Press

Grace, G.R. 1994. Urban education and the culture of contentment: the politics, culture and economics of inner city schooling. In *Education in Urban Areas: cross-national dimensions*, ed. N.P. Stromquist, Westport, CT: Praeger

—. 1995. *School Leadership: Beyond Education Management*. Lewes: Falmer

—. 2002. *Catholic Schools: Mission, Markets and Morality*. Abingdon: RoutledgeFalmer

Greenleaf, R.K. 1977. *Servant Leadership: A Journey into the Nature of Legitimate Power and Greatness*. New York: Paulist Press

Grint, K. 2002. Management or leadership. *Journal of Health Service Research and Policy* 7 (4) (October): 248-51

Groome, T.H. 1999. *Christian Religious Education: Sharing Our Story and Vision*. San Francisco, CA: Jossey-Bass

Guignon, C. 2004. *On Being Authentic*. London: Routledge

Gula, R. 1996. *Ethics in Pastoral Ministry*. New York: Paulist Press

Gunter, H. 2001. *Leaders and Leadership in Education*. London: Paul Chapman

Haldane, J. 2003. On the very idea of spiritual values. In *Spirituality, Philosophy and Education*, eds D. Carr and J. Haldane, 11-25. London: Routledge

Halpin, D. 2003. *Hope and Education: The Role of the Utopian Imagination*. London: RoutledgeFalmer

Halstead, J.M. 2003. Metaphor, cognition and spiritual reality. In *Spirituality, Philosophy and Education*, eds D. Carr and J. Haldane, 83-96. London: Routledge

Hanvey, J. 2008. *The Spirituality of Leadership*. London: Heythrop Institute for Religion, Ethics and Public Life

Hargreaves, A. 2003. *Teaching in a Knowledge Society: Education in an Age of Insecurity*. Buckingham: Open University Press

Hargreaves, A. and D. Fink. 2005. *Sustainable Leadership*. San Francisco, CA: Jossey-Bass

Harries, R. 2002. *God Outside the Box: Why Spiritual People Object to Christianity*. London: SPCK

Harris, A. 2002a. Distributed leadership in schools: leading or misleading? Paper presented at BELMAS Annual Conference, 20 September

—. 2002b. Effective leadership in schools facing challenging contexts. *School Leadership and Management* 22 (1): 15-26

Harris, A. and C. Chapman. 2002. *Effective Leadership in Schools Facing Challenging Circumstances*. Nottingham: National College for School Leadership

Hauser, M.D. 2007. *Moral Minds: How Nature Designed Our Universal Sense of Right and Wrong*. London: Little Brown

Hay, D. and K. Hunt. 2000. *Understanding the Spirituality of People Who Don't Go To Church*. Research Report of the Adult Spirituality Project. Nottingham: University of Nottingham

Hay Group/HTI (Heads, Teachers and Industry). 2002. *No Barriers, No Boundaries: Breakthrough Leadership that Transforms*. Warwick: HTI

Healey, D. 1990. *The Time of My Life*. London: Penguin

Heaney, S. 1990. *The Cure at Troy: A Version of Sophocles' Philocetes*. London: Faber

Heifetz, R.A and M. Linsky. 2002. *Leadership on the Line: Staying Alive Through the Dangers of Leading*. Boston, MA: Harvard Business School Press

Hick, J. 1999. *The Fifth Dimension: An Exploration of the Spiritual Realm*. Oxford: One World

Hicks, T. 2008. Sonnet on the rock. Poem written for ordinations in the Diocese of Derby, 28 June

Himmelfarb, G. 1995. *The Demoralization of Society: From Victorian Virtues to Modern Values*. New York: Knopf

Hodgkinson, C. 1993. *The Philosophy of Leadership*. Oxford: Blackwell

Holloway, R. 1999. *Godless Morality: Keeping Religion out of Ethics*. Edinburgh: Canongate

Hoyle, E. and M. Wallace. 2007. Beyond metaphors of management: the case for metaphoric redescription in education. *British Journal of Educational Studies* 55 (4): 426-42

HTI (Heads, Teachers and Industry). 2004. *Secondment Almanac*. Warwick: HTI

Hyman, P. 2005. *1 Out of 10: From Downing Street Vision to Classroom Reality*. London: Vintage

Ingate, C. 2006. *Should I Stay Or Should I Go? Perspectives on Middle Headship*. NCSL Practitioner Enquiry Report. Nottingham: National College for School Leadership

James Report. 1972. *Teacher Education and Training*. Report by a Committee of Inquiry appointed by the Secretary of State for Education and Science under the Chairmanship of Lord James of Rusholme. London: HMSO

Julian of Norwich. 1373 (reprinted 2003). *Revelations of Divine Love*. London: Penguin

Keenan, J.F. 1998. Virtue ethics. In *Christian Ethics: An Introduction*, ed. B. Hoose, 84-94. London: Cassell

Keys, W., C. Sharp, K. Greene and H. Grayson. 2003. *Successful Leadership of Schools in Urban and Challenging Contexts*. Nottingham: National College for School Leadership

Layder, D. 1993. *New Strategies in Social Research*. Cambridge, Polity Press

Lee, T. 2005. *Far From the Madding Crowd? How Can Hard-pressed Headteachers Find Sanctuary to Prepare for the Future Whilst Coping With Daily Operational Challenges?* NCSL Practitioner Enquiry Report. Nottingham: National College for School Leadership

Leithwood, K. 1992. The move towards transformational leadership. *Educational Leadership* 49 (5): 8-9

Leithwood, K., D. Jantzi and R. Steinbach. 1999. *Changing Leadership for Changing Times*. Buckingham: Open University Press

Loader, D. 1997. *The Inner Principal*. London: Falmer

Luckcock, T.R.S. 2004. Church school leadership and the theology of education: integrating spirituality, ministry and administrative philosophy in the practice of the headteacher. Unpublished PhD thesis, University of Liverpool

—. 2007. Appreciative Inquiry and spiritual practice. Paper presented to the Theology and Religious Studies Research Group, Liverpool Hope University, 25 April

Luther King, Martin. 1963. I have a Dream speech. Washington DC, 28 August

Lynch, G. and D. Willows. 2000. Telling tales: the narrative dimension of pastoral care and counselling. In *Spiritual Dimensions of Pastoral Care: Practical Theology in a Multidisciplinary Context*, eds D. Willows and J. Swinton, 181-7. London: Jessica Kingsley Publishers

MacIntyre, A. 1981. *After Virtue: A Study in Moral Theory*. London: Duckworth

Macquarrie, J. 1977. *Principles of Christian Theology*, revised edition. London: SCM

—. 1992. *Paths in Spirituality*. Harrisburg, PA: Morehouse

—. 1998. *Christology Revisited*. Harrisburg, PA: Trinity Press

McClendon, J.W. 1974. *Biography as Theology: How Life Stories Can Remake Today's Theology*. Nashville: Abignon Press

McGrath, A.E. 1997. *Christian Theology: An Introduction*, 2nd edn. Oxford: Blackwell

—. 1999. *Christian Spirituality*. Oxford: Blackwell

McLaughlin, T.H. 2003. Education, spirituality and the common school. In *Spirituality, Philosophy and Education*, eds D. Carr and J. Haldane, 185-99. London: Routledge

McLeod, J. 1998. *An Introduction to Counselling*, 2nd edn. Buckingham: Open University Press

Maden, M. and J. Hillman. 1996. *Success Against the Odds*. London: Routledge

Mander, M. 2008. *Critical Incidents: Effective Responses and the Factors Behind Them*. NCSL Practitioner Enquiry Report. Nottingham: National College for School Leadership

Manning, Bishop Kevin. 2007. Address delivered at Diocesan Education Mass, Diocese of Parramatta, Blacktown, Australia, 14 March

Milacci, F.A. 2006. Moving towards faith: an inquiry into spirituality in adult education. *Christian Higher Education* 5 (3): 211-33

Mohler, A. 2005. In End of the Enlightenment, D. MacKenzie. *New Scientist* 8 October: 42

Moltmann, J. 1967. *Theology of Hope*. London: SCM

—. 1972. Report of seminar contribution. In *Hope and the Future of Man*, ed. E.H. Cousins. Philadelphia: Fortress Press

—. 2002. *Theology of Hope*. London: SCM Press

Moody, C. 1992. *Eccentric Ministry: Pastoral Care and Leadership in the Parish*. London: Darton Longman & Todd

Moran, G. 2002. *Reflections on Leadership*, NCSL Leading Edge Seminar. Nottingham: National College for School Leadership

Morgan, G. 1986. *Images of Organisation*. Newbury Park, CA: Sage Publications

Mowlam, M. 2002. *Momentum: The Struggle for Peace, Politics and the People*. London: Hodder & Stoughton

Moxley, R. 2000. *Leadership and Spirit: Breathing New Vitality and Energy into Individuals and Organisations*. San Francisco, CA: Jossey-Bass

Muijs, D., M. Ainscow, A. Dyson, C. Raffo, S. Goldrick, K. Kerr, C. Lennie and M. Miles. 2007. *Leading Under Pressure: Leadership for Social Inclusion*. Summary Report. Nottingham: National College for School Leadership

Munby, S. 2005. Growing the future together. Paper presented at NCSL Regional Seminar, Nottingham, 7 July

Murphy-O'Connor, Cardinal Cormac. 2008. Interview on BBC Radio 4 Today Programme, 9 May

Murray, R.B. and J.P. Zentner. 1988. *Nursing Concepts for Health Promotion*. London: Prentice Hall

NCSL (National College for School Leadership). 2002. *Making the Difference: Successful Leadership in Challenging Circumstances: A Practical Guide to What School Leaders Can Do to Improve and Energise Their Schools*. NCSL Leading Practice Workshop. Nottingham: NCSL

—. 2006a. *Growing Tomorrow's Leaders*. Nottingham: NCSL

—. 2006b. Leadership programme for serving headteachers: analysis of the data. Unpublished report. Nottingham: NCSL

—. 2007. *What We Know about School Leadership*. Nottingham: NCSL

—. 2008. *LDR Magazine* 29 (January): 28

—. 2009. *Developing Outstanding Leaders: Professional Life Histories of Outstanding Headteachers*. Nottingham: NCSL

Newman, T. and C. Koerner. 2010. *Small, school-based sabbaticals in CPD provision*. National College Research Associate Report. Nottingham: National College

Neylan, A. 2005. Pathways to spirituality. Unpublished workbook. Sydney: Archdiocese of Sydney Catholic Spirituality Team

Northouse, P.G. 2000. *Leadership: Theory and Practice*. Thousand Oaks, CA: Sage Publications

Nouwen, H.J.M. 1994. *The Wounded Healer: Ministry in Contemporary Society*. London: Darton Longman & Todd

Nye, J.S. 2008. *The Powers to Lead*. Oxford: Oxford University Press

O'Collins, G. 1983. *Interpreting Jesus*. London: Mowbray

—. 1995. *Second Journey: Spiritual Awareness and the Mid-Life Crisis*. Leominster: Gracewing

—. 2000. Redemption. In *Oxford Companion to Christian Thought*, eds A. Hastings, M. Mason and P. Pyper, 598-601. Oxford: Oxford University Press

O'Connell, S. 2008. Time Out. *Managing Schools Today* 17 (4): 13-15

Ofsted (Office for Standards in Education). 2000. *Improving City Schools*. London: Ofsted

—. 2002. *The Annual Report of Her Majesty's Chief Inspector of Schools 2000/01: Standards and Quality in Education*. London: Ofsted

Osmer, R.R. 2008. *Practical Theology: An Introduction*. Grand Rapids, MI: Eerdmans

Palmer, P.J. 1998. *The Courage to Teach: Exploring the Inner Landscape of a Teacher's Life*. San Francisco, CA: Jossey-Bass

Pannenberg, W. 1968. *Jesus: God and Man*. London: SCM

Parker, R. 2002. *Passion and Intuition: The Impact of Life History on Leadership*. NCSL Practitioner Enquiry Report. Nottingham: National College for School Leadership

Pass, J. 2009. *It's Life...But Not As We Know It: Towards a Programme for Lifestyle Development to Enhance Personal Effectiveness and Well-being for School Leaders*. National College Research Associate report. Nottingham: National College

Pinker, S. 2007. *The Stuff of Thought: Language as a Window into Human Nature*. London: Allen Lane

Polkinghorne, D.E. 1989. Phenomenological research methods. In *Existential-Phenomenological Perspectives in Psychology*, eds R.S. Valle and S. Halling, 41-60. New York: Plenum

Polkinghorne, J. 1994. *Science and Christian Belief*. London: SPCK

Pope Benedict XVI. 2006. *The Guardian* 9 September

—. 2007. Encyclical letter. *Spe Salvi* 30 November

Putnam, R.D. 2000. *Bowling Alone*. New York: Simon & Schuster

Putnam, R.D., L. Feldstein and D. Cohen. 2003. *Better Together: Restoring the American Community*. New York: Simon & Schuster

Reed, B., J. Bazalgette, H. Hutton and I. Kehoe. 2002. *Becoming Fit for Purpose: Leading Transformation in Church Schools*. London: Grubb Institute of Behavioural Studies

Robinson, J.A.T. 1963. *Honest to God*. London: SCM Press

Rokeach, M. 1973. *The Nature of Human Values*. New York: The Free Press

Sage Publications. 2010. 50 most cited articles in *Management in Education*. http://mie.sagepub.com/reports/mfc_all_7.dtl

Saulwick, I. and D. Muller. 2004. *The Privilege and the Price: A Study of Principal Class Workload and Its Impact on Health and Wellbeing, Final Report*. State Government of Victoria: Department of Education

Savage, S. 2005. In Meeting of minds, M. Brooks. *New Scientist* 8 October: 45

Schillebeeckx, E. 1979. *Jesus: An Experiment in Christology*, trans. H. Hoskins. New York: Crossroad

Schneiders, S.M. 1990. Spirituality in the Academy. In *Modern Christian Spirituality: Methodological and Historical Essays*, ed. B.C. Hanson, 15-37. Atlanta, GA: Scholars Press

School Curriculum and Assessment Authority. 1995. *Spiritual and Moral Development*. COM/95/311. London: School Curriculum and Assessment Authority

Schweizer, E. 1968. Pneuma, pneumatikos. *Theological Dictionary of the New Testament Vol. 6*, 332-455. Grand Rapids, MI: Eerdmans

Senge, P. 1990. *The Fifth Discipline*. New York: Doubleday

Sergiovanni, T.J. 1991. *The Principalship: A Reflective Practice Perspective*. Needham Heights, MA: Allyn & Bacon

—. 1992. *Moral Leadership: Getting to the Heart of School Improvement*. San Francisco, CA: Jossey-Bass

—. 1997. Organisations or communities? Changing the metaphor changes the theory. In *Organisational Effectiveness and Improvement in Education*, eds A. Harris, B. Bennett and M. Preedy. Buckingham: Open University Press

—. 2001. *Leadership: What's In It For Schools?* London: RoutledgeFalmer

Sheldrake, P. 1992. *Spirituality and History: Questions of Interpretation and Method*. New York: Crossroad Books

Smith, D. 1999. *Making Sense of Spiritual Development*. Nottingham: The Stapleford Centre

Smithells, A. 1921. Professors and practical men. In *From a Modern University: Some Aims and Aspirations of Science*, A. Smithells, 25-39. London: Oxford University Press

Southworth, G. 2002. Instructional leadership in schools: reflections and empirical evidence. *School Leadership and Management* 22 (1): 73-92

Spears, L. 1998. *Insights on Leadership*. New York: John Wiley

Stamp, G. and N. Todd. 1996. Pastoral theology re-defined. In *Management and Ministry: Appreciating Contemporary Issues*, ed. J. Nelson, 37-58. Norwich: Canterbury Press

Stark, M. 1998. No slow fixes either: how failing schools in England are being restored to health. In *No Quick Fixes: Perspectives on Schools in Difficulty*, eds L. Stoll and K. Myers, 34-44. London: Falmer

Starratt, R.J. 1993. *The Drama of Leadership*. London: Falmer

—. 2003. *Centering Educational Administration: Cultivating Meaning, Community, Responsibility*. Hillsdale, NJ: Lawrence Erlbaum

Stebbins, G.D. 2002. The public school principal: elements for successfully surviving and thriving in the system. Unpublished Ed.D dissertation, Fielding Graduate Institute, USA

Stephenson, J. 2000. *Corporate Capability: Implications for the Style and Direction of Work-based Learning*. Working Paper 99-14. Sydney: University of Technology

Storr, A. 1988. *Solitude: A Return to the Self*. New York: Simon & Schuster

Straw, J. 2010. G2 Interview with Stephen Moss. *The Guardian* 29 March: 7-10

Sullivan, J. 1997. Leading values and casting shadows: moral dimensions of school leadership. *Pastoral Care* September: 8-12

—. 2002. Living logos. *Networking* 3 (March): 28-31

—. 2003. The skills based approach to school leadership. In *Religion and Education*, vol. 4, eds W. Kay and L. Francis. Leominster: Gracewing

—. 2008a. Philosophy of Catholic education. In *Exploring Religious Education: Catholic Religious Education in an Intercultural Europe*, eds P. Kieran and A. Hession. Dublin: Veritas

—. 2008b. Education and evangelisation. Paper delivered to Hope Theological Society, Liverpool Hope University, 4 December

—. 2010. Religious speech in the public square. In *Communicating Faith*, ed. J. Sullivan. Washington, DC: Catholic University of America Press

Swinton, J. 2000. *From Bedlam to Shalom: Towards a Practical Theology of Human Nature, Interpersonal Relationships and Mental Health Care*. New York: Peter Lang Press

Taylor, C. 1991. *The Ethics of Authenticity*. Cambridge, MA: Harvard University Press

—. 2007. *A Secular Age*. Cambridge, MA: Harvard University Press

Taylor, W.S. no date. *The Far Side of Reason*. London: G.R. Welch

Terry, I.A. 2005. The distinctive religious and cultural values of Church of England primary schools. Unpublished PhD thesis, University of Surrey

Tillich, P. 1952. *The Courage to Be*. New Haven, CT: Yale University Press

—. 1957. *The Protestant Era*, abridged. Chicago, IL: University of Chicago Press

Tisdall, E. 2000. Spirituality and emancipatory adult education in women adult educators for social change. *Adult Education Quarterly* 50 (4): 308-35

Tourish, D and N. Tourish. 2010. Spirituality at work, and its implications for leadership and followership: a post-structuralist perspective. *Leadership* 6 (2): 207-24

Tracy, D. 1994. *On Naming the Present: God, Hermeneutics and the Church*. Maryknoll, NY: Orbis

Travis, S.H. 1980. *Christian Hope and the Future of Man*. Leicester: Inter-Varsity Press

Tripp, D. 1993. *Critical Incidents in Teaching: Developing Professional Judgement*. London: Routledge

Tuohy, D. 1999. *The Inner World of Teaching: Exploring Assumptions Which Promote Change and Development*. London: Falmer

Tutu, D. 1991. Grace upon grace. *Journal for Preachers* 15 (1) Advent

—. 1998. *The Wisdom of Desmond Tutu*, compiled by Michael Battle. Louisville, KY: Knox

—. 1999. No Future without Forgiveness. New York: Doubleday

University of Western Sydney. 2007. *Teaching and Leading for Quality in Australian Schools: A Review and Synthesis of Research-based Knowledge*. Sydney: University of Western Sydney

Veling, T.A. 2005. *Practical Theology: On Earth As It Is In Heaven*. Maryknoll, NY: Orbis

Verity, K. 2005. School Mentor. www.mentus.co.uk

Vine, W. 1966. *An Expository Dictionary of New Testament Words With Their Precise Meaning for English Readers, Vol. 4*. Old Tappen, NJ: Fleming H Revell Company

Volf, M. 1991. *Work in the Spirit: Towards a Theology of Work*. Eugene, OR: Wipf & Stock

Wakefield, G.S. 1983. *The Westminster Dictionary of Christian Spirituality*. Louisville, KY: Westminster John Knox

—. 2000. Spirituality. In *Oxford Companion to Christian Thought*, eds A. Hastings, A. Mason and H. Pyper, 685-6. Oxford: Oxford University Press

Walker, K. 2005. *Fostering Hope: A Leader's First and Last Task.* Monograph 37. Sydney: Australian Council for Educational Leaders

Watts, F.N. 2002. *Theology and Psychology.* Aldershot: Ashgate

West-Burnham, J. 1997. *Managing Quality in Schools.* London: Pitman

—. 2000. *Moral Leadership.* New Visions Thinkpiece. Nottingham: National College for School Leadership

—. 2001. *Interpersonal Leadership.* Leading Edge Seminar Thinkpiece. Nottingham: National College for School Leadership

—. 2002. *Leadership and Spirituality.* Leading Edge Seminar Thinkpiece. Nottingham: National College for School Leadership

—. 2009. *Rethinking Educational Leadership: From Improvement to Transformation.* London: Continuum

West-Burnham, J. and G. Ireson. 2005. *Leadership Development and Personal Effectiveness.* Nottingham: National College for School Leadership

Wheatley, M. 2002. The servant leader: from hero to host. Unpublished interview. Indianapolis, IN: Greenleaf Center for Servant Leadership

Williams, C. 2001. *Interpersonal Leadership.* Leading Edge Seminar. Nottingham: National College for School Leadership

Williams, Archbishop Rowan. 2008. Interview with Stuart Jeffries. *The Guardian* 8 October

Willows, D. and J. Swinton, eds. 2000. *Spiritual Dimensions of Pastoral Care: Practical Theology in a Multidisciplinary Context.* London: Jessica Kingsley Publishers

Wittgenstein, L.J.J. 1922. *Tractatus Logico-Philosophicus,* trans. C.K.Ogden (1981 edition). London: Routledge and Kegan Paul

Woodhead, C., former HM Chief Inspector of Schools. 2003. *Nottingham Evening Post* 28 November

Woods, G. 2007. The 'bigger feeling': the importance of spiritual experience in educational leadership. *Educational Management, Administration and Leadership* 35 (1): 135-55

Woods, R. 2002. *Enchanted Headteachers: Sustainability in Primary School Headship.* NCSL Practitioner Enquiry Report. Nottingham: National College for School Leadership

Yeats, W.B. 1921. The Second Coming. In *The Collected Poems of W.B. Yeats,* 1994 edition. London: Wordsworth

Yukl, G.A. 2002. *Leadership in Organisations.* Upper Saddle River, NJ: Prentice Hall

Zohar, D. and I. Marshall. 2000. *Spiritual Intelligence: The Ultimate Intelligence,* London: Bloomsbury.

INDEX